HAD ENOUGH?

A HANDBOOK
FOR FIGHTING BACK

JAMES CARVILLE

WITH JEFF NUSSBAUM

SIMON & SCHUSTER
NEW YORK ■ LONDON ■ TORONTO ■ SYDNEY

SIMON & SCHUSTER
Rockefeller Center
1230 Avenue of the Americas
New York, NY 10020

SIMON & SCHUSTER and colophon are registered trademarks
of Simon & Schuster, Inc.

For information regarding special discounts for bulk purchases,
please contact Simon & Schuster Special Sales at 1-800-456-6798
or business@simonandschuster.com

Designed by Dana Sloan

Manufactured in the United States of America

10   9   8   7   6   5   4   3   2   1

Library of Congress Cataloging-in-Publication Data has been
applied for.

ISBN 978-1-4516-1358-2

For Bill Carville (1950–2003)
Life dealt him a tough hand, and he played it into a winning one.

For Uncle Lloyd (1923–2003)
*The best man at my wedding and, other than
my daddy, the best man I ever knew.*

ACKNOWLEDGMENTS

One of the great fictional Louisianans of all time, Blanche DuBois, said famously that she always depended on the kindness of strangers. This real Louisianan has always depended on the kindness of friends.

More friends than I can possibly name here contributed their time, energy, intelligence, and insight to this book. To try to recognize all of you would inevitably mean that I would slight one of you, and that is something I never want to do.

So I'll just say that y'all know who you are, and I know who you are, and that I'm grateful for your help and blessed by your friendship.

CONTENTS

PROLOGUE

I don't know about you, but I've had enough of the whole damn thing.

I've had enough of losing elections.

I've had enough of losing arguments.

I've had enough of seeing Americans losing their jobs.

Heck, I've had enough of losing my hair.

I've had enough of calling some B-rate cowboy my commander in chief.

I've had enough of the broken promises, the unnecessary secrecy, and the lying to the American people.

I've had enough of people saying government doesn't work—when, for them, it's working like a charm.

I've had enough of giving millionaires like Dick Cheney and myself tax breaks and giving America's kids a mountain of debt.

I've had enough of being hated around the world because I'm an American.

Oh, but my frustration is an equal-opportunity thing.

I've had enough of Democrats rolling over and thinking that you can appease George Bush, Dick Cheney, Tom DeLay, and that whole gang of Keystone Kops who are running America today.

I've had enough of seeing our ideas stolen, then bastardized, then used to beat us over the head so hard that we stop thinking straight and what should be cries of outrage become pitiful whimpers.

I've had enough of people coming up to me on street corners, in hotel lobbies, in airports, and whining to me about how bad things are. Believe me, I know.

I've had enough of a press too scared and pathetic to ask a follow-up question.

I've had enough of the blowhards on cable TV and the self-righteous anger I hear from people whose only accomplishment in life is their ability to turn the dial on an AM radio.

Tell you what, I've had enough of having enough.

In fact, there's only one thing in this world aside from the love of my wife and two daughters that gives me comfort right now, and it is this: If you're picking up this book, you've probably had enough, too.*

Rest assured, there are a lot of people who are as fed up as you and me. And most of them want to do something about it. But here's the problem: they're just sitting there, taking it. Sure, maybe you throw your shoe at the TV sometimes. But that doesn't accomplish anything, unless you count seeing a tread mark on Bill O'Reilly's face as progress.

---

*Now there's a slight chance that you're picking up this book just to see what kind of burr I've got under my saddle, but you're not nearly as PO'd as I am. That would probably make you a Republican. Once you discount my lovely wife, the odds that you, a Republican, intend to read or purchase this book are even slimmer. However, I'm a big-tent kind of guy, and you're still welcome to read the guide and come along for the ride. There's not a church in the world that won't take a converted sinner— and the church of the Ragin' Cajun is no different. Maybe you'll even learn something.

It's time to quit stewing, steaming, and taking abuse and start taking action.

We need to take back our country from the tax-cutting, environment-desecrating, secret-keeping, influence-peddling, warmongering, free-speech-hating, hypocritical right-wing goofballs who are running things today.

We need to say, "Enough is enough." We want our country back, and we intend to get it back.

That's what this book is: it's a guide for taking back Congress, the White House, and America from the people running our country—and running it into the ditch—today. And we're not just going to rant, and rave, and criticize. We're going to put forward some fresh new ideas to make progressives stronger, and our country better.

So consider the following pages a constructive outlet for your case of political road rage, and read on.

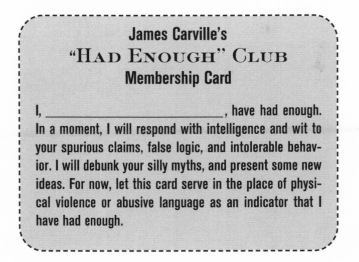

James Carville's
"HAD ENOUGH" CLUB
Membership Card

I, _____, have had enough. In a moment, I will respond with intelligence and wit to your spurious claims, false logic, and intolerable behavior. I will debunk your silly myths, and present some new ideas. For now, let this card serve in the place of physical violence or abusive language as an indicator that I have had enough.

INTRODUCTION

THE LESSON OF THE
TRANSGENDER AMENDMENT

The only time anyone ever calls me "smart" is when it's paired with the word "mouth." Such is my lot in life. I've seen my speeches called "fanatical ravings," "foam-at-the-mouth rants," and—my favorite—"scattershot barrages of verbal silage." One editorial went so far as to talk about a national "poverty of spirit induced by . . . James Carville's mouth."

The supposed power of my mouth got me to thinking. If my mouth can induce a national poverty of spirit, maybe it could help me test a growing concern I've been having about the Democratic Party.

You see, there are a lot of allegations made against Democrats that are complete and total BS—we burn American flags for sport, we'd make America's military look like France's in World War II if given the chance, we never met a government program we didn't like, we coddle criminals. The list goes on and on. We're going to put the lie to those spurious, ridiculous claims in the following pages.

To be honest, there *is* one charge made of the Democratic Party that makes me wince. It is that the Democratic Party as we know it has become more of an accumulation of interest groups than a national party with something concrete to offer the entire American public. How can this be? How can the party that won two world wars, rebuilt Europe, fought for civil rights, created Social Security and Medicare, gave us a cleaner environment, and built the strongest economic engine the world has ever seen be wincing at the accusation that we don't have something to offer all Americans? I didn't want to believe it. So I decided to use this mouth of mine to test it out.

I chose as my focus group a large gathering of Democrats at an annual dinner in a state that shall remain nameless. I stepped up to the podium, looked out at the crowd, and started them off with a little joke:

"You know, back in 2000 a Republican friend of mine warned me that if I voted for Al Gore and he won, the stock market would tank, we'd lose millions of jobs, and our military would be totally overstretched. You know what: I did vote for Al Gore, he did win, and I'll be damned if all those things didn't come true."

Then I got a little serious.

"This is truly a historic time. But historic doesn't necessarily mean good. With the exception of one brief year, this is the first time since Eisenhower was president that we do not hold power in the Senate, the House, or the executive branch.

"Look anywhere and you'll find a statistic or story about how bad this is for average Americans. I can only see the slimmest of silver linings here, and it is that America will finally see what we all know—that when you look at a right-wing agenda that is unvarnished, untempered by moderation, amendment, or debate, and fundamentally unstoppable, it's pretty damn scary."

I saw some heads beginning to nod, and I continued on:

"What do you do in the face of such an agenda? Well, for starters, you quit sniping about the little things that divide Democrat from Democrat, progressive from progressive, even centrist from liberal. You know the difference between a Democrat and a cannibal? Cannibals don't eat their own. Stop chewing on each other, and start chewing on the people who deserve it."

There was some laughter and applause, and I started to get comfortable.

"They are trying to make big, bad changes to this country, changes that will fundamentally alter the role of government and the shape of our nation for years if not generations to come. We're not going to stop this steamroller by putting pebbles in its path. We need to be unified and disciplined and visionary and smart."

More nodding heads and a hum of murmured *uh-huh*s.

"We shouldn't be afraid to agree when we can and compromise if it's in America's interest. But they've got to know, and you've got to be ready, because some things are only gonna get settled in a fight."

I was getting good and lathered.

"We have got to tell America what we are for, as well as what we are against. In 1992, we came together and, against the odds, we won. It was a big victory, and made a mighty big difference for this country. All those promises we made—about a smaller, smarter government, about an economy that gives people a chance to succeed, about investing in the talents of the American people—we kept 'em. And eight years and twenty million new jobs, the lowest unemployment rate, the highest home ownership rate in history, the lowest crime rate, reduced welfare rolls, and the first balanced budget in decades later—I'll put our record against anybody's. Heck, so many people did so well under the Clinton-Gore economy that we created a pretty decent number of Republicans."

A few people in the crowd said, "Amen to that."

"Now we've got to come together again. We've got to come together for a strong economy that allows people to earn a decent living. We need schools that give the children the skills they need to get the jobs of tomorrow . . . and to guarantee a retirement of dignity after a lifetime of work."

Applause.

"We stand for clean air to breathe, clean water to drink, and a clean government that gives a damn."

More applause.

"Whether it's women's rights, or civil rights, or workers' rights, we are the only party that speaks to the hopes of *all* Americans."

Then just when I had them whipped into a good frenzy, I hit them with it. "And I'll be got-damned if we are going to let them stop us from passing the transgender amendment."

Cheers and applause. People were out of their seats. It was thunderous.

There's only one problem. There is *no* transgender amendment.* I don't even know what would be *in* a transgender amendment.

That's when it really hit me. People went wild because it sounded like something Democrats are for. I almost felt guilty. After all, it wasn't that audience's fault for being gullible. It was our fault for sounding like

---

*I've since been told that there is a transgender amendment. There was one in Australia and one in New York. I'm sure I support it, whatever it is. But I wasn't speaking in either of those places, and my point stands.

a party that is a sum of different things targeted to different groups. Maybe someday someone will write a transgender amendment—and we will stand for it. But we need to stand for more than that.

Let's hold up right there for a second. You picked up this book because you wanted someone to kick the ever-living piss out of George W. Bush, not just be another self-hating Democrat. Don't worry, you won't be disappointed. Beating up on George W. Bush is like being a mosquito at a nudist colony—the only question is where to start. But this book isn't (just) about how much I hate the president, his cronies and what they're doing to this country—it's about how much I love America, how much I love the Democratic Party, and the things we need to do to make both stronger.

FEAR THE DONKEY, ASK NOT WHAT YOU CAN DO FOR YOUR COUNTRY

The symbol of my party is the donkey. It began with Andrew Jackson, whose opponents labeled him a jackass for adopting the slogan "Let the people rule." Republicans thought that self-rule was a silly concept then. They still do.

But Jackson turned it to his advantage, and it came to represent his stubbornness and willingness to stick by his principles.

Republicans have as a mascot the elephant, a creature Adlai Stevenson described as one that has "a thick skin, a head full of ivory, and as everyone who has seen a circus parade knows, proceeds best by grasping the tail of its predecessor."

It was Sam Rayburn who, unwittingly, described the main failing of the jackass—which is that "any old jackass can kick down a barn, but it takes a carpenter to build one."

For the entire history of our party, Democrats have been not only jackasses but carpenters. We're not afraid to kick down a bad idea or two, but we've also been relentless in our commitment to build a better America.

That is why Americans have always turned to us in times of national challenge. We're the ones with vision, a sense of creativity, and a willingness to experiment boldly and to use the government to do big things that make us all better off.

Whether it was Woodrow Wilson cracking down on unfair business by creating the Federal Trade Commission, FDR's sweeping New Deal and the creation of Social Security, Truman's Fair Deal and the expansion of Social Security, Kennedy staring down the Cuban missile crisis and creating the Peace Corps, Johnson's signing of sweeping civil rights legislation and the creation of Medicare, Carter's much maligned passion for energy conservation, or Clinton's commitment to reduce the deficit and make the economy work for millions of Americans who had never before been given a fair chance, Democrats have always identified national challenges and issued national calls to action to meet them.

Americans were looking for that call to action in the days after September 11. People lined up at the blood banks until the blood banks said, "No more!" People donated work gloves and search equipment, and whatever else they could muster—and not a few of them hopped in their cars and trucks and actually drove it to New York and Washington.

People wanted to make a sacrifice; they were *begging* to make a sacrifice. They just wanted to be told what was needed and where. Yet our president asked nothing of us.

President Bush could have called for a new wave of national service, to send American volunteers to other countries where they could help people understand our good intentions, and teach the world that the country with the fastest growing freely worshiping Muslim population is the United States.

He could have said, "You know what, the only reason we do 'bidness' in the Middle East is because we're in a marriage of convenience, and the dowry is oil. So let's try to save some energy, and stop relying on Saudi Arabia, the country that not only gives us oil, but gave us fifteen of the nineteen September 11 hijackers."

He could have said, "This attack really helped push a teetering economy over the edge, and now the war on terror is going to call for new resources to make our country safer. So maybe you millionaires could hold off on that $53,000 I decided to give you each and every year in a tax cut."

Instead, in his speech before a joint session of Congress, this is what he said: "Americans are asking, 'What is expected of us?' I ask you to live your lives and hug your children."

Live your lives and hug your children? If you feel like you're giving up something by living your life, you probably need professional help. And if hugging your child is a sacrifice, maybe parenting isn't your thing.

Later, when asked if there were sacrifices other than living and hugging that Americans could make, Bush answered, "Get on the airlines, get about the business of America."

Okay, we've got it. Live, hug, travel, shop.

Just to make sure we got the travel/shop message. Bush lent his image to a $20 million travel industry–sponsored TV advertisement (which seemed aimed at helping George W. Bush as much as our economy).

You know, Mary and I once did a couple of commercials for Heineken beer. Basically, it involved some footage of our house, with us arguing in the background, which we do very well. The point was that Heineken beer is as real as our household arguments.

I would call those commercials a lot of things: fun, easy, good-spirited, and a quick payday. However, I would not call them an economic stimulus program for Amsterdam or a personal sacrifice on behalf of the Netherlands.

Bush compared September 11 to Pearl Harbor. Look at what Franklin Roosevelt had to say to the American people after Pearl Harbor:

> Not all of us can have the privilege of fighting our enemies in distant parts of the world. Not all of us can have the privilege of working in a munitions factory or a shipyard, or on the farms or in oil fields or mines, producing the weapons or the raw materials that are needed by our armed forces.
>
> But there is one front and one battle where everyone in the United States—every man, woman, and child—is in action, and will be privileged to remain in action throughout this war. That front is right here at home, in our daily lives, in our daily tasks. Here at home everyone will have the privilege of making whatever self-denial is necessary, not only to supply our fighting men, but to keep the economic structure of our country fortified and secure during the war and after the war.

Then FDR went on to lay out seven sacrifices that the American people would have to make—everything from raising taxes to rationing commodities. He continued:

> *The blunt fact is that every single person in the United States is going to be affected by this program. Some of you will be affected more directly by one or two of these restrictive measures, but all of you will be affected indirectly by all of them.*
>
> *Are you a businessman, or do you own stock in a business corporation? Well, your profits are going to be cut down to a reasonably low level by taxation. Your income will be subject to higher taxes. . . .*
>
> *Are you a retailer or a wholesaler or a manufacturer or a farmer or a landlord? Ceilings are being placed on the prices at which you can sell your goods or rent your property.*
>
> *Do you work for wages? You will have to forgo higher wages for your particular job for the duration of the war.*
>
> *All of us are used to spending money for things that we want, things, however, which are not absolutely essential. We will all have to forgo that kind of spending. Because we must put every dime and every dollar we can possibly spare out of our earnings into war bonds and stamps. Because the demands of the war effort require the rationing of goods of which there is not enough to go around. Because the stopping of purchases of nonessentials will release thousands of workers who are needed in the war effort.*
>
> *As I told the Congress yesterday, "sacrifice" is not exactly the proper word with which to describe this program of self-denial. When, at the end of this great struggle, we shall have saved our free way of life, we shall have made no "sacrifice."* [1]

No, I didn't know Franklin Roosevelt, Franklin Roosevelt was not a friend of mine, but I feel entirely comfortable in saying: George W. Bush, you're no Franklin Roosevelt.

Did George W. Bush lead by calling out the best in us? No. Instead, with one breath he tells our men and women in uniform that they may have to give it all and then tells every other American that they can have it all. Next to a president like FDR, Bush looks and sounds like a pissant.

George W. Bush will never get it. Greatness isn't measured in the number of American flag lapel pins we wear, or the number of GOD BLESS THE USA stickers we have on our SUVs, or even how much we shop. Leadership isn't about doing all you can to stop a train from leaving the station, then jumping on board and pretending you're the conductor (as he does on every issue that average Americans like but he doesn't). It's about rising together to meet shared challenges. It's about doing collectively what none of us could do alone.

That attitude explains why the quintessential Republican question, "Are *you* better off now than you were four years ago?," is so flawed.

Now, I'll wager that even they aren't dumb enough to be asking that question this time around, because there's not more than a handful of Americans who can answer in the affirmative, much less a majority. But it's because they insisted on asking that question so much, for so long, that we're in the mess we're in today.

If Republicans insist on asking questions about how we're doing as individuals, the Democratic question needs to be about something larger—it needs to be about where we're headed together, as a nation. If you hear a Republican stupid enough to ask: "Are you better off now than you were four years ago?" you need to shoot right back at them: "Is *America* better off now than it was four years ago?"

The answer, I'm sad to say, is that it is not.

But did Democrats offer the bold, visionary solutions that are the hallmark of our party? Sadly, we did not.

.167 REPUBLICANS

Oh, but have faith. No matter how bad things are for Democrats, no matter how weak or divided our party may seem, we need to remember that even failure is relative, and in the last three years, Republicans have failed the American people in every way that leaders can fail the folks they're supposed to serve. You don't have to take my word for it. After all, everyone knows I'm a partisan, dyed-in-the-wool, liberal pitbull. If George W. Bush walked on water, I'd be the guy out there yelling that the man can't swim. Let's try to come up with a measure other than the Carville commonsense standard by which to judge the success or failure of our government under Republican control. Somewhere, it must be written what our government is supposed to do. Someone must have laid out a government's responsibilities. Wait, I vaguely remember a minor document in our history that tells us exactly what our government is supposed to do. I believe it's called the Constitution—and its Preamble lays it out.

Let's take a look and see what the Preamble to our Constitution says about how to measure the success or failure of those who govern. If you don't have your own copy, I'm sure you can find one in the trash outside of John Ashcroft's office. If you do have a copy, start reading. You'll quickly see that there are basically six things the United States government is supposed to do:

1. "Form a more perfect Union"
2. "Establish justice"
3. "Insure domestic tranquility"
4. "Provide for the common defense"
5. "Promote the general welfare"
6. "Secure the blessings of liberty to ourselves and our posterity"

You don't even need to read the whole Constitution to see this. It's all right there in the Preamble. Six things—the rest is just process. So, if you count tough talk and a willingness to invade countries for no apparent (or honest) reason as "providing for the common defense," then the way I see it, the folks in charge right now are batting 1 for 6. That's a batting average of .167. In baseball, that doesn't just get you sent to the showers, it doesn't just get you sent to the minors—it gets you sent into a new line of work. One sixty-seven isn't good enough for America, either.

Provide for the common defense? As I said, I'm being really generous in giving them this one—and I'm only giving it to them because they talk about it so damn much. In all honesty, this is like those first 200 points on the SAT—you get them basically for signing your name. That's because talking tough, wrapping yourself in the flag, and turning America into the playground bully that nobody likes is one thing, but taking the steps militarily, diplomatically, and domestically to make America safer is another. We'll discuss this at greater length in the next section.

Promote the general welfare? The key word here is "general." They've certainly promoted the welfare of the well-off, but average Americans have actually seen their incomes decline.[2] Poverty has risen for two straight years[3] and, after declining for the two years before Bush came to office, the number of Americans without health insurance has grown by 3.8 million.[4] They haven't promoted the general welfare; they've guaranteed that a lot more people will need welfare!

Secure the blessings of liberty to ourselves and our posterity? Let's see here, the only thing that we seem to be intent on leaving our children these days is a mountain of debt. We're not going to leave them clean water, or healthy forests, or a commitment to their education. At this rate, the only thing we're going to secure for our children is a roll of duct tape and a world that hates them because they were born American. Then we're going to saddle them with debt and ride them like pack mules into the sunset of our lives.

Establish justice? Please. Two words: John Ashcroft. This man wants a small government all right. He wants it so small that it can fit into your bedroom, your computer, and your phone. To John Ashcroft, the Constitution isn't a sacred document. It isn't even a road map. It's a speed bump. I wouldn't be surprised if he tried to lock me up for just saying that. Then add some right-wing judges who want to roll back decades of progress on civil rights and women's rights and workers' rights to the mix—and you see that establishing justice is not a priority for these guys.

How about ensuring domestic tranquility? George W. Bush came to office promising to "change the tone"—but he's succeeded in polarizing our nation like never before: rich against poor, young against old, urban versus rural. Thanks to George W. Bush, America is angry and divided. The only tranquility this administration has achieved is the fact that more than 3 million people who had jobs when President Bush took office are now sitting tranquilly on their couches.[5]

Form a more perfect Union? The income gap between rich and poor is growing. A smaller percentage of Americans has a greater percentage of the wealth than at any time in recent history,[6] and Republicans are proposing to make that gulf even wider. Republicans have fought hard against reforms that would guarantee that every vote is counted, and race relations have been strained by a president who believes the only type of affirmative action we need is the kind that gets the underachieving sons of important people into Yale.

☆ ☆ ☆

This is the result of three short years of governing by .167 Republicans. So, if Republicans aren't working for any of the goals our founders laid out, what are they working for?

In a word: power.

They are the power party. They serve solely in the interest of power. Their entire political machine—including the institutions of government—has been set to work trying to gain power, consolidate it, expand it, and use it, and not to the benefit of the country as a whole.

Since they've been in office we've seen an incredible transfer of power and wealth to powerful and wealthy people.

They've been working for the people who cut down the forests, not the families that enjoy them. They side with the drug companies, not the people who need the medicine. Their rules benefit the finance companies, not the retirees who depend on them. They seek to make things easier for the energy companies, not the people who work for them.

It's about accumulating ever greater power and wealth in the hands of the wealthy and powerful through tax cuts, deregulation, and flat-out crony capitalism.

When people ask me what the difference is between the Democratic and Republican parties, this is the crux of it:

A Republican is willing to take on people in the interest of power.

A Democrat should *never* be afraid to take on power in the interest of people.

When you take the Republican predilection for power to its logical conclusion, you get a vision of American society where the only good regulation is a dead one, where the best rate of taxation is none, and where the heavy hand of government will no longer press down upon the populace.

Recently, we've seen such a place. A place where all regulation was a thing of the past, where all taxes were gone, and where people were free to pursue their hopes and dreams unfettered by a government that held them back. The date was April 2003. The place was Baghdad, Iraq.

WHAT CAN WE DO?

There is only one entity that has any ability to stand up to the power the right-wingers are accumulating, and that is a more aggressive federal government. The only explanation I've come up with as to why the right hates the federal government is that they don't want anything to be more powerful than their friends and contributors. I believe, and I'm not afraid to say it, that the government should always be the most powerful interest in our country. Of course, right-wingers will rant and rave that our founders wanted smaller government, and that's not untrue. They wanted smaller government because, in those days, the government was the biggest threat to citizen power. Today, corporations are the great threat to citizen power. They have the ability to abuse em-

CARVILLE'S TEN RULES FOR PROGRESSIVES TO LIVE BY

1. **Stop Apologizing for Everything.** You are a member of the party that beat the Depression, won two world wars, cut elderly poverty by two-thirds, and is responsible for the greatest periods of economic growth since World War II. Democrats wake up and start looking for someone to apologize to. Stop it. You've got nothing to apologize for.

2. **Quit Conceding That the Other Side Has a Point.** I taught school for a little while, and guess what? There is such a thing as a stupid question. The same goes for opinions. Not everyone has a valid point. The next time a right-wing nut tells you that the Bush plan gives the poor a lot of incentive to get rich, don't say, "Well, you've got a point." They don't have a point. What they're saying is stupid. Sometimes a mind is like a mouth: you just got to shut it.

3. **Be Big:** Think only of, and talk only about, big things. When I advise candidates, I tell them it is okay to have an opinion on everything, it is just not okay to render said opinion on everything. I may favor a transgender amendment. But if I were running for president, I would not make that part of my core platform of ideas.

4. **Be Positive.** I grew up in the town of Carville, Louisiana—so named because my family provided the town with its most indispensable federal employee, its postmaster. When I was growing up, my daddy convinced me that I was living in the best place in the world. He always made sure I remembered that we had the best climate, the best people, the best family, the best soil, the best peaches—the best everything. "Of any place that you could live in the world," he'd tell me, "you're living right here in Carville, Louisiana." Man, I thought it was the garden spot of the uni-

verse. Did I know that there were places where the heat index wasn't a hundred gazillion on an August day? No. Did I know that there was a Broadway or a Michigan Avenue or a Rodeo Drive? No. And I didn't give a damn. Progressives are genetically inclined to talk about how bad things are. We'd rather be the skunk than enjoy the garden party. We need to be able to see the good—and make a case for making it better. In short, we need more of my daddy's Carville attitude in Washington and less of our liberal activist carping one.

5. **Use Their Weapons Against Them.** Republicans love to talk about right and wrong. They do so with an absolutely religious fervor—and that makes sense because more than a small number of them use their religion as a justification for their policies. If they're going to do that, it's fair for us to ask questions like "Is cutting funds for the schools that educate the kids of the people fighting for us in Iraq a bad, stupid right-wing policy, or is it an affront to God?" "Is rolling back clean water protections so your rich contributors can blight the environment bad policy, or is it a sin for which you can burn in hell?" For more on this, see the discussion of Alabama governor Bob Riley in Part Five.

6. **Attack Their Lack of True Patriotism.** There are actually some people who will buy a used car from the dealer with the biggest flag. He's usually the guy with the biggest mouth, too. The same goes for politics. We shouldn't look for the biggest flag or listen to the biggest mouth—we should look for the real patriots, the ones who are willing to tell the truth and make America stronger. It is completely antithetical to the American ideal of generational promise to burden future generations with a massive amount of debt. Every American child has heard the story from his or her parents or grandparents about how they worked hard to make things better for the next generation. They struggled to be the first in their family to finish high school, so that the next generation could be the first to finish college, so that the next could be the first to finish graduate

school. And whether our family came here on the *Mayflower* in 1620 or from Manila in 2003, we all share the belief that America is not just a good place today, but is going to be a better place tomorrow. Republicans have destroyed that. Being an American, honoring the flag, is much more than some trumped-up staged landing on an aircraft carrier. Just having a lot of red, white, and blue bunting at your convention isn't patriotic. Their lack of understanding of what this country is really about demonstrates a total lack of patriotism. We need to call them out on it.

7. **Never Just Oppose, Always Propose.** I can tell you with absolute certainty that back in 680 B.C., the first sentence of the first speech in the first campaign of the first Athenian running for City-State Council was this: This election presents a choice. Every election is a choice, and as progressives, our goal must be to ensure that the choice isn't between bad and nothing; the choice needs to be between bad and good. We progressives need to define our vision of America, not just react to the right wing's vision of America. We don't like the America they want to build, we need to show Americans something better.

8. **Don't Let the Little Crap Get in the Way of the Big Shit.** You have to pardon my language, but I just don't know a better way of saying it. As progressives we need to do more than fight symbolic battles, we need to be driving toward a larger goal. For example, the big shit is energy independence. The little crap is drilling in the Arctic National Wildlife Refuge. (For more on this, see chapter 6 on the environment and energy.) I once asked a friend of mine who was very active in the environmental movement, "Would you trade off a fuel standard that freed us from Middle Eastern oil for drilling in ANWR?" He said no. To me, that's an example of the little crap getting in the way of the big shit. Would you trade off late-term abortions for universal health care? To me, the great gain of universal health care is far more important than the largely symbolic battle over a little-used procedure. Don't get me wrong; symbolic fights are periodically worth fighting.

I have nothing against them, and I'm not saying we should abandon our principles. What I'm saying is that we should be willing to make trade-offs to advance them.

9. **Sometimes You've Got to Be Willing to Fight. Period.** Why is it that Democrats were calling on Al Gore to concede the election when no Republicans called on George Bush to concede? Why didn't we want to fight as badly as they did? Why didn't we call on *Bush* to concede? Because our nature is not to be tough. If I've said it once, I've said it a million times: America will never trust a party to defend America that fails to defend itself.

10. **Stop Brown-nosing the Elites.** I believe that in the 180 days prior to any election, candidates should be required to stay away from cocktail parties, dinner parties, or any social event that occurs in the following areas:
   - Georgetown
   - Foxhall
   - Spring Valley
   - Bethesda
   - Old Town Alexandria (where Mary and I live)
   - McLean
   - Chevy Chase . . .

. . . and other bastions of stupidity inside the Washington Beltway.

One of the reasons that Tom DeLay is so successful is that he doesn't give a damn what any people in any of these neighborhoods think. Democrats tend to become completely paralyzed by it. I can't tell you the number of times in a Democratic meeting where someone says that such-and-such was said at so-and-so's dinner party, and that the deputy assistant to the associate editorial page editor at *The Washington Post* rolled her eyes. Everybody freaks out. For reasons not completely understandable to me, the effect is far greater on Democrats than on Republicans. This is a disease we must cure ourselves of.

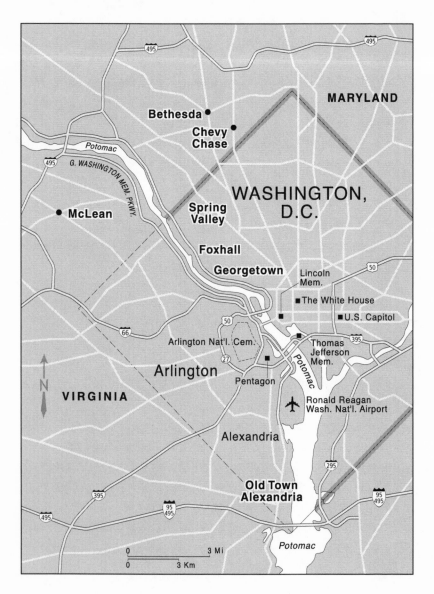

ployees, shareholders, customers, neighbors, and the environment. The only force powerful enough to stop that abuse is government, which is why rich people and corporations either want to shrink our government or own it. Republicans are helping them do both.

Republicans talk sanctimoniously about small government as if obsequious praise for small government were proof of their virtue—even though there's nothing virtuous about it. Republicans want smaller government for the same reason crooks want fewer cops: it's easier to get away with murder.

"But James," you ask, "you say with one breath that you are skeptical of power, but with your next breath you say that you want a more active federal government to stand up to that power. Can't the government be an instrument of tyranny?"

Most assuredly so.

But, here's the key difference: in our government, we can change the board of directors, we can change the management.

We couldn't change the people in charge of Enron . . . or WorldCom . . . or any of the places that bankrupted millions of Americans—at least not until they'd screwed the stockholders and employees and everybody else. We can't change the lobbyists and influence-peddlers who do their bidding.

But we can decidedly change the way the federal government does business. That's what elections are for. And that's why we've got to start winning them. It is long past time for the American people to say that we've had enough, and that we're going to fight back, and we're going to take back the White House, the Congress, and the country.

☆   ☆   ☆

Here's how this book is going to work: we're going to take some of the most important issues facing our country today, outline each problem, and take a look at what President Bush has done about it. Then we're going to write up some real answers to the problem that makes sense. In some cases, that means outlining a solution that already exists. In others, it means coming up with some fresh new ideas. The bottom line is that we're going to be real jackasses, but we're going to do more than kick down some right-wing barns . . . we're going to get back into the business of building as well.

Through it all, we're going to spice it up with some other thoughts I have, some stories I want to share, and, of course, what would a Carville rant be without a Carville recipe or two?

At the end of the day, we'll have a nice little progressive playbook that you can flash at people when they tell you how great George W. Bush is, that you can reference when people say that Democrats have no ideas, and that you can throw at people when you've truly had enough.

COOKING WITH GAS

I'm proud to say that I'm not the only Ragin' Cajun in Democratic politics today. My friend Donna Brazile is from Kenner, Louisiana, just about an hour from my hometown of Carville. (Donna's actually a Ragin' Creole. We once got in heated discussion about the difference between Cajun and Creole. Donna distilled the difference down to this: "Creoles put butter on our sausage, and you all just eat the stuff plain.") Despite the Cajun-Creole difference, we do have a lot in common. We both grew up on waterfront property, which, in Bayou country, means that the minute it starts raining, you get the Mississippi River in your front yard. We were both raised to believe that the four seasons are mardi gras, crawfish, shrimp, and crab. We both know our third, fourth, and fifth cousins by name. And we also both went to LSU.

Donna ran Al Gore's campaign, and won every vote she needed except the five on the Supreme Court. She helped Mary Landrieu win her Senate seat in Louisiana and give life to the demoralized Democrats. She's got a saying that when things are really moving, you're cooking with gas.

You're about to get a headful of good arguments and good information, and I don't believe you should try to fill a head without first filling a stomach. So since we're about to get things moving in this book, I think it's only fitting that we do some cooking with gas, too.

Red Bean Soup

This is a red bean soup recipe that my momma, Miss Nippy, and one of her best friends, Mrs. Abbie Hasten, concocted. While all my Jewish friends' mothers were serving them chicken soup, my momma was serving me this. And if chicken soup cures a cold, I'll wager that this'll cure cancer.

> 1 pound dried kidney beans
> 2 smoked ham hocks or ham bone or 1 pound salt or pickled meat
> 1 large onion, chopped
> 3 cloves garlic, chopped
> A couple of tablespoons of my brother Bill's seasoning mix
>   (3 teaspoons ground red pepper, 1 teaspoon thyme,
>   2 teaspoons chili powder, 2 teaspoons oregano, 2 teaspoons
>   white pepper, 4 teaspoons paprika, 2 teaspoons salt)
> 3 quarts water
> 1 pound smoked sausage (sorry, Donna, no butter)

The following are all optional:

> **½ bunch of green onions, chopped**
> **Worcestershire sauce, to taste**
> **½ bunch parsley, chopped**
> **Juice of 1 lemon**
> **Sherry or red wine**
> **1 lemon, sliced**
> **Hard-boiled eggs, sliced**
> **Croutons**

1. In a large heavy Dutch oven, soak beans in water overnight. (An alternate method is to cover the beans with water and bring to a boil. Turn off heat and let stand 1 hour to tenderize.) Drain. Return to pot and cover with water.
2. Add ham hocks (or ham bone or salt or pickled meat), onions, garlic, and seasoning mix to taste.
3. Cover and simmer over medium heat for 2 hours or until beans are tender.
4. Pulverize beans in a food processor. Remove and set aside.
5. Skin sausage and pulverize in food processor or blender.
6. Return beans and sausage mixture to pot. Add 2 quarts water.
7. If desired, add green onions. Cook an additional 20 minutes.
8. For additional flavor, Worcestershire sauce can be added.
9. When serving, sprinkle parsley, add lemon juice and red wine or sherry, if desired. Garnish with lemon slices and sliced hard-boiled eggs and top with croutons, if desired.

Yield: 12 servings

When I tell you this soup is good, it's *ridiculously* good.

★ PART ONE ★

"THE COMMON DEFENSE"

✶   ✶   ✶

A couple of months ago, I went to speak to the Panetta Institute. It's a public policy study center run by Leon Panetta and his wife, Sylvia. Leon Panetta is one of my favorite people in public service. Leon was an eight-term member of Congress from California, head of the Office of Management and Budget, and, later, President Clinton's chief of staff. I have nothing but respect for the guy. In fact, I was the unwanted, unpaid, unappreciated campaign manager trying to get Al Gore to pick Leon to be his running mate in 2000.

Now he runs this public policy center, and as part of my visit, he brought in a bunch of policy students to ask me questions. The first question I was asked out of the box was: "If the 2004 election comes down to the Bush folks saying it's about defense and the Democrats saying it's about the economy, who do you think will win?"

I get asked questions like this a lot, so I've thought about it a bit. My response was that the Democrat would have to be awfully stupid to let that happen, and here's why: The president has hundreds of thousands of people who work for him. He's got the Treasury Department, the State Department, the Defense Department, the Justice Department, the Agriculture Department, the Labor Department, and all the other departments and agencies. He can call on any cabinet secretary at any time, and they can call on the thousands of people who work for them. He has a big airplane. The airplane has an office in it. He has a big house, and the National Park Service takes care of it for him. He gets wake-up calls in the morning. People do his schedule for him. They write his speeches for him. He has someone drive him around, and when he's on the road, he doesn't encounter other traffic or have to stop for red lights.

Will the election be about foreign policy or the economy? You know what—he's the president; he's supposed to be able to do *both*.

Oh, and by the way, he should be able to handle health care, and education, and the environment, and crime and all that other stuff, too. If he can't or won't, he should be out on his ass.

Nobody ever got drafted into the job of being president of the United States. Every SOB who occupied that office got there by fighting for it, clawing for it, working through eighteen-hour campaign days, having reporters pick apart their résumés, disrupting their family, raising money, kissing ass, begging for votes.

So if a Democrat is going to do all of those things to become president, if they're going to scramble for every advantage so that they and their ideas have a chance to influence the direction of America, why would they ever cede a single issue of importance? Would FDR have said, "I think I can whip this Great Depression thing, but we'd better let somebody else have at the Nazis"? Heck, no. So why would you say that you'd be better on the economy, and then concede that George W. Bush is doing foreign policy better than you could anyway—especially when my two dogs could handle our foreign policy better than George W. Bush has.

If Democrats find themselves saying that this upcoming election is a choice between foreign policy and the economy, then we've *already* made a stupid, ignorant, jackass choice. I, for one, won't stand for seeing my party be silent on a single issue that matters to the American people.

I will, however, tell you exactly where this fallacy that we have nothing to say on issues of national security comes from. One of the things that happens in Washington, D.C., is that there are a number of times a year where the entire party apparatus goes away to some fancy resort and has a big retreat. Both Democrats and Republicans do this. They bring pollsters and consultants and media people out to give speeches and do demonstrations for the elected officials, who are sup-posed to absorb this wisdom and return to Washington as better public servants. This has been going on for many years. There are sessions on policy, and direct mail, and all the other nuts and bolts of politics. You hear what the national committee is doing, how the fund-raising is going, who the exciting new candidates are—all that stuff. Of course, there's plenty of time for nice meals and a round or two of golf.

Now I can't tell you for sure what happens at the Republican re-treats, but at the Democratic retreats, some pollster—and these guys are my friends, so it's not entirely their fault, because pollsters can only empirically tell you what people think—gets up in front of a screen and shows you a lot of graphs and charts which can, year after year, be summed up like this: "The public agrees with us on X, therefore we need to talk about X." X is usually prescription drugs, or Social Security, or education. Just as predictably, they will say: "Republicans have a pretty big advantage on Y, therefore we shouldn't be emphasizing Y very much." Y is almost always national defense. As a result, years of assem-bled Democratic wisdom has convinced us that people are unwilling to hear what we have to say on national security issues. The result? We look weak and stupid because we heard some PowerPoint presentation on a mountain in Virginia.

For years I've heard too many political professionals say that voters care more about the economy than foreign policy, and I've bitten my tongue—which is not an easy thing for me to do. After all, I'm just some rube from the South who didn't run a winning campaign until I was forty-two—so maybe the assembled wisdom of the Beltway graybeards is true. But I simply can't bite my tongue anymore—because here's something else that's true. There are about 50 million voters in this country who are either military veterans or retirees or their spouses. I've made a decent living off interpreting polls, but here's a case where I don't give a rat's ass what a poll says. When you've got 50 million Americans connected in some way to our military, defense and national security is always a top issue—especially after what happened to this country on 9/11. No Democrat should ever, ever forget that. And no Democrat should cede the issue of defense, not one damn inch.

That's why, in the first part of this book, we're going to take it into this administration's supposed wheelhouse. We're going to start with the issues that fall under the scope of "providing for the common defense"—homeland security and foreign policy, including the war in Iraq. We're going to take a real good look at what Republicans and the administration are doing on these issues, and we're going to do it not because we don't love this country (as they will certainly claim) but because we do.

I

HOMELAND SECURITY

E very time someone asks me, "What's wrong with the Democratic Party today?" I say, "Got a week?" It's a flip answer, it gets a laugh, and then I sneak away without really responding. The truth is, everything you need to know that's wrong with the Democratic Party can be found in one, big, cautionary tale: the debate over a Department of Homeland Security. Why homeland security? For starters, this debate could have and should have been about everything that is *right* about the Democratic Party. It was an example of a new and grave challenge that called for a new and innovative solution. Democrats came up with such a solution and pushed for it. Public opinion was in our favor. Yet faster than you can say "lily liver," our party ended up on the defensive, looking like we were obstructing, having to answer claims that we were weak, and ultimately getting creamed at the polls. It came to symbolize everything that is wrong with the way Democrats are doing business.

It's a cautionary story, a difficult one to tell and a painful one to hear. But it's worth listening to. So, kids, come gather 'round. Uncle James is going to tell you a homeland security fairy tale.

A Homeland Security Fairy Tale

Once upon a time there was a kingdom that was the strongest, richest kingdom in all the land. It was ruled by a young and untested king named King George the Second, and his loyal and ruthless adviser, Turdblossom.*

George II and Turdblossom had reclaimed the family throne from King Bubba, and while the villagers had loved King Bubba, he had made the village so safe and so wealthy that they figured King George couldn't screw it up too bad. Plus, King George seemed to want to give them a lot of their money back, which the villagers liked.

One horrible day, the kingdom was ruthlessly attacked, and thousands of villagers lost their lives. It was a sad day in the kingdom.

Now, the people of the kingdom were scared. They didn't know if more attacks were coming, and they wanted the kingdom to be safe, so they looked to King George the Second. King George II knew he had to do something, so he huddled with Turdblossom, and issued a declaration. "Each day, I will raise a different color flag over the kingdom," George II decreed proudly. "The color of the flag will tell you how safe you are."

The people asked, "How will this make us safer?"

*A turdblossom is an expression for a flower that grows out of a cow pie. It is also one of George W. Bush's nicknames for Karl Rove. Of course, any resemblance between characters in this story and actual people is completely coincidental.

King George replied, "Because on different days, the color will be different, and when the color is different, you will know to behave differently. For example, an orange flag means to be more scared than a green flag. And a red flag means that you should hide under a table or a bale of hay for a day or two." (Sometimes the questions the villagers asked infuriated King George.)

Not surprisingly, the villagers were not satisfied, so they asked the village council to help them think of ways other than variously colored flags to make the kingdom safer.

They sought out the advice of the wise elders, Sir Gary of Hart and Sir Warren of Rudman, who had been thinking of ways to make the kingdom safer for years. Sir Gary and Sir Warren dusted off an old report that they had tried to give to King George, but which King George had ignored, and began to read it to the villagers:

"The guards are very good at guarding," the two elders told the villagers. "But they only guard their own area. They do not talk to each other. And they don't talk to the gatekeepers. And the gatekeepers don't talk to the boiling tarmakers, and the boiling tarmakers don't talk to the drawbridge operators, and the draw-bridge operators don't talk to the moat-tenders. It is a royal mess.

"Here is what you must do," said Sir Gary and Sir Warren. "You must bring all of these people together and create one group in charge of kingdom security. Then you must give those people some new equipment—telescopes, anti-battering-ram technology, that sort of thing—so that they can do this new job even better."

One of the members of the village council, Joe the Saint, said, "This idea is good. I will bring it before the village council."

King George and Turdblossom were watching all of this with displeasure.

"Why don't they like the flags?" asked King George.

"We've got a bigger problem than that," said Turdblossom. "They will listen to Joe the Saint, and they'll like his plan . . . and maybe they'll even want him to be king. We must come up with something."

So King George and Turdblossom dispatched their trusty servants to a dungeon deep below the castle to come up with their own kingdom security plan.

Meanwhile, Joe the Saint and the village council agreed on their kingdom security plan and asked King George to consider it.

"Never shall this pass," said King George II.

"Please reconsider," said Joe the Saint and the members of the village council. "It is a good idea, we all agree it should be done, and those colored flags just leave everyone confused."

"Never shall this pass!" repeated King George II. And his anger grew at the village council. He wanted them banished for questioning him. But he knew they were right.

At that moment, the trusty servants emerged from the dungeon with their plan. When George and Turdblossom looked at it, they saw that it was almost the exact same plan as that of the village council.

And so the next day, King George called all the people of the kingdom together. With much fanfare, and great blaring of trumpets, King George announced his kingdom security plan. "A new day of kingdom security is upon us!" he declared.

But the village council had some concerns. They saw that the plan required some of the guards to shift their posts. And it said that some of them might have to wear less armor, so they could move more quickly. And because the village council spoke for the guards, too—they were the ones who now said, "Never shall this pass"—they did not approve the plan.

And as the village council sought to see that the guards were not mistreated, Turdblossom and King George saw their opportunity to get revenge on the village councillors who had questioned them.

Every day, King George came to speak from his balcony. "The village council does not want you to be safe," he proclaimed.

"The village council must be working for the people who attacked us!" he cried.

"The village council is weak and unpatriotic!" he bellowed.

"The village council cannot be trusted with the safety of the kingdom!" he declared.

As the days passed without a kingdom security plan, the villagers began to agree. Many of them took up the cry themselves.

After many weeks of hearing the king, new elections for village council were held, and only the candidates supported by the king won. The former village councillors were banished from the kingdom.

Turdblossom smiled. And his picture appeared on the cover of *Kingdomweek* magazine.

The king was happy.

The confusing, multicolored flags continued to fly.

The village councillors did not live happily ever after.

✮   ✮   ✮

You all get the picture. The president first took no action aside from appointing toothless Tom Ridge to create a nice threat-level color scheme for our nation. Soon, having a homeland security plan that an interior decorator could have come up with became unsustainable, especially given the fact that Joe Lieberman's committee—on a party-line vote, which is to say that no Republicans supported it—had passed a bill creating a Department of Homeland Security. That's when the president completely reversed course, took a Democratic idea, made it worse, and then beat us to a pulp with it.

It was a cynical, ugly, mean-spirited ploy—and it worked better than Turdblossom, er, Karl Rove ever could have hoped. Just look at what happened in the Senate race of Max Cleland of Georgia. Max Cleland is a war hero and an inspiration. He is a Bronze and Silver Star winner who lost three limbs to a grenade explosion in Vietnam. After the war, he willed himself to health and eventually won office as a Georgia state senator. President Carter made him his head of Veterans Affairs. While he was there, Max not only improved the lives of America's veterans, he personally won an award for reducing waste in government. See, his new position entitled him to a government car and a government driver. And even if his position hadn't allowed for that, certainly his disability would have. Max was having none of it. He had a seven-year-old Oldsmobile specially fitted so he could drive it himself and save the government a little money. War hero, solid Georgian, not wasteful of the government's money, centrist enough to support the president on a number of issues—you think George Bush gave a damn? Heck, no. Bush worked to unseat him by helping Saxby Chambliss of Georgia run the dirtiest, meanest campaign in recent memory. (Of course, that recent memory is pretty recent, because the campaign George W. Bush ran against John McCain in South Carolina was pretty damn dirty.) The centerpiece of the campaign involved Chambliss— a man who was unable to serve his country because of a bum knee even though he was a star baseball player at the University of Georgia (and remained a regular pickup basketball player as a member of Congress)—questioning Cleland's patriotism. At the heart of that strategy was a campaign commercial that featured a picture of Osama bin Laden and claimed that Max had stood with that guy by "voting against homeland security 11 times." Never mind that Max hadn't been voting *against* anything. In fact, he'd been voting for the department at a time when both Chambliss and Bush opposed it. Pretty unpatriotic, huh?

"Okay," you say. "So the guy's making a political issue out of a policy issue—nothing new there. After all, shouldn't good policy be good politics?" Here's the twist. Bush is making a policy issue into a political issue—and *ignoring* the policy. See, the work on homeland security shouldn't end with the creation of a new government department, it should *begin* there—and that's where Americans who actually care about our safety have an opening.

So, let's use the homeland security debate as the template for how we're going to deal with a lot of the big issues facing America today. We're going to lay out the problem, lay out the Bush solution, demonstrate how totally cockamamie it is, and then put forward a real solution—a strong, smart, winning solution that progressives can be for.

The Problem: On September 11, 2001, America suffered a devastating attack that took thousands of lives and laid bare the holes in the systems we rely upon to protect our nation and our people.

The Bush Response: Reject and then later support proposals for a unified Department of Homeland Security. Create a color-coded alert-level meter. Block homeland security funding. Blame others.

The "Had Enough" Solution: Create a unified homeland security agency, give police officers, firefighters, and local health officials the tools and training they need in case of emergency, and not only provide the funding but also do the creative thinking necessary to secure ports, borders, bridges, tunnels, food and water supplies, and the rest of the stuff we rely on.

THE PROBLEM IN DEPTH

It's a scary world out there.

● Today, out of every one hundred cargo containers that enter U.S. ports, somewhere between three and five are inspected. Six hundred thousand such containers arrive in the United States every day.

● Canadian intelligence sources estimate that fifty terrorist groups operate within their borders, including al Qaeda and Hamas. Yet, until recently we had only three hundred agents working the one hundred ports of entry along the three-thousand-mile U.S.-Canadian border. Not too long ago, only half of all ports of entry were staffed twenty-four hours a day.

● In the 1980s, South Africa stockpiled and weaponized a number of biological hazards, including forty-five types of anthrax as well as the bacteria that cause cholera and plague—many of which are now in private hands and some of which can no longer be accounted for.[1]

● Russia cannot account for some of its highly enriched uranium, and there have been forteen confirmed cases of trafficking in fissile material in that country.

● North Korea just admitted that it has nuclear weapons, and Iran is on its way. These aren't rich countries, so if they have something to sell, they've got no problem selling it, especially to folks that hate America.

● According to EPA figures, there are 125 chemical facilities in the United States where an accident could affect 1 million people; and 3,700 other facilities where an accident could endanger tens of thousands. And those numbers reflect the risk of what might happen if there's an *ac-*

cident, not a directed terrorist attack. Still, there haven't been any systematic efforts to provide greater chemical plant security.[2]

We know these threats. We know these weaknesses. We know al Qaeda is looking to exploit them. Not doing everything in our power to address them is nothing short of shameful.

When you run through all the bad things out there and the bad people who want to introduce us to those bad things, it makes me want to take my daughters inside and stay there. When enough sane people feel so insecure that they react this way, your homeland security problem becomes an economic problem, too. For both our safety and our economic security it is important we address this in the right way. Unfortunately, that's not what President Bush is doing.

THE BUSH RESPONSE IN DEPTH

1. Reject, then later accept a Department of Homeland Security.
2. Reject homeland security money.
3. Shortchange first responders.
4. Blame others.

Really, that's pretty much it. When I go and tell people that George W. Bush rejected Democratic efforts to strengthen homeland security, they can't believe it. They think, There goes ol' James again, shooting from the hip, holding another one of his dissertations without the benefit of any information. More than a few of them have asked me to prove it. So I went and did a little research, and came up with every time that George

W. Bush has rejected Democratic efforts to strengthen homeland security. Here's the secret history that George W. Bush doesn't want you to know:

November 14, 2001: Senate Democrats propose $15 billion for homeland security in an economic stimulus package. The White House warns of "permanent spending on other projects that have nothing to do with stimulus and that will only expand the size of government." (Just out of curiosity, which would you rather have: a $2.248 trillion government that doesn't keep you safe, or a $2.253 trillion government that does? I thought so.)

December 4, 2001: The Senate Appropriations Committee votes 29–0 for a bill that includes $13.1 billion for homeland security programs. One day later, President Bush threatens to veto it.

December 6, 2001: Senate Republicans reduce homeland security funding in the Defense Appropriations bill by $4.6 billion.

December 19, 2001: Under further pressure from the White House, conferees reduce funds by an additional $200 million. This reduction comes from the areas of airport security, port security, nuclear facility security, and postal security.

June 7, 2002: The Senate, by a bipartisan vote of 71–22, passes a spending bill that includes $8.3 billion for homeland security. The next day, the president's senior advisers recommend a veto of this *"excessive homeland security spending."*

July 19, 2002: Under pressure from the White House, homeland defense funding is reduced again. This time, the money comes out of food safety, cyber security, efforts so that police and fire radios can work together, nuclear security, increased lab capacity to determine whether biological or chemical weapons have been used, airport security, port security, and water security. Who cares about that stuff, anyway?

August 13, 2002: President Bush decides not to spend the $2.5 billion in emergency funding for homeland security. He casts his decision as one of "fiscal responsibility." The spineless press, which just saw him call for a tax cut 200 times that size, lauds him for his firm stand.

January 16, 2003: The White House reacts to Democratic efforts to in-crease homeland security funding by issuing a statement saying, "The Administration strongly opposes amendments to add new ex-traneous spending to the package." Later that day, Senate Republi-cans follow suit, voting against additional funds to implement the president's smallpox vaccine plan, among other things.

January 23, 2003: The Republican Senate cuts security programs in the Federal Emergency Management Agency, the FBI, the Immigration and Naturalization Service, the National Nuclear Security Admin-istration, and Transportation Security Administration and Coast Guard operations.

February 3, 2003: President Bush submits his 2004 budget. It reduces the budget for homeland security programs by 1.9 percent.

February 14, 2003: Senate Democrats introduce their economic recov-ery act. It includes money to fund the smallpox vaccine program, to get police and fire communications systems to work together, and to protect public transportation. No Republicans support it.

March 21, 2003: Republicans defeat a series of four amendments aimed at increasing security.

March 25, 2003: Republicans defeat three more amendments aimed at strengthening homeland security.

April 2, 2003: Senator Fritz Hollings of South Carolina offers an amendment to provide $1 billion for port security programs. Republicans reject the amendment by a vote of 47–52.

April 3, 2003: Republicans reject five more pro–homeland security amendments, including one to protect commercial aircraft from the threat of shoulder-fired missiles.

June 2003: In the House Appropriations Committee and later on the House floor, Republicans reject a Democratic amendment to add $1 billion for homeland defense, paid for by trimming a piece of the recently enacted tax break for two hundred thousand millionaires from $88,000 each to $83,000.

✷ ✷ ✷

By my count, that is twenty-one times that George W. Bush and congressional Republicans restricted or rejected the resources necessary to make us safer.

And how did Bush explain this behavior? He blamed others for being weak on homeland security. He would have gotten away with it completely, except that a high partisan voice rose to speak the truth and call Bush to account. This partisan charged that the Bush White House has been "factually inaccurate" in its attempts to blame Congress for the shameful failure to properly fund heroes like the firemen who rushed into two burning towers on September 11. He said that Bush should "move on from this pointless and harmful debate." Who was this un-American pinko who dared criticize this president during a time of war? It was the Republican chair of the House Appropriations Committee—Congressman Bill Young.

I guess Mr. Young got a little fed up with George W. blaming Congress for all of those rejections we talked about earlier. In a letter that was leaked to *The Washington Post*, he wrote: "You can choose to continue the debate on this issue in this fashion, or we can be responsible and address the real issues facing first responders."

I guess Bush chose the former, because three weeks later, talking to the new employees of the Department of Homeland Security, he said, "I proposed record funding for the first responders. . . . Unfortunately the Congress . . . reduced my total request for state and local law enforcement and emergency personnel by $1 billion and designated part of the funding to go to other priorities."[3] This prompted another member of the House Republican leadership to fume, "If the president wanted the money, he should have asked for it. He never did."[4]

Basically, what Bush said right there was a lie. It was not a little lie about a little thing like sex. It was a big lie about a big thing—our safety and what he is doing about it.

The other thing we need to remember is that homeland security isn't a problem that is solved just by throwing money at it. I like to think of it this way: Not enough money can guarantee you a poorly protected nation, but a lot of money doesn't guarantee you a well-protected one. There's another ingredient, and that ingredient is creative thinking. Unfortunately, the White House is coming up short in this area as well. In a speech at John Jay College of Criminal Justice, Hillary Clinton described the Bush homeland security phenomenon pretty well in: "We have relied on a myth of homeland security, a myth written in rhetoric, inadequate resources, and a new bureaucracy, instead of relying on good old fashioned American ingenuity, might and muscle."[5]

You know why right-wingers hate her so much? Not because her book sold a million copies and my *Crossfire* co-host had to eat his shoe because of it, but because she knows what she's talking about.

THE "HAD ENOUGH" SOLUTION

When you've had enough of the empty rhetoric and the political posturing, it's time to get down and dirty and actually take some action. Homeland security is about more than reorganizing existing bureaucracies. It's about having the right focus and the right resources.

I bet I can tell you what's going to happen right now. We're going to get lazy. We're going to stop being vigilant. We're going to let down our guard. These things are inevitable. Equally inevitable is the fact that we will be attacked again. The folks who bombed the World Trade Center in 1993 didn't give up until they took it down in 2001. The folks who tried to take out an airplane with a shoulder-fired missile in Kenya in November 2002 missed. Do you think they're just going to pack up and give up? What are we waiting for? A passenger plane shot down as it leaves the runway? A mushroom cloud over one of our cities? We need to get serious about this, now.

I'll give President Bush some credit—we've done a decent job in working to prevent a repeat of the September 11 airplane attacks. By securing cockpit doors and improving the screening process, we took away the terrorists' ability to use the same tactics they used before (sure, those were Democrats' ideas, but one thing you come to accept in politics is that he who signs the bill gets the credit). In military circles, that's called being prepared to refight the same war. But we need to remember that al Qaeda is an entrepreneurial organization, and they aren't going to try to refight the same war. They're going to try to come up with something new and creative, and devastating. Al Qaeda was initially rocked back on its heels by our response in Afghanistan and elsewhere. Recently, however, we saw evidence that they are regrouping with the sophisticated attacks in Saudi Arabia and Morocco just days apart from one another. We have an increasingly limited time to put in place the systems that will prevent terrorists from doing what we know they want to do, keep them from getting their hands on the things they want to get their hands on, and make it difficult for them to attack things we know they want to attack.

Because no defense is perfect, we also need to have in place the systems to respond to any future attack with speed, sureness, and authority. If we don't use this feeling of urgency to put in place the systems to do those things now, we never will. And at some point, someday, we will pay the price.

Now, I'm no expert on this. But it seems to me that Democrats can take this issue back by calling up all of the smart people in Washington and asking them to sit down and make a list of things we need to do a better job of protecting. I'm just spinning these off the top of my head, but my guess is the list would look something like this:

Things to protect: ports, borders, bridges, tunnels, rails, water supply, food supply, computer systems, power grids, power plants (nuclear ones especially), chemical plants, supplies of biological agents.

Things to prevent: selling of nuclear materials, proliferation of chemical and nuclear weapons, information disconnects between the FBI and CIA, and between local and federal law enforcement.

Things to prepare: firefighters, police, and EMTs to deal with biological, chemical, and radiological attacks. Prepare the tools public health workers need to deal with outbreaks.

Once you have that list of things, we should go to experts in each of those areas and ask them how we can best protect, prevent, and prepare.

Protecting against rockets is rocket science. Protecting against terrorists isn't.

Michael O'Hanlon and Peter Orszag are both Brookings Institution
scholars who have been doing some creative thinking on this issue, and
here are some of the ideas they've come up with. These are things that
will protect America, that aren't being done, and that we should be
pushing to get down now.

Incentives to protect private sector infrastructure. Some of the
juiciest targets for terrorists are not "government" structures, like
bridges or tunnels or army installations. They are privately held things
like food-processing facilities, power grids, and chemical plants. Let's
go with the example of chemical plants for a second. I said before that
according to Environmental Protection Agency (EPA) figures, there are
125 chemical facilities in the United States where an accident could affect 1 million people, and 3,700 other facilities where an accident could
endanger tens of thousands. If those numbers reflect the risk of *accident*,
just think how devastating a terrorist *attack* on any one of these plants
could be. However, if you're a plant owner and you're trying to beat your
competitors, the odds that your plant is going to be the one out of thousands across the country that becomes the target of attack are so low
that it's not worth taking on any extra security costs. Of course, that's
not in the interest of the millions of people living near your plant. This is
a classic case in which the vaunted market, which Republicans love so
much, is providing you no incentive to beef up security around your
plant. At the same time, the government, which is run by a guy named
George W. Bush (whom a lot of these big plant owners gave money to)
doesn't want to hit you with burdensome regulations—after all, if you

give him a choice between rewarding campaign contributors versus protecting public safety, he'll need some time to think about it.

So what can we do? One creative idea is to require all chemical facilities to carry terrorism insurance. That imposes a certain cost on everyone—keeping the competitive playing field level. Of course, if you take safety measures, your insurance rates will go down—so this proposal provides a free market incentive to keep these plants safer. That's something progressives can and should get behind.

Cargo inspection. Ever driven by the port of New York and New Jersey and seen acres and acres of shipping containers? Well, 600,000 of those containers arrive every day in 361 seaports around America. Somewhere between 3 and 5 percent of them ever get inspected—which leaves, at best, 570,000 uninspected containers that arrive at a port, get offloaded, and hit the roads and tracks of this country every day.

At the same time, we know that Osama bin Laden has access to dozens of container ships, some of which delivered the explosives that were used to bomb our embassies in Kenya and Tanzania. We also know that a suspected member of al Qaeda attempted to stow away in a shipping container heading to Toronto. His container was nicer than my first apartment. It was furnished with a bed, a toilet, its own power source, a global satellite telephone, a laptop computer, an airline mechanic's certificate, and security passes for airports in Canada, Thailand, and Egypt. If that guy wasn't arrested at a port stop in Italy, where would he have showed up next?

Experts say they'd feel a lot more comfortable if we got that inspection number up to 10–20 percent of containers. If that's what the experts want, that should be our goal. One way we can do it is by securing megaports abroad. Over half of all the cargo we receive comes in from eight ports around the world. There are machines capable of sensing any radioactive material in any one of those ports. I'm no scientist, but they've been described to me as a kind of radar that sweeps the ports looking for radiation. But these machines aren't cheap. It would cost about $20 million to equip each port. So do the math. Eight ports at $20 million a port guarantees that half of all cargo doesn't have a dirty bomb in it—seventeen times more than our current level. To do that costs $160 million. By refusing to fund the container security initiative, President Bush is saying we don't have the money for it. Are you kidding me? For about one ten-thousandth the cost of his tax cuts, we could make ourselves 47 percent safer from dirty bombs than we are today. This is a misplaced priority of the highest order, and the man needs to be made to pay for it.

Surface-to-air missiles (SAMs). Again, we know al Qaeda wants to use SAMs to take down commercial jets. They tried to down an Israeli jet with shoulder-fired missiles in Kenya in November 2002. We've seen lots of shoulder-fired missiles floating around in Saudi Arabia. It's estimated that it would cost between $1 and $2 million per plane to equip our commercial fleet with countermeasures.[6] Other ideas include having planes constantly in the air looking for these little missiles. At the very least, there should be some increased perimeter patrols around airports. Each of these solutions is complicated. Each is expensive. But doing *something* is necessary, and it shouldn't take losing an American plane as it lifts off the runway before we take action.

Federal-state-local information sharing. One of the big problems on September 11 was a failure to "connect the dots." Say that over the course of a week, ten local police departments arrest people who are trespassing on the grounds of airports. To any one of those local police depart-

LOOKING FOR TERRORISTS,
OR DEMOCRATS?

What do Democratic state representatives from Texas have in common with terrorists hiding in America? The Department of Homeland Security has dedicated its resources to finding both of them.

When the Democratic Texas legislators left Austin in the summer of 2003 to protest Tom DeLay's attempts to rig Texas's congressional districts to gain seats for Republicans—the plan would have created such bizarre districts that one street in Austin would be divided into four congressional districts, one of which would have been connected by a milewide strip of land with the Mexican border about three hundred miles away—a couple of them took former Democratic Speaker Pete Laney's private plane to go to Oklahoma.

Someone (Rove? Bush? Tom Ridge? Governor Rick Perry?—we don't know, because the Texas Department of Public Safety destroyed all of the pertinent records) ordered the Air and Marine Interdiction Coordination Center, a federal Homeland Security agency, to track the plane, which it did.

Presumably the Department of Homeland Security should be spending its time looking for terrorists, not Democrats.

I don't know what scares me more: the stunning abuse of power that a federal Homeland Security agency was used for political espionage or that the agency was too incompetent to find the plane.[7]

ments, it's just one lone guy behaving oddly. Put all ten of them together, and you see a different picture: a coordinated attempt to scout out airports. That's the dot connecting that didn't happen before September 11 with a bunch of strange people attending flight schools. By coordinating computer systems and crime-tracking databases, we can connect the dots—and learn from the failures of September 11.

Coast Guard. Until September 11, our Coast Guard had roughly five missions: boater safety, drug interdiction, waterway usage monitoring, icebreaking, and navy fleet protection in wartime. After September 11, we added one more, but it was a biggie—homeland security functions. As a result, we've increased the Coast Guard's activity level by nearly half. However, we haven't increased its staffing, funding, or support by that much. That's a mistake that, unless we remedy it, will bite us in the collective ass.

✫　✫　✫

Those are just some of the good ideas out there that are being largely ignored by the Bush administration. So, you've got your good policy. We should write it up in a bill. The goal is to make America safer and get that bill passed. But, in the meantime, Democrats should be going out and making relentlessly good politics of it. See, if we are again to be a truly national party with a national message, we need to embrace these issues, not run from them. Part of the problem in 2000 was that even though we were right on the issue, we didn't want to talk about it. People are concerned about an uncertain world. That is the reality. It may not always be the most dominant concern at any given time; but it will now and forever be a concern. A national party needs to respond to the concerns of the American people. That's why people will listen to someone who sounds strong, even if they happen to be strong and wrong. In the last election, Republicans sounded like they had big ideas for making America safer— even though they were actually cutting homeland defense and using the war on terror to push for more tax cuts for their friends. The very fact that Democrats wanted to change the subject made Democrats less viable not only on this issue but on other national issues as well.

That's why we should take our new homeland security bill that we just wrote and wave it in President Bush's face at every opportunity. We should be hammering George Bush and the Republicans every day of the week—and twice on Sundays—until they decide to pass the thing. They're so happy to have the White House and both houses of Congress—we need to make people realize that if they're not going to use those pretty buildings to make Americans safer, they don't deserve offices in them. They're in charge. They've been pretty good at knocking government; it's now their job to run it. If they fail to govern, we have to make them pay. If George Bush looks at our bill we just wrote and wants to change something, we call him weak on homeland security. If he delays, you have people dressed up as terrorists waving signs that say: *Thank you for making sure that America remains an easy target.* Over the top? Yes. Tasteless? Yes. Is it any more over the top or tasteless than what they did to Max Cleland? Hell, no. And because of those tasteless, false attacks, Max isn't in the Senate anymore to join in the fight. They're not afraid to make strong claims that are false. We can't be afraid to make strong claims that are true. Because when you've had enough, you learn that you can't get tough on security issues by being weak in advocating your ideas.

2

MILITARY AND FOREIGN POLICY

All you ever needed to know about George Bush's foreign policy you saw when he landed on the aircraft carrier USS *Abraham Lincoln*.

I want to be totally clear here. I have no problem with George Bush visiting an aircraft carrier. I firmly believe that any U.S. commander in chief has the right to visit U.S. military personnel at any United States military installation, anytime, anywhere.

I do have a problem with the fact that the spectacular landing had as its premise a lie (the boat was too far out to take a helicopter), and that the speech he gave there was both triumphalist and deceptive (the battle of Iraq is over, we've won a victory in the war on terror).

I don't know what amazes me more, that the White House had the balls to pull it off or that the media bought it—tailhook, line, and sinker.

SUPPORT OUR TROOPS

George W. Bush loves our troops. He loves them as backdrops for his speeches. He loves them as props for his political events. Any chance he gets, he'll go and stand in front of them. The problem is that he won't stand behind them.

While our men and women in uniform have been fighting overseas, George W. Bush has been fighting to cut the things that matter to them and their families when they get home. President Bush and his Republican lackeys in Congress have proposed:

- $1.5 billion in cuts to military family housing, schools, and child care centers;
- $200 million in cuts to Impact Aid, the program that funds schools near military bases;
- Doubling the prices that veterans will pay for prescription drugs;
- Cutting veterans' medical care by suspending enrollments at VA health centers.

Heck, Bush has even tried to cut pay to soldiers in harm's way—proposing to roll back recent increases in monthly "imminent danger pay" (from $225 to $150) and family separation allowance (from $250 to $100).

That's right, the man who says we can afford trillions of dollars in tax cuts says that we can't afford $225 a month for people who are getting shot at. It just goes to show that when faced with the choice between supporting our troops or supporting his fat cat contributors, our commander in chief will take the Benjamins over the Joes any day of the week.

"I PROPOSE A TOAST"

So, with Mary Matalin as my witness, I hereby propose a toast to George W. Bush, our flyboy president:

Mr. President, I raise my glass of fine French wine to you. That landing was great political theater. Especially compared to the fact that the next day, John Kerry—a man who was earning his Silver Star, Bronze Star, and three Purple Hearts while you were earning your yellow beret—had to sit down and look presidential while debating Dennis Kucinich and Al Sharpton.

You had media outlets gushing about whether or not, while flying to the aircraft carrier, you would "take the stick." Never once did anyone mention that the last time you "took the stick" was in the Texas Air National Guard, and you disappeared for a year.

This was the photo-op of the century, no question. Michael Deaver on acid couldn't have conjured up this one. From now on, when people talk about pictures of politicians in military hardware, this is what everyone will think of. Somewhere in Massachusetts, Michael Dukakis is relieved.

When you got out of that plane, in that flight suit, with that swagger, even Rick Santorum found himself oddly drawn to you.

The U.S. Navy went to the trouble of stenciling *Navy One* on the side of your S-3B Viking. They might as well have written *Testoster One*. You could practically hear America's soccer moms swoon.

You were America's Top Gun, and—for a moment—you made America forget that your ego is writing checks that the U.S. Treasury can't cash.

Kudos, Mr. President. This was your day. I give you all the credit in the world. You were a star. You were like Harrison Ford in the movie *Air Force One*. Just like him, you were a pilot. Just like him, you played the part of a president. There's just one thing to remember: People liked that movie because, in the end, he got the terrorists.

WHAT TYPE OF LEADER LIKES WEARING
A MILITARY UNIFORM?

All children love to play dress up. Most people grow out of that phase. Some don't: J. Edgar Hoover, for example. Lots of little boys love to play soldier. Unless they actually become soldiers, most grow out of that phase, too. In fact, there's one group of people who almost never plays dress up and almost never plays soldier. Those people are democratically elected heads of state. So what type of leader likes playing dress up *and* playing soldier? Take a look at these photographs and see what they have in common.

Let's go through our drill.

The Problem: America's standing in the world is at an all-time low. The war on terrorism is unfinished. We've screwed up the rebuilding in Afghanistan and have a quagmire in Iraq.

The Bush Response: Pull out of international agreements, antagonize nations that don't agree with us (France, Germany, somehow we weren't even able to bribe Turkey), waltz into wars without planning for their aftermath, ignore threats like North Korea—do I need to go on?

The "Had Enough" Solution: True Leadership—a tough, strong America that tells the truth and leads the world rather than ignores it, making it easier to deal with all the other challenges we face.

THE PROBLEM IN DEPTH

It is a dangerous world out there. With the Cold War over (yes, Republicans, it is over, though I hate to be the one to break it to you), the fear of a common enemy no longer keeps allies by our side. At the same time, there are a whole bunch of new threats—terrorism, al Qaeda, proliferation, weapons of mass destruction—and we need allies more than ever to help us stamp these things out before they end up here. Somehow, we need to figure out how to use our strength in a way that protects our own interests, but also advances a common interest. Only then will we return to being respected, instead of what President Bush has made us, which is resented.

THE BUSH RESPONSE IN DEPTH

I gave the president credit for that landing because we should celebrate the man's one great foreign policy accomplishment—that he didn't look entirely foolish in a flight suit.

But Democrats, progressives, multilateralists, Francophiles, Francophobes—heck, even isolationists—should be deeply concerned about the course of America's foreign policy, the significance of diminishing America's standing in the world, the lies that led to war with Iraq, the fact that there was a plan to get us in but no plan for once we were in, and what our quagmire there means for our ability to rally allies and fight the war on terrorism.

I also want to be clear on another point. I am not a peacenik Democrat—nor do I think that's the way the Democratic Party needs to go. I was a corporal in the Marines, which, for a time, made me the highest-ranking military officer in the Clinton White House. Do I think we should avoid war wherever possible? Yes. But I also think that intelligent use of American military power can accomplish things—and we need to be clear about the things worth accomplishing.

I recently heard a story that made my skin crawl. It was about Karl Rove going around speaking to a bunch of Republicans and getting laughs when he talks about people who have come up to him in the supermarket and said, "I'm a Democrat, but I'm sure glad your boy won instead of mine."

The worst part of that story is that I believe it. I believe that there are self-hating Democrats who buy into that theory because I've seen them. So, in case you're one of those people who's inclined to say, "Golly, I sure love Democrats, but I want a tough-as-nails Republican in charge

NOT READY FOR DUTY?

There's a story that's been going around that at one of these fancy-schmancy black-tie Washington dinners, my buddy Al Franken walked up to Deputy Secretary of Defense Paul Wolfowitz and said, "Clinton's military did pretty well in Iraq, huh?" Reportedly, Wolfowitz responded by telling Al to go perform an anatomically impossible act.

The truth is, Al deserved a serious answer. After all, America's military performed brilliantly in both Afghanistan and Iraq. That's pretty impressive given that during his party's nomination speech, Bush said that military morale and readiness had plunged so far that "If called on by the Commander-in-Chief, two entire divisions of the Army would have to report, 'Not ready for duty, sir!' "

Did George W. Bush, the disappearing reservist, whip them into shape in record time? Or could this stunning display of military competence be attributed to something else? Let's ask Dick Cheney. Here's what he said in August 2000, before he was vice president: "A commander-in-chief leads the military built by those who came before him. There is little that he or his defense secretary can do to improve the force they have to deploy. It is all the work of previous administrations. Decisions made today shape the force of tomorrow . . . when that [first Persian Gulf] war ended, the first thing I did was to place a call to California, and say thank you to President Ronald Reagan . . ."[8]

Al Franken is still waiting for his answer, and Bill Clinton and Al Gore are still waiting for that call.

when the world gets ugly," let me remind you of one thing: To believe that we are better off in terms of foreign policy because George W. Bush is president is to believe that the smarter and more experienced man— Al Gore—would have put together an administration that would have done a worse job relating to the world and responding to the attacks of September 11.

In fact, I'll go a step further and say that I think if Al Gore was president, it is significantly less likely that the attacks of September 11 would have happened in the first place. Here's why. As vice president, Al Gore actually read all of his daily intelligence briefings, and made notes of questions he wanted answered in the margins. Gore was the one who had waiting for him, should he have been elected president, an actual plan to target and take out Osama bin Laden and his al Qaeda henchmen—the same plan that was given to Condoleezza Rice by Dick Clarke, the White House counterterrorism coordinator, and promptly put on the shelf, only to reappear again—according to the White House—on September 10.

Gore's national security adviser probably wouldn't have ignored Clinton's national security adviser, Sandy Berger, when he said that they should "spend more time on terrorism generally, and on al Qaeda specifically, than any other subject."[9]

Since Gore was one of the people urging the incoming Bush officials to consider using predator drones equipped with hellfire missiles against bin Laden, he probably wouldn't have pooh-poohed the idea— as the Bush folks did—only to realize after September 11 how effective it was.

Gore was a guy who wouldn't have taken a record number of days of vacation in the first year of his presidency, making it harder for him to get his briefings—including that fateful briefing Bush got in August while on his "ranch" * in Crawford that is alleged to have warned of terrorists seeking to smash planes into buildings.

---

*It's technically a farm—but this is another myth-making lie that the press swallowed whole. You need cattle to have a ranch.

I could make that argument, but I won't. Instead, let me just say this. Foreign policy has never been the sole province of Republicans. In fact, America's foreign policy vision has been largely and permanently shaped by Democrats. And Democratic presidents haven't been afraid of the title "Commander in Chief"; they've used it to commit American troops to fighting wars and keeping the peace. They have done it unabashedly and unashamedly.

It was Woodrow Wilson who shaped a new internationalism by committing U.S. troops abroad, but not as a conquering force. That was the first time our country ever did that. He saw the United States as a country that could lead and influence the world. Up until that point, America wasn't a world power.

Roosevelt wasn't afraid to lead America into World War II, and Harry Truman wasn't afraid to win it. Truman then went on to create organizations like the International Monetary Fund, the World Bank, and NATO—international bodies, of which the United States would be a leader—that advanced America's interests while solving international problems.

Yes, Vietnam divided and chastened our party, and gave rise to a skepticism that America is not a force for good. (Too often, that thinking still infects the left.) But, with the possible exception of what George W. Bush blundered into in Iraq, we haven't repeated the mistakes of Vietnam. And in 1992, it *was* the economy, stupid; but a lot of Democrats have forgotten that Bill Clinton took the foreign policy issue to George Bush—on the Balkans, for example. George W. Bush derided Clinton's "nation building" during the campaign, but he seems to rely on it now—even if he's doing a crappy job of it.

The point is we have a vision for America and for the world. Most people—even Republicans—agree with it, whether they admit it or not. We should not hide it, soft-pedal it, deny it, or walk away from it. Bill Clinton said it best in a speech to the Democratic Leadership Council in December 2002: ". . . we've got to be strong. When we look weak in a time where people feel insecure, we lose. When people feel uncertain, they'd rather have somebody who's strong and wrong than somebody who's weak and right."

Let me add the Carville corollary to President Clinton's words. You've got strong and wrong. You've got weak and right. Where is it written that we can't be strong and right?

It's like when I was at LSU, I'd go to all the basketball games, without fail. In fact, my unfailing support of the basketball team contributed to my failing grades. My friends would give me a hard time about it. They'd say, "Carville, this is a football school. Why do you spend all your time watching basketball at the field house?" I always wondered where it was written that we couldn't be a football school and a basketball school. Why couldn't LSU be both? My point is that Democrats need to be both. We need to be strong in addition to being right. Because George Bush may talk tough and sound strong, but he is most definitely wrong.

WRONG FROM THE START

In his first big foreign policy speech as a presidential candidate, George Bush said, "To be relied upon when they are needed, our allies must be respected when they are not. We have partners, not satellites." The speech was titled "A Distinctly American Internationalism." It should have been called "A Distinctly Egregious Lie," because no sooner did he take office than he started crapping all over our allies and the international agreements we had entered with them. It's worth remembering that the dislike and distrust the world now feels toward America didn't just happen. It was the result of a concerted effort by this administration to piss off everyone in the world on just about every issue. Heck, if George Bush could build coalitions half as well as he burns bridges, we wouldn't be in this mess to begin with.

Now, I'm not saying that we need to go along with every agreement that every other country reaches, but we can't just cooperate only when it suits us, either. If I cooperated with Mary only when it suited my interests, we wouldn't be married. If Keyshawn Johnson cooperated only when the ball got thrown to him, he wouldn't be wearing a Super Bowl ring. And if William Procter and James Gamble cooperated only when it suited them, well, you get my point.

Not every agreement suits your interests directly, but it often pays to be in rather than out. Which is why it was so amazing to see George Bush take the United States out of six big international agreements in his first six months of office.

Here's what they were, what Bush did, and why it was stupid.

● **The Kyoto Protocol.** *Signed by the United States, November 12, 1998. Abandoned by George Bush, March 2001.*

The Kyoto treaty is about global warming. (For more on this, see the environment and energy chapter.) It acknowledges what all but the most crackpot scientists now admit—global warming is occurring, it isn't good, and it's being caused by greenhouse gases. The Kyoto treaty would commit the United States to reducing greenhouse gases to below our 1990 levels. Rather than use it as an opportunity to push for a better energy policy, George Bush said it would "wreck" the economy and walked away. (He seems to have done a good job of wrecking the economy without this treaty, but I digress.) In Bonn, Germany, where 178 other countries endorsed the Kyoto accords, our delegates were literally booed out of the room. That's a nice image of American leadership. It was also an example of how not to sustain alliances, because by embarrassing Prime Minister Gerhard Schröder at an important meeting in his country, we gave him no incentive to be "willing" when we came knocking for allies in our "coalition of the willing." By the way, when Bush realized how much people didn't like his decision, he promised a cabinet-level review of climate policy and a new proposal in the fall. If we had all held our collective breath, it probably would have solved the carbon dioxide problem, because it's been two years, and we're still waiting.

● **The Comprehensive Test Ban Treaty (CTBT).** *Signed by Bill Clinton, 1996. Opposed by George Bush, from day one.*

The Comprehensive Test Ban Treaty (CTBT) would ban all nuclear explosions. Clinton signed it in 1996 and sent it to the Senate in 1997. The Republican Senate rejected it in 1999. To enter into force, forty-four named nations, including the United States, need to ratify the treaty. Back in 1961, Dwight Eisenhower said that not achieving a nuclear test ban "would have to be classed as the greatest disappointment of any administration, of any decade, of any time and of any party." George W. Bush could have made it happen. Instead, he called it "unenforceable" and paid it no more mind. So, as of today, George Bush's refusal to support this treaty leaves the United States in the company of North Korea, India, and Pakistan. As my momma used to say, "Tell me who you go with, and I'll tell you who you are." Are these the countries we really want to "go with"?

● **Anti-Ballistic Missile Treaty.** *In force since 1972. Abandoned by George Bush, May 1, 2001.*

Ballistic missiles are the real bad boys out there. They can carry nuclear warheads and other weapons of mass destruction, and because the long-range ones go through outer space, they can get just about anywhere in the world in a matter of minutes. This treaty limited the United States and the Soviets to deploying a single, land-based system to defend against long-range ballistic missiles. George Bush didn't like it, because it wouldn't allow him to go forward with his national missile defense system. This is a system that, in addition to being the most expensive solution to the least likely threat we face (the Pentagon estimates it would cost over $150 billion to build), has also been demonstrated to be capable of knocking down an actual missile exactly *zero* times.

By tearing up this treaty before we have a proven missile defense (something we may never have), George W. Bush managed to piss off Russia and China and send them a message that if they intend to be able to stay in a mutually assured destruction standoff with us, they have one thing they can do—build more ballistic missiles. That's what's called an arms race. Kudos to George Bush for potentially restarting one.

● **Nuclear Non-Proliferation Treaty (NPT).** *In force since 1970. Undermined by George Bush since 2001.*

The Nuclear Non-Proliferation Treaty (NPT) says that states without nuclear weapons will refrain from acquiring nuclear weapons. In exchange, countries that have nuclear weapons promise to make progress on nuclear disarmament. Although the administration theoretically supports the NPT, it has done everything possible to undermine it. For example, it published a report called the *Nuclear Posture Review* that talks about a bunch of situations in which the administration could envision us having to use nuclear weapons; it has repealed the ban on low-yield nuclear weapons; and it has supported research and development into a weapon called the Robust Nuclear Earth Penetrator. It may sound like some kind of kinky toy—it ain't. And the NPT might sound like some unimportant international agreement—but it ain't either.

● **Protocol to the Biological Weapons Convention.** *Negotiated by the United States for ten years. Abandoned by George Bush, July 2001.*

The Biological Weapons Convention is a treaty banning the production, possession, or use of germ warfare agents. Even though 143 countries have signed the thing, the problem is that the original treaty doesn't have any provisions to prevent cheating. For the last ten years, the United States had participated in an effort to negotiate an addendum (what those bow-tie-wearing diplomats call a "protocol to the convention") that would get tough on cheaters. In July 2001, the Bush administration announced that it opposed the draft rules that had resulted from those negotiations. A lot of folks hoped that they'd come up with a stronger alternative—after all, America was terrorized by anthrax just three months after this announcement. Two years later, nada.

● **International Criminal Court (ICC).** *Supported by every American administration since World War II. The Bush administration withdrew our signature from the treaty, May 6, 2002.*

Because of long delays and expenses involved with setting up new tribunals every time we want to try people accused of genocide, war crimes, and crimes against humanity, the United States and the rest of the world set out to establish a permanent forum, the International Criminal Court (ICC), to try individuals for these heinous crimes.

During the negotiations surrounding the ICC, the United States made sure there were important safeguards to protect U.S. troops from politically motivated prosecutions. Instead of working with key allies such as Britain, Israel, and Japan to advance U.S. interests and improve the court, the Bush administration unilaterally withdrew from the treaty. The court is going to happen, with or without us. All that George Bush accomplished was removing officials from the Pentagon and the State Department from the ongoing negotiations on the court—preventing them from working to protect U.S. national security priorities during these talks.

● **Conference on the Illicit Trade in Small Arms and Light Weapons in All Its Aspects.** *Conceived July 2001. Rejected by George W. Bush—outright.*

This was the first attempt by the international community to address the illegal trade of small arms and light weapons—the weapons that fuel civil wars, terrorism, and the international drug trade. These are the kinds of weapons used to kill our troops in Somalia, Afghanistan, and Iraq. The Bush folks immediately made it clear that they would not support language in the plan of action that would be unacceptable to domestic opponents of gun control.

With U.S. negotiators actively opposing these efforts, the thing is pretty much toothless. It's kinda ironic—here we are begging and, in some cases, forcing Iraqis to give up their guns, but Bush refused to do anything that would stop them from having them in the first place.

☆ ☆ ☆

When it comes to agreements with other countries—this administration doesn't practice abstinence. They practice pulling out. What's the difference? If you pull out, you're still getting screwed.

Now, smart, reasonable people can disagree about the merits of each of these agreements, but don't tell me that there aren't consequences to tearing up each one of them. There are.

For example, the chart on page 70 is a disturbing look at what other countries now think of us.

Remember after September 11, the whole world essentially said, "We're all Americans"—in fact, it was France's largest newspaper, *Le Monde*, that ran a headline, in English, that said: "We Are All Americans."

Now the majority of them hate Americans. This isn't just about people sneering and occasionally spitting on Americans when we go abroad (though they do). If governments bend to the will of their people, which they do, we're going to have more and more governments that are unfriendly to the United States. When people hate America, their leaders can stay popular by pledging not to work with America. And you saw that when it was time for us to round up the posse to head into Iraq—nobody was home. And that's part of why this thing is such a disaster.

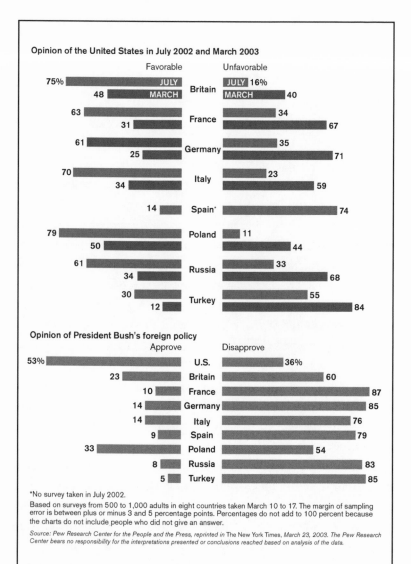

Opinion of the United States in July 2002 and March 2003

Favorable — Unfavorable

	Favorable (July)	Favorable (March)		Unfavorable (July)	Unfavorable (March)
Britain	75%	48		16%	40
France	63	31		34	67
Germany	61	25		35	71
Italy	70	34		23	59
Spain*		14			74
Poland	79	50		11	44
Russia	61	34		33	68
Turkey	30	12		55	84

Opinion of President Bush's foreign policy

Approve — Disapprove

	Approve	Disapprove
U.S.	53%	36%
Britain	23	60
France	10	87
Germany	14	85
Italy	14	76
Spain	9	79
Poland	33	54
Russia	8	83
Turkey	5	85

*No survey taken in July 2002.

Based on surveys from 500 to 1,000 adults in eight countries taken March 10 to 17. The margin of sampling error is between plus or minus 3 and 5 percentage points. Percentages do not add to 100 percent because the charts do not include people who did not give an answer.

Source: Pew Research Center for the People and the Press, reprinted in The New York Times, *March 23, 2003. The Pew Research Center bears no responsibility for the interpretations presented or conclusions reached based on analysis of the data.*

IRAQ

Here's my two cents on Iraq. Iraq is like an affair—it's a lot easier to get into than to get out of. Twenty years from now, you mark my words, people are going to look back and say, "What the hell were we thinking, invading that country?"

And here's my advice for Democrats. We shouldn't make this anything more than it is. We ought not to exaggerate the charges about the Bush administration and Iraq. We should only just state what is obvious to everyone.

First—that they lied repeatedly about the justification for war.

Second—that they were thoroughly unprepared for the aftermath of war.

Now, intrinsic to those two claims is that they're just a pack of liars, and it's not just that they're liars—they're stupid, too. But you don't need to say that explicitly.

Lied to get us in: This soil's been pretty well tilled, but let's just go over the basics.

In a speech on August 26, 2002, to the Veterans of Foreign Wars, Dick Cheney declared that he had "no doubt" that Saddam Hussein was preparing to use weapons of mass destruction against the United States, and that "the risks of inaction are far greater than the risks of action." Those who might disagree, he said, were victims of "wishful thinking or willful blindness." The headline of the next day's *New York Times* read: "Cheney Says Peril of a Nuclear Iraq Justifies Attack."

It looks like the wishful thinking and willful blindness were Cheney's.

In his State of the Union address in January 2003, Bush shocked the

world by announcing that the British had discovered that "Saddam Hussein recently sought significant quantities of uranium from Africa."
Now, the discovery that that line was based on known flawed intelligence caused an uproar, and after weeks of flailing around, blaming the
CIA (even though the CIA took a similar line out of a previous speech),
claiming that the line wasn't substantively untrue (even though Colin
Powell thought it was such junk that he refused to use it in his presentation to the United Nations), and finally saying that maybe Bush
shouldn't have used it in the speech—what's the big deal? Joe Cirin-
cione, a senior analyst at the Carnegie Endowment for International
Peace and a frequent guest of mine on *Crossfire*, described the big deal
best: "We did not go to war because of mustard gas or Scuds. We went to
war because President Bush told the nation that Saddam had, or might
already have, a nuclear bomb, and we could not afford to wait. Now it's
obvious that's not true and there was no solid evidence it was true at the
time. . . . We wouldn't have gone to war without the nuclear threat. The
President's case for war was centered on the nuclear threat."[10]

Ergo, they lied to get us in.

The problem is, that threat wasn't really real. In early 2002, Joseph
C. Wilson, a retired U.S. ambassador, was sent by Cheney's office on a
mission to Niger to find out if that statement was true. He interviewed
dozens of people who had access to years of records and concluded it
wasn't true. He told folks as much and wrote up his conclusion in a report that went to Cheney's office. So, imagine his surprise when he
heard those words come out of the president's mouth. Unable to keep
silent, he ultimately wrote an op-ed in *The New York Times* and told *The
Washington Post*: "It really comes down to the administration misrepre-
senting the facts on an issue that was a fundamental justification for

going to war."[11] To sum up, one dedicated public servant does an exhaustive search to verify or debunk a truly terrifying claim—that Iraq was trying to restart a nuclear program. In a sane administration, the fact that the claim was debunked—that Iraq was *not* trying to buy uranium from Niger—would be a relief. Of course, the truth is never a relief when it hurts your cause.

I actually got a letter from an officer of our armed forces in Iraq saying among other things that his men were "pretty pissed" about being lied to about the weapons of mass destruction.

I'm pretty pissed, too.

Now there's been all kinds of speculation about how that line got into the speech, seeing as how CIA director George Tenet and Secretary of State Colin Powell knew it shouldn't have been there—in fact, it's kind of become Washington's own version of the game "Clue." "It was Condi Rice, in the situation room, with the speechwriter . . ." "It was Dick Cheney, in the Oval Office, with a pen . . ." or, "It was Paul Wolfowitz, in the Pentagon, with his ego . . ."

Of course, playing that game is a pointless exercise. The thing that's really important, as Wilson himself wrote, is that "it begs the question, what else are they lying about?"[12]

The answer is that they're lying about the fact that Iraq is somehow linked to al Qaeda.

Back in October 2002, President Bush said that "Iraq could decide on any given day to provide a biological or chemical weapon to a terrorist group or individual terrorists." And that "alliance with terrorists could allow the Iraqi regime to attack America without leaving any fingerprints." At a rally in New Hampshire, he was even more blunt, saying, "We know he's [Saddam] got ties with Al Qaeda."[13]

The only problem with that statement is that it is another lie. In fact, declassified elements of our National Intelligence Estimate made exactly the opposite argument to what Bush was saying—they judged that the only way it would be likely that Saddam Hussein would form any alliance with al Qaeda would be if he was facing death or capture at the hands of the United States. To quote from the report: "Saddam, if sufficiently desperate, might decide that only an organization such as al Qaeda . . . already engaged in a life-or-death struggle against the United States, could perpetrate the type of terrorist attack that he would hope to conduct." [14]

Isn't that ironic? There was no al Qaeda presence in Iraq before, but there might be now.

When you lie and make stuff up as the basis for a war, you really, really hurt our credibility. And when you say people are going to be throwing flowers at us, and they're throwing grenades, it ain't going to be easy to get some other countries to come in and help out and lend some legitimacy to this occupation.

Unprepared to get us out: I was recently speaking to a bunch of executives with Newt Gingrich, and he said that by the middle of 1942, we had a four-hundred-page plan of what we'd do in Europe after World War II was over. He was stunned—stunned—that there seems to have been no similar thinking in Iraq. This is Newt Gingrich we're talking about here.

The only reason not to have a plan for the victory is if you don't think you're going to win. Honestly, did they think that maybe we wouldn't win? No, Paul Wolfowitz and his academic chicken-hawk buddies acted all along as if we'd topple Saddam and the Iraqi people would immediately go build a stock market.

THE PURPOSE OF PLANNING

More Americans have been killed in Iraq after the president stood on the deck of the USS *Abraham Lincoln* and declared "major combat operations" over than were killed during "major combat operations." What do you think was the *combined* number of postconflict American combat casualties in our engagements in Germany, Japan, Haiti, Bosnia, and Kosovo?

> **A:** 1,320
> **B:** 256
> **C:** 35
> **D:** None of the above

The correct answer is *D*, because the correct answer is zero.[15] Zero postconflict combat casualties in all those other engagements combined. What a difference a little postcombat planning makes, huh?

Did they for a moment consider that these people might, oh, loot everything that wasn't nailed down? Nope. Did they consider that ethnic or tribal fighting might ensue? Nope. Did they consider that maybe if we came in and said we were in charge, people might actually expect us to be in charge, by providing electricity, food, and running water? Doesn't look that way.

As far as I can tell, all they had was a theory. And as far as I can tell, that theory was essentially the domino theory in reverse—win the war in Iraq, and everything else will fall into place. It looks to be about as sound as the original domino theory. Except in dominoes, the first one's got to fall *forward*.

And then, of course, our decapitation strategy failed to decapitate

SHOOT THE MESSENGER

No group of soldiers has gotten jerked around more than the 16,500 troops of the Third Infantry Division. They were the ones who led the charge on Baghdad in the early days of the invasion of Iraq and suffered more fatalities than any other division. Since then, they've been trying to keep the peace, sweltering in the 110-degree heat. Initially, they were told they'd be headed home in June 2003. In July, the Pentagon announced that their stay in Iraq had been extended again, indefinitely.

When reporters asked them about their situation in Iraq, one soldier said, "If Donald Rumsfeld was here, I'd ask for his resignation." All of this was reported on ABC News by Jeffrey Kofman. What was the administration response to this stunning display of poor morale? First, they said that the soldiers would be punished. Then, they realized that people were much more sympathetic to the soldiers in Iraq than the desk jockeys in their air-conditioned offices in Washington. So they tried a different approach—they decided to punish the messenger. Someone in the White House (they won't say who, and the press secretary says he won't try to find out) pointed cybergossip Matt Drudge to a news story noting that Kofman was not only gay but also Canadian. This prompted a headline on Drudge's site: ABC NEWS REPORTER WHO FILED TROOP COMPLAINTS STORY—OPENLY GAY CANADIAN. As Maureen Dowd said, this was a twofer of a demonstration—it showed the "baser nature of President Bush's base" and "how ugly it can get when control freaks start losing control."[16]

Sure, those soldiers probably shouldn't have said what they did. But their commander in chief probably shouldn't have sent them into Iraq without a plan to get them out, either. And you can't blame gay people or Canada for that.

Saddam, so we've got bands of his loyalists going around killing more Americans *after* Bush declared victory than we lost during the war. When asked about that, here's what Bush had to say. "There are some who feel like that if they attack us, that we may decide to leave prematurely," he said. "My answer is: bring them on."

I've got a news flash for you, cowboy. Our boys over there are already getting their asses shot off—they don't need you egging the shooters on. Are you a president, or are you the guy who insists on taunting players from the opposing team because he knows he's never going to have to get off the bench?

All in all, do I think there's a chance that the average Iraqi will be better off because of this? Yeah, they couldn't be that much worse off. And if that was the goal, Bush should have said so in the first place.

But do I think the world is a safer place today than it was a month ago—or that it will be safer three years from now? No. And that's a problem, because that—in addition to nuclear weapons they don't have and the connection with al Qaeda that isn't there—was the justification for going there in the first place. And remember, when we say "going there," we're not talking about a road trip, we're talking about a *war.* By the way, if anyone ever asks you what the fifty-first state is, it ain't Puerto Rico, or any of those islands in the Pacific. It's Iraq. It's our problem now. Except that there are no states that cost us $87 billion a year to run where the people who live there insist on shooting at American soldiers.

Like I said, we shouldn't make more of this than it is. He lied to get us in and had no plan to get us out. Thank you, President Bush.

THE WAR ON TERROR

Just two weeks after he hung that MISSION ACCOMPLISHED sign from the aircraft carrier and declared that the battle of Iraq was "a victory in the war on terror," more than twenty people, including seven Americans, were killed by synchronized bombings in Saudi Arabia, bombings that Colin Powell called "a well-planned terrorist attack, obviously." Mission accomplished? Mission accomplished, my ass.

Unlike Saddam Hussein—who, as of this writing, has begun recording messages and inciting his supporters to kill American troops—Osama bin Laden was directly responsible for taking nearly three thousand American lives. He, too, is still recording messages and inciting his supporters to kill Americans. And he's got no shortage of people who can answer his call. According to terrorism experts at the International Institute for Strategic Studies, about twenty thousand jihadic soldiers had graduated from al Qaeda's training camps by October 2001. They estimate that around two thousand have been captured or killed as part of the war on terror. That means that 90 percent of bin Laden's forces, and more than half of his top commanders, remain free. Let me repeat—mission accomplished, my ass.[17]

In sum, George W. Bush took a country that had no interest in killing Americans and got them very excited about killing Americans. At the same time, he took a terrorist group that had actually attacked America and somehow decided that it was no longer America's number one target. Don't try to tell me with a straight face that Democrats couldn't have done a better job.

THE "HAD ENOUGH" SOLUTION

Get back in the game, lead the world in solving shared problems, be a good neighbor, practice True Leadership. Remember that famous question from the movie *A Bronx Tale*, in which Calogero asks Sonny, "Is it better to be loved or feared?" The answer, when it comes to foreign policy, is that it's best to be both. Being loved gets people to do what you want them to do because they want to. That's the cheapest, safest foreign policy there is. Being feared, of course, helps convince people to do what you want them to do, even when they don't want to. Our foreign policy needs to be a balance of both.

That's why, first, we need to get back in the game on all the agreements Bush walked away from. It's that simple.

Second, we need to lead the world in solving shared problems. That means helping to confront threats that don't involve terrorism or war—but also things like AIDS and global warming. Sure, we may have the nicest house in the world neighborhood—but if we don't join the neighborhood watch, or stop throwing our trash on other people's lawns, or do the other stuff to improve the neighborhood, we're going to reduce our own property value.

Third, we need to get muscular. Remember I said that there's strong and wrong and weak and right, but I haven't seen it written anywhere that progressives can't be strong and right. Basically, I think that if you're going to be strong and right, it would look something like True Leadership. Now I know it's a stupid catchphrase, but you need to remember that leadership means having others to lead. And true means being honest about the threats and the risks.

Rather than try to give you some academic definition of what I mean, let me give you an example of a huge threat, an area where the Bush folks have really screwed the pooch, and an area where true, strong leadership is the only answer: North Korea.

One of the things President Bush said in his State of the Union address that wasn't a lie was: "the gravest danger in the war on terror . . . is outlaw regimes that seek and possess nuclear, chemical, and biological weapons."

George W. Bush meet North Korea.

The very day Secretary of State Colin Powell succumbed to administration arm-twisting and made the case for war with Iraq at the United Nations, North Korea flipped the switch and restarted a power plant used to produce plutonium for nuclear weapons. Basically, North Korea has told us that they have nuclear weapons and they're making more. At the UN, Colin Powell talked about the fact that someday, Iraq could build a missile that would travel 1,200 kilometers. In 1998, North Korea fired a multistage rocket over Japan, proving that they are capable of hitting one of our closest allies and, soon, us.

Also, remember that everything North Korea makes, they sell. Those Scuds we intercepted on a ship to Yemen—and then, inexplicably, returned—weren't a gift. They were an example of business as usual from the world's worst proliferator.

This news is alarming. More alarming is what the administration has done about all of this—nothing.

Now, the traditional liberal response would be a kind of wobbly multilateralism. In other words, we'd say that what other nations think is more important than what we think. It's a "let's do what our allies want" view of the world that a lot of Democrats have to get away from. In this case, it would involve saying something like "If the South Koreans and the Chinese don't worry about it too much, then we shouldn't either."

Clearly, when a country is building missiles that can hit us, and that can be topped with nuclear weapons that they have, that approach is unacceptable.

Equally unacceptable is Bushian unilateralism. Bushian unilateralism involves calling someone a member of the "axis of evil," pissing them off, and leaving our allies in the lurch. Think about how South Korea felt when Bush said that. It was throwing a rock at a beehive that your friend happens to be standing next to. You're not the one who gets stung.

Here's why the unilateral approach fails. If you want to get tough with North Korea, and you don't have South Korea, Japan, and China on board, whatever you try to do is going to fail. If we try to strangle North Korea's economy and China isn't on board, North Korea will just smuggle stuff through China as they have for years. If Japan and South Korea aren't involved, they don't feel any pressure from their neighbors to change their behavior. Unilaterism doesn't work morally or practically.

So what would you, a newly minted True Leaderist, do? You get South Korea, and China, and Japan, and Russia all together, and you lay out for North Korea some of the good things that can happen to them if they get rid of their nukes and missiles—ending trade sanctions, diplomatic relations, help with food for the millions who are starving there, good stuff like that. So you've got everyone together saying, "Give this a try, North Korea." That has two advantages. First, it often works. Second, if it doesn't work, and North Korea gives everyone the finger—everyone is now pissed off. You've got all these countries who now have to say, "We tried diplomacy, now I'm open to trying something tougher." It puts us in a much better position of moral authority to use our muscular authority.

★ PART TWO ★

"THE GENERAL WELFARE"

George W. Bush was sworn into office on January 20, 2001. Every day that he has been in office, including the remarkable number of days that he's been on vacation, here's what's happened to America under his leadership:[1]

The stock market has lost $3.6 billion in shareholder value a day.[2] That's right, every day that this man strutted into the Oval Office, Americans saw the value of their savings, pensions, and investments decrease by $3.6 billion.

Our fiscal situation has worsened by $9.5 billion a day. Let's see that with all the zeroes: $9,500,000,000. That's right, in going from a $5.6 trillion projected surplus to $3.2 trillion of projected deficits (just for sport, and unlike the White House, we're going to estimate continuing the tax cuts that Bush wants to continue. To be conservative, however, we didn't include the cost of fixing the Alternative Minimum Tax, which would have upped Bush's losses by about a billion dollars a day), the man has lost nine and a half billion dollars . . . *every day*. Even Bill Bennett can't lose that much money that fast.

But that's just a big number that doesn't mean anything, right? Well, actually it does mean something. This kind of fiscal irresponsibility puts huge burdens on working families—burdens that are a lot heavier than the "relief" those families get from Bush's tax cuts. According to a study put out by Citizens for Tax Justice, the middle 20 percent of

Americans ranked by income will get $3,791 in tax cuts between 2001 and 2006. At the same time, thanks to President Bush's policies, their share of the federal debt will grow by $24,859. Robert McIntyre, the director of Citizens for Tax Justice, explained it best, saying, "The government is basically borrowing $1,000 in your name and then handing you $250 of it." He's right, and the problem is that average Americans are left holding a $24,000 IOU. The only people whose share of the Bush tax cuts is greater than the new debt they face? You got it—the top 1 percent.[3]

As a result of those deficits, national savings will go down and long-term interest rates will go up, which will have the effect of slowly lowering people's incomes. Of course, that's like the story of the frog and the hot water. Throw a frog in a pot of boiling water, and it'll have the good sense to jump out. Put a frog in a pot of cold water and slowly raise the heat, and it'll end up on your plate because it doesn't have the sense to get out before it gets cooked. The point is, people don't feel the slowly rising heat of a bad economy. But they do feel jobs. And that's another front where George W. Bush has thrown us into some pretty hot water.

Every day he's been in office, 3,409 private sector jobs went down the drain.

Every day, 5,114 more people started working part time, because they couldn't find a full-time job.

Every day, another 250 people have stopped being counted among the unemployed because they've just plain given up on trying to find a job.[4]

Right now, George W. Bush is on track for the worst job creation in seventy years. The last president to lose jobs over the course of his term in office was Herbert Hoover, and that was during the Great Depression. Some people have called him the worst president for the economy since Hoover. Frankly, I think that's an insult to Herbert Hoover's good name. At least he *tried* to put a chicken in every pot.

Republicans are forever saying that if we do this or that, "we'll hurt the economy."

You'd think we'd be able to trust them; after all, if there's one thing they know about—it's hurting the economy. I'm not just mouthing off here, either. That statement is empirically true. If you take the last fourteen presidents, you have eight Republicans and six Democrats. Below is a chart of the annual rate of job loss or gain, from best to worst, by every president since Calvin Coolidge.

	President	Rate of Job Gain (or Loss)
	Roosevelt (1933–45)	5.3
	Johnson (1963–69)	3.8
	Carter (1977–81)	3.1
	Truman (1945–53)	2.5
	Clinton (1993–2001)	2.4
	Kennedy (1961–63)	2.3
	Nixon (1969–74)	2.2
	Reagan (1981–89)	2.1
	Coolidge (1923–29)	1.1
	Ford (1974–77)	1.1
	Eisenhower (1953–61)	0.9
	G. Bush (1989–93)	0.6
	G. W. Bush (2001–present)	−0.7
	Hoover (1929–33)	−9.0

Notice something? Every single Democrat has a better record of job creation than any single Republican. I went and had a couple of statisticians calculate the odds of this happening randomly; it turns out that it's 3 in 10,000. So, when someone tells you that Republicans do a better job of the economy, just shove this chart in their face. If you don't feel like doing that, you can simply tell them that the odds are 1 in 3,003 that they're right and would they care to bet?

When you look closely at this, you'll also notice something else. With the exception of Herbert "Great Depression" Hoover, the worst presidents when it comes to jobs are the Bush boys. As of this writing, if you combine both Bush administrations, they haven't created a single American job. That's amazing, when you consider that just about every president can claim to have created jobs because even the smallest amount of economic growth will create *some* jobs. Not these two.

Now, of course, Republicans will tell you that I'm not being fair. They'll tell you that George Bush *inherited* a recession.

First of all, I'm not getting paid to be fair. I'll settle for being right. Second of all, George W. Bush never seemed to have a problem with inheriting anything else before. Third of all, wasn't he the guy who said that he'd be the MBA president, he'd restore responsibility to the White House? Doesn't that mean taking responsibility for little things like, oh, the economy? Fourth of all, none of that matters because he's *lying.* He didn't inherit a recession at all. This is one of the most repeated, most egregious lies of this administration. Let's debunk that little myth right now.

For all of Washington and most businesses, business cycles are defined by the National Bureau of Economic Research (NBER)—a private, nonpartisan, nonprofit research organization whose job is to monitor and define U.S. economic business cycles. (This isn't some hole-in-the-wall nonprofit, either; they're made up of twelve of the thirty-one American Nobel Prize winners in economics, and count as their researchers more than six hundred professors of economics and business.) I'm sure George Bush would like to believe that the recession began in January 2001—twenty days before he took office—but it didn't. According to NBER, the recession began in March 2001, two months *after* he took office.

This put George W. Bush in a little bind, because he wanted to say that he inherited a recession when the NBER was saying that we *weren't* in a recession. Sometimes he hedged his language just enough to cloud the issue. That's what he did in November 2001 when a reporter asked him, pointedly, if we were in a recession. Remember, at that point, NBER was saying that we weren't. Here's how Bush responded: "You let the number-crunchers tell us that."

Of course, that sounded . . . Clintonian. So Bush began just lying outright. For example, talking to Republican governors in September 2002, he said, "I want you all to remember that when Dick Cheney and I got sworn in, the country was in a recession."

He must've liked the sound of that, because he started saying it all the time. In just about every speech he gives on the economy, you can bet on him using some variation of the line "we inherited an economy in recession."

Let me say this again: the economic consensus as represented by the National Bureau of Economic Research is that we entered a recession in 2001, two months *after* George W. Bush took office. In fact, the NBER put out a report in November 2001 that stated that "a peak in business activity occurred in the U.S. economy in March, 2001."[5] In other words, when Bush came into office we weren't in a recession. We weren't sliding into one. We weren't diving into one. And Bush sure as hell didn't inherit one. It's that simple.

When you hit Republicans with this argument, they will invariably start sweating, stammering, and turning red. The smart ones will probably say something like "Well, so maybe the recession did start when he was in office—what was he supposed to do in two months?" That's your cue to remind them that by March of 2001, most of the components of Bush's tax cuts had *already passed* out of committee in the House of Representatives. He had already started us down his treacherous economic path. Plain and simple, it's his recession.

Speaking to the New Jersey business community in June 2003, George Bush famously said, "There are some who would like to rewrite history—revisionist historians is what I like to call them." To quote my eight-year-old daughter—it takes one to know one.

☆ ☆ ☆

If the jobs chart and the recession argument tell you anything, they tell you that it's time for progressives to stand proud and tell Republicans to keep their wacky economic ideas to themselves, because if there's one thing that they shouldn't be lecturing Democrats about, it's the economy.

See, we know how to make the economy strong. We know how to

make it work for everyone. We've done it. And once you read the following pages, you'll be stunned to know just how badly wrong they've gotten it, and how we can go about getting it righted.

After all, it *is* the economy, stupid—and we just can't afford to have these stupid people running our economy anymore.

3

DEFICITS MATTER, DEBTS MATTER, AND THEY MATTER A LOT

The Lie: "We will not deny, we will not ignore, we will not pass along our problems to other Congresses, other presidents, and other generations. We will confront them with focus, and clarity, and courage."

—*George W. Bush, State of the Union address, January 2003*

The Truth: George Bush is on pace to leave "other Congresses, other presidents, and other generations" more debt than any president in history.

—*OMB Historical Tables, fiscal year 2004*

Deficits and debts are like drinks. Having one every once in a while can be good for your health. Have a lot of them every day and you've got a problem. Thanks to George Bush, America has a debt problem. What we need is a debt intervention.

Can you imagine what a George Bush debt intervention would look like?

Laura: George, whatever happened to that $5.6 trillion that you were going to keep next door at the Treasury Department?

George: I don't know.

Laura: Is it still on its way there?

George: No.

Laura: Where'd it go?

George: I spent it on some stuff.

Laura: What type of stuff?

George: Tax cuts, mostly. Oh, and some cool new toys.

Laura: Did you at least keep the money we had promised for retirees, for Social Security, because that's money we're just holding on to for them for when they retire?

George: Ummm . . .

Laura: George, there are some people here who love you, and worry about you, and want to talk to you.

(Laura escorts George into the Cabinet Room, where a collection of friends and family are waiting.)

George: Oh, man, not another one of these.

Well, now America is saying, "Oh, man, not more of these interest-rate-raising, economy-stifling deficits." Unfortunately, thanks to President Bush, we got 'em. Let's go through the drill:

The Problem: The federal government has seen a $9 trillion reversal in its projected fiscal situation. What were supposed to be surpluses are now growing deficits. What was supposed to be debt reduction is now going to be debt increases.[6]

The Bush Response: Deficits and debt don't matter.

The "Had Enough" Solution: Stanch the bleeding, stop the digging, tell the truth, and invest in new ideas that will grow the economy well into the future.

THE PROBLEM IN DEPTH

The scope of the fiscal mismanagement of this country is truly mind-boggling. In 2001, when President Bush came to office, the nonpartisan Congressional Budget Office (CBO) predicted a $5.6 trillion surplus for 2002–2011. Today, that $5.6 trillion projected surplus is now a projected deficit of $1.4 trillion. I don't want to bore you with technicalities here, but the CBO is only allowed to calculate the effect of things that are in law now. They can base their estimates only on the stuff that's already there, not on the future tax cuts that we all know Bush wants, not on the cost of rebuilding Iraq that we all know has been grossly underestimated. When you add in those things, you're looking at a *deficit* of about $5 trillion. This president has made close to $10 trillion disappear in two years. That's the worst fiscal turnaround in our nation's history.[7]

I'm no genius, but $5 trillion seems to be a lot bigger than the zero-trillion-dollar debt some economists were actually worried we were headed toward just a couple of years ago.

In an address to Congress in February 2001, President Bush said, "My plan pays down an unprecedented amount of our national debt." He was lying, plain and simple. In the months following that speech, it became clear to everyone that he was lying. And now, when confronted with their lying, the administration is squirming.

THE BUSH RESPONSE IN DEPTH

During the campaign, when people questioned the size of Bush's proposed tax cuts and spending programs, he made a point of claiming that he wouldn't run deficits. Period.

Then, when he actually started running deficits in 2002, his recollection changed. For example, when he was speaking in June to a group in Houston, he said, "When I was one time campaigning in Chicago, a reporter said, 'Would you ever have a deficit?' I said, 'I can't imagine it, but there would be one if we had a war, or a national emergency, or a recession.' Never did I dream we'd get the trifecta."

I happen to think that's a sick joke, but it's a line Bush has been playing for laughs all over the country.

Here's the problem with George W. Bush: he doesn't remember things that did happen, but he *does* remember things that *didn't.* Because in this case, he's very clearly remembering something he never said. Not once. *New Republic* magazine did an investigation, and they found that no reporter who covered the 2000 campaign remembers him ever having said it; no records of any campaign event in Chicago—or anywhere else, for that matter—caught it, and despite repeated inquiries from the media, the White House has never produced any evidence that he did.

In fact, the first public mention of Bush's exceptions came, conve-

STATE YOUR CASE

When the federal government cuts spending, states are the ones who really feel the pinch. They rely on the federal government for everything from highway funding to health care help. Today, states find themselves $80 billion in the hole, and George Bush's tax cuts promise them no help. When you're trying to get away with running massive deficits and making massive cuts, state governors and officials are not your friends. In February 2003, the nation's governors came to Washington to complain about the inadequate federal funding that they were getting. As their evidence, they cited an annual report put out by the Office of Management and Budget called *Budget Information for States*. *Budget Information for States* is a four-hundred-page document that tells states how much money each state gets under each federal program. How did George Bush respond to these complaints? He stopped printing the report. Knowledge may be power, and this president is intent on keeping his power, even if it means taking away not only states' funding, but also their knowledge.[8]

niently enough, in August 2001—before September 11—just as it became evident that the tax cuts and slowing economy would likely force him to dip into Social Security.[9]

Ironically, there *was* one candidate during the 2000 election who did say, "Barring an economic reversal, a national emergency, or a foreign crisis, we should balance the budget this year, next year, and every year." That candidate was Al Gore.[10]

So, when the deficits could no longer be denied, the Bush response was to say that at least they're small and temporary. In April 2002, speaking, ironically enough, to the Fiscal Responsibility Coalition, Bush said, "We have a temporary deficit in our budget . . . we can return to a balanced budget, something I want, as early as 2004."

When people started to realize that debt wouldn't be paid down, but rather run up, and that it would be neither small *nor* temporary, the administration started making a new argument: Deficits don't matter. Here's Dick Cheney speaking to the U.S. Chamber of Commerce in January 2003. "Eliminating the deficit is an important goal . . . but we also need to put the current deficit in perspective. The recession, the declining stock market, and the ongoing war on terror have combined to turn budget surpluses into deficits. Even so, the deficit in the last fiscal year was only 1.5 percent of our national economy, well below the average the government has incurred coming out of recessions during the last several decades." Let me summarize that very sophisticated argument for Mr. Cheney. As far as I can tell, he's saying that deficits don't matter. Others in and around the administration don't mince words nearly as much. Here's Mitch Daniels, the former director of the President's Office of Management and Budget, in March 2003: "They [deficits] didn't produce disaster before. They won't this time, either."

So, with denial being the public response, what's the programmatic response? You got it, more tax cuts.

THE "HAD ENOUGH" SOLUTION

Ask anybody on the street if deficits matter, and they'll say yes. Intuitively, we know that deficits matter, because it doesn't take an economic rocket scientist to tell you that it's not generally a good idea to spend what you don't have. But this is a case where Paducah and Princeton are on the same page, because some economic rocket scientists did take a look at this, and guess what they figured out—deficits do matter.

During the Clinton administration, deficit reduction contributed lower long-term interest rates even as the economy grew. Those lower interest rates led to a national first: seven consecutive years of double-digit investment growth. That investment growth led to both increased productivity and new job creation, and so on and so forth in a happy cycle. Just as small deficits free up capital for investment, larger deficits mean that the government is borrowing more money, which leaves less money available for other people who want to invest and innovate. It's estimated that within ten years, these deficits will effectively take $1,000 out of the pocket of each working American because increasing deficits will decrease national savings and increase long-term interest rates, which have the effect of lowering incomes. As the Committee for Economic Development concluded, massive deficits actually reduce our future standard of living.[11]

In political consulting, when you're working for a challenger, one of the things you often do is put together a poll where you run a "generic" candidate against the guy (or gal) currently in office. You don't give your generic candidate a name; you just give them a list of qualifications and positions on the issues and see how people think they stack up against the competition. That started me wondering what would happen if you made the United States a "generic" country and listed our economic "positions." What would be the world opinion about us? Well, I was reading The New Yorker (Mary lets me read it in my office, but I'm not allowed to bring it into the house) and I came across this quote from Kenneth Rogoff, the chief economist at the International Monetary Fund. Here's what he had to say: "Suppose for a minute that we were talking about a developing country that had gaping current account deficits year after year ... budget ink spinning from black into red ... open ended security costs, and a real exchange rate that had been inflated by capital inflows. With all that, I think it's fair to say we would be pretty concerned." John Cassidy, who wrote the article, summarized it best: "When I.M.F. types start talking about the United States as if it were a banana republic on a bad day, it's probably time to change course."[12]

That's why the first step here is to do something that this administration is unwilling to do: admit that the types of deficits we're talking about here do matter, and they matter a lot.

Now I'll be the first to tell you that a little or temporary deficit isn't necessarily a bad thing. People go into deficit all the time, and it's okay. Families borrow money to buy a car, or a house, or to send a kid to college. But when you borrow money to go to college today, you have a reasonable expectation it will improve your financial situation tomorrow. The same can be said about buying a house. Even a car can be a "good" deficit if it's getting you to a job that will pay you more. And in each of those cases, it is clear that debt will be paid off in a prescribed time frame. That's why those deficits aren't necessarily bad; and they can even be good. It's when the deficit is large, long lasting, and your future financial situation is uncertain that a deficit becomes a bad thing. That's where America is.

When we borrow money today, we are not borrowing against some future windfall. We're not borrowing money now in order to earn more money later. In fact, it's the opposite. We're borrowing money now with the retirement of the baby boom coming later. At age fifty-eight, I'm at the leading edge of that group. About 77 million of my closest buddies will be following me shortly. When it comes to government policy, we're not baby boomers, we're budget sappers. Today, there are 3.2 workers

A HOT PLACE FOR THE HYPOCRITES

Dante wrote that the hottest place in hell is reserved for people who, in times of moral crisis, maintain their neutrality. If that's true, the second hottest place has got to be reserved for people who say one thing and do another—the hypocrites. And there's no better demonstration of political hypocrisy than the people who said that our Constitution ought to be amended to require a balanced budget, and then voted for massive tax cuts that will keep us from seeing a balanced budget for decades. Here are some of the sixty-two House of Representatives hypocrites who voted for a balanced budget amendment in 1992, 1994, and 1995 and then voted for tax cuts for the rich in 2001 and 2003. Below them are some of the twenty-five senators who voted for a balanced budget amendment in 1996 and then voted to pass tax cuts in 2001 and 2003. Put a thermometer on these guys, because there's a hot place waiting for them!

Some of the sixty-two House hypocrites:

Rep. Michael Bilirakis, R-FL	Rep. Amo Houghton, R-NY
Rep. Sherwood L. Boehlert, R-NY	Rep. Henry Hyde, R-IL
Rep. Mary Bono, R-CA	Rep. Nancy Johnson, R-CT
Rep. Dan Burton, R-IN	Rep. Jim Kolbe, R-AZ
Rep. Michael N. Castle, R-DE	Rep. Jim Nussle, R-IA
Rep. Christopher Cox, R-CA	Rep. Michael G. Oxley, R-OH
Rep. Tom DeLay, R-TX	Rep. Thomas Petri, R-WI
Rep. John Doolittle, R-CA	Rep. Ralph Regula, R-OH
Rep. David Dreier, R-CA	Rep. Dana Rohrabacher, R-CA
Rep. Wayne Gilchrest, R-MD	Rep. F. James Sensenbrenner, R-WI
Rep. Porter Goss, R-FL	Rep. Christopher Shays, R-CT
Rep. Dennis Hastert, R-IL	Rep. Billy Tauzin, R-LA
Rep. Joel Hefley, R-CO	Rep. Bill Thomas, R-CA

Rep. Jim Walsh, R-NY	Rep. Frank Wolf, R-VA
Rep. Curt Weldon, R-PA	Rep. C. W. Bill Young, R-FL

And here are some of the more better-known shameless senators:

Sen. Christopher Bond, R-MO	Sen. James Inhofe, R-OK
Sen. Conrad Burns, R-MT	Sen. Jon Kyl, R-AZ
Sen. Larry Craig, R-ID	Sen. Trent Lott, R-MS
Sen. Mike DeWine, R-OH	Sen. Richard Lugar, R-IN
Sen. Pete Domenici, R-NM	Sen. Mitch McConnell, R-KY
Sen. Bill Frist, R-TN	Sen. Don Nickles, R-OK
Sen. Charles Grassley, R-IA	Sen. Rick Santorum, R-PA
Sen. Judd Gregg, R-NH	Sen. Richard Shelby, R-AL
Sen. Orrin Hatch, R-UT	Sen. Arlen Specter, R-PA
Sen. Kay Bailey Hutchison, R-TX	Sen. Craig Thomas, R-WY

contributing to support each of the 39 million retirees; by 2035, there will only be 2 workers supporting each of an estimated 76 million retirees, all of whom deserve and have been promised a retirement of dignity after a lifetime of work. If there's a light at the end of this deficit tunnel, it's an oncoming freight train.

What's a tax-cut-happy president to do? Easy, let our children pay for it. Or let them pass it on to their children. If this sounds like a ridiculous abdication of responsibility that makes Bush's promise to "not pass along our problems to other Congresses, other presidents, and other generations" look like one of the most hypocritical things ever said by an American president, it is—but it's exactly what the Bush administration is calling for.

Earlier, I mentioned a guy named Robert McIntyre. He runs an organization called Citizens for Tax Justice, and he's one of the smartest, hardest working, most devoted, most dedicated men in Washington. A while ago, he was on a Philadelphia public radio program with Bruce Bartlett, head of the rabidly antitax National Center for Policy Analysis. Bartlett was a policy adviser in the Reagan White House and wrote the page-turner *Reaganomics: Supply-Side Economics in Action*. Now he's an influential ideas man in the Bush administration.

On the radio show, Bartlett argued that complaints about Bush leaving a crushing tax burden on our children were "not correct" since our children can just pass on the debt to their kids, who will pass it on to their kids, etc. "We'll simply pass this on forever," he said. That's a jaw-dropping thing to admit, but it's basically what Mitch Daniels was saying, too. Of course, Bartlett, Daniels, and the other members of their economic lunatic fringe are forgetting (or ignoring) one thing. The money is borrowed, and we need to pay interest on it.

So McIntyre decided to try a little experiment to test what would happen if we actually followed this crackpot idea to its logical conclusion, and funded everything the government does (with the exception of Social Security) by borrowing the money. Here's what he concluded:

> Ignoring the likely economic meltdown, making heroically low assumptions about interest rates, and keeping total federal spending (including interest) at the same share of the economy as it is today, here's what I found.
>
> Within eight years, interest on the ballooning national debt would cost more than all other federal outlays combined. About a decade later, the

entire non–Social Security budget would be devoted to interest payments.
Not a single penny would be available for defense, homeland security, roads,
education, or anything else.

After that, well, after that I had to relax my constraint on the size of
total federal spending because interest payments would continue to sky-
rocket. Another decade or so later, federal spending, entirely on interest,
would be twice as high as it is now as a share of the economy—assuming we
still had an economy.

A government that can do nothing at all but pay interest on the debt
is not a pretty picture, but it's one that Republicans today are danger-
ously close to painting . . . or are they?

As McIntyre concludes, "The revisionist theory that deficits don't
matter is really a cover up. [The Republicans] hope that big deficits will
force major cuts in public services, cuts that would be hugely unpopular
and politically impossible otherwise." [13]

He's right. There are two types of people who believe that these
deficits don't matter. The first group is people who are just plain stupid.
That group includes people like Larry Lindsey and John Snow. The second group worries me more, because they are crazy . . . like a fox. It includes people like Dick Cheney, Bruce Bartlett, and Grover Norquist,
president of Americans for Tax Reform, a group whose mission statement says, "The Government's power to control one's life derives from
its power to tax. We believe that power should be minimized." As I said
before, their vision for a perfect America is one with virtually no taxes,
virtually no services, and virtually no regulation. When that's your goal,
ballooning, unsustainable deficits are the fastest way there.

So what's a progressive who's had enough to do? Well, like the intervention calls for, it's a multistep program:

Step 1: Admit the Problem
Step 2: Stop the Digging
Step 3: Grow the economy in the short term and the long term.

First, level with us, the American people. We're not stupid. We can handle the truth. When the White House press secretary comes out and says that the deficit "is one that's manageable and it's one that we are addressing," or, "it's not something that's harming the economy,"[14] you insult our collective intelligence. Progressives need to trust the American people by telling them the truth.

The first rule of holes is when you find that you're in one, stop digging. So our second step is for progressives to say clearly, "Stop the damn digging!"

Most important, deficits are one of those problems that you fix by solving other problems—like by getting the economy growing. Dick Cheney himself said that a 1 percent difference in economy growth over two years can mean an $800 billion difference in America's fiscal situation.[15] And here's where progressives need fresh new ideas. To get the economy growing, what you want to have is short-term stimulus and long-term growth. It's like lighting a charcoal grill—you need some lighter fluid up front but what you really want is good sustained heat afterwards. The problem with the Bush plans in general is that by cutting taxes in the future and calling it economic stimulus today, they provide virtually no spark up front and end up pissing away a lot of lighter fluid in the future.

For too long in this debate, Democrats have looked at Bush's "economic plans" and said, "We need an alternative." Recently, the alternative has been Bush's plan, but less of it. Bush Lite is bad beer and even worse politics. Progressives need to change the shape of the debate. That's why it's time for us to put forward two economic plans—one plan for jobs today and one for growth tomorrow.

A plan for jobs today: Unlike President Bush, who calls a tax cut a jobs plan, we need an economic plan that will actually provide jobs and give the economy a shot in the arm—now. A couple of months after September 11, when it became clear that those attacks had kneecapped an economy Bush had already driven into recession, Democrats and Republicans in Congress met with experts like Federal Reserve chairman Alan Greenspan and former Treasury secretary Robert Rubin and asked them what would be the most effective steps that we could take to shore up our economy.

The answer they got was pretty clear. Put money into the hands of low- and middle-income workers; they're the ones who will spend it quickly. Make sure that workers who have lost their jobs receive unemployment benefits. And cut taxes for businesses—but limit the tax cuts to those that actually help create jobs. They also reminded the congressional leaders that any plan to stimulate the economy should help people regain the sense of security they need to shop, travel, and invest. That essentially meant that homeland security investments would be a twofer—they'd not only increase safety, they'd also increase the confidence that is so important to the economy.

They added that with the baby boomers about to start retiring in less than a decade, any plan should be affordable and temporary.[16]

Two years later—and one Bush tax cut later—there has been

no plan passed that vaguely resembles that advice. Democrats in both the Senate and the House have one. We need to start talking about it.

A new idea for growth tomorrow—American Stakeholder Accounts: To provide, real, sustained, long-term growth into the future, you need to have more Americans contributing to the economy, going to college, starting businesses, getting jobs, and creating jobs. That's no small order when you consider that by the end of the 1990s, the bottom 40 percent of Americans earned just 10 percent of the nation's income and owned less than 1 percent of the nation's wealth. As progressives, we know that if we don't bring those people into the fold, we'll create an America that is even more separate and unequal. As pragmatists, we know that without the contributions of 40 percent of our country, we'll never get the kind of sustained growth we need.

That's where progressives can champion and win on an idea called asset building. Owning assets—a house, land, a business, a savings or investment account—is what we want to encourage in this country, because owning assets allows people to build wealth, plan for the future, and contribute to our economy. Throughout history, America's asset-building programs have been some of the most successful federal programs—we just haven't called them asset building. Take the Homestead Act, which offered an asset—160 acres of free land—to anyone willing to work it for five years. Or the GI Bill, which offered an asset—a college education or a first home—in thanks for service in the armed forces. Both programs had huge, positive impacts on our country. They equalized the distribution of wealth in America—not by making rich people less wealthy, but by making poor people more wealthy. That's our goal, and that's why progressives should introduce to America the idea of American Stakeholder Accounts.

One of the people who's been doing a lot of thinking on this issue is Ray Boshara. He's the director of the asset-building program at the New America Foundation—a foundation that brings a lot of smart people and new ideas into Washington. He's come up with a plan for American Stakeholder Accounts that is not just great policy, but could be pretty darn good politics, too. Here's how he described those accounts in the *Atlantic Monthly* in January 2003:

> *Every one of the four million babies born in America each year would receive an endowment of $6,000 in an American Stakeholder Account. If invested in a relatively safe portfolio that yielded a 7 percent annual return, this sum would grow to more than $20,000 by the time the child graduated from high school, and to $45,000 by the time he or she reached thirty (assuming that the account had not yet been used). Funds in the American Stakeholder Account would be restricted to such asset-building uses as paying for the cost of higher education or vocational training, buying a first home, starting a small business, making investments, and, eventually, creating a nest egg for retirement. Withdrawals would of course decrease the account; work and saving would build it back up. Family members and others could also add money to the account.*
>
> *Although the program would be universal, giving every American child a tool to help meet his or her lifelong asset needs, it would especially benefit the 26 percent of white children, the 52 percent of black children, and the 54 percent of Hispanic children who start life in households without any resources whatsoever for investment. For these children and others, an asset*

stake would provide choice, a ticket to the middle class, and, most impor-
tant, hope.[17]

Of course, Republicans will tell you to go back to Sweden, and raise hell about how much it will cost. So here's my (not Ray's) proposal. This program is estimated to cost about $24 billion a year. In fact, it could cost less if you make it an incentive-based thing (say you get $3,000 at birth and the second $3,000 when you graduate high school, vocational school, or do some sort of national service). That would allow us to make these accounts reward responsibility as well.

One of the most anti-progressive, anti-American things the Republican Party wants to do is report what is called the estate tax—or what they like to call the "death tax"—a tax that only 2 percent of the wealthiest taxpayers ever have to worry about, but one that is responsible for promoting a huge amount of charitable giving (to reduce the size of estates) and one that states rely on to pay for services.

I propose that instead of repealing the estate tax, we modify it so that only estates over $3.5 million are taxed. That means that only one-half of 1 percent of all estates would be taxed—the richest of the rich. By the way, Warren Buffett agrees with me on this, and he's worth about $32 billion. So that makes the average net worth of the two of us about $16 billion, and two guys with an average worth of $16 billion must be pretty smart.

Modifying instead of repealing the estate tax saves America an average of $46 billion a year, more than enough to pay for this program. Then you make it a simple choice: Do we want to reward the shiftless scions of American royalty, or do we want to modestly tax their inherited wealth in order to encourage a new generation of kids to go out and learn and work and innovate and thereby truly level the playing field in America? To me, that's no choice at all.

By encouraging college, homeownership, national service, and a bunch of other positive outcomes, American Stakeholder Accounts are a way to grow us out of debt and make America a more equal place in the process.

A real plan for jobs today, and American Stakeholder Accounts for growth tomorrow—those are new ideas and good ideas for progressives who have had enough.

4

TAX CUTS: THE BIG LIE

"Nothing is more important in the face of a war than cutting taxes."

—HOUSE MAJORITY LEADER TOM DELAY,
THE NEW YORK TIMES, APRIL 3, 2003

Tax cuts—their size, their cost, who benefits from them, and how well they work—are the biggest lies in the conservative movement today. Tax cuts are like those games at the carnivals—they look so easy, and the prizes look so great. All you need to do is hit a balloon with a dart, or hit a free throw, or aim a squirt gun, and you'll win a stuffed animal the size of a small car. But it's a sucker's game. The dart is dull, the rim is tight and the ball overinflated, and the squirt gun doesn't shoot straight. And even if by some miracle you do win, the prize is never that huge stuffed animal you see; it's some cheap, rock-hard, mangy-looking piece of felt that my daughters wouldn't put in their rooms if I paid them. Ultimately, it's never worth what you end up paying to get it.

Tax cuts—at least the ones Republicans talk about—are a sucker's game, too. They're a snake oil solution, and Republicans have been hawking them like carnival barkers for as long as I can remember.

The loudest carnival barker of them all? George W. Bush. This man has never seen a tax cut he didn't like, although I'd wager that he'd even like a tax cut he hasn't seen.

The love affair began back in Texas, when he was governor. In fact, the very first bill that Governor Bush signed in the 1999 session of the Texas State Legislature was an emergency tax break for oil wells.[18] On the heels of that inspirational victory for the people of Texas, he passed an additional $1.7 billion in tax cuts, most of which was a property tax cut.

So, whatever happened with those tax cuts down there in Texas? Well, by the time George Bush moved to Washington, it took about $750 million of Texas's $1 billion surplus to keep the state budget out of the red.[19] Today, Texas has the third largest deficit in the nation (it's the eighth largest deficit of any state as a percentage of spending).[20]

When Governor Bush was asked on the campaign trail about his state's fiscal situation, he actually said, "I hope I'm not here to have to deal with it."[21]

Well, he's not in Texas to deal with it, but he didn't leave the mess in Texas, either. It's now America's mess, too.

The fact that his tax cutting failed the people of Texas so miserably should have made us all pretty suspicious when the love affair between Bush and tax cuts sparked back up. Then again, we shouldn't have been too surprised. In this man's world, tax cuts are the answer to everything.

Here's a brief history:

Back in the New Hampshire primaries, when he thought he was going to be challenged by Steve Forbes, then-governor Bush thought if he was going to win the Republican nomination, he had to be the biggest tax-cutting wheel in the field, so he said: I know what we need—a $1.6 trillion tax cut.

Then, once he won the nomination, and the economy was going gangbusters and it looked like we had repealed the business cycle, Republican nominee Bush said: I know what we need—a $1.6 trillion tax cut.

And then, when the economy started slowing, and we needed to provide some stimulus and middle-class tax relief, President Bush said: I know what we need—a $1.6 trillion tax cut.

And then guess what happened? President Bush made that tax cut his first order of business. He pushed for it and focused on it. Heck, he even managed to lose Jim Jeffords and the Senate in the process because of it. But the tax cut passed. And things kept going downhill.

Then came the attacks of September 11, 2001, which shocked our nation and our economy. What did President Bush say? We must get our economy moving again and I know what we need: *another* $1.6 trillion tax cut.[22] Honestly, I can't make this stuff up.

And when corporate scandal after corporate scandal shook investor confidence, President Bush said: I know what the markets need: another $1.6 trillion tax cut.

And once the markets lost $7 trillion in shareholder value,[23] and 8.5 million Americans were out of work,[24] President Bush said that he had a new stimulus plan: another $1.6 trillion tax cut.

I guess the old saying really is true: when the only thing you've got is a hammer, everything starts looking like a nail.

But tax cuts rarely work as advertised. In my fifty-eight years on this earth, the only thing tax cuts have worked to do is get people elected who don't have a single other idea in their heads.

So let's go through our drill—the problem, the Bush solution, and a real solution for progressives who have had enough.

The Problem: The economy is floundering, the tax code is confusing, and (some) people feel they pay too much in taxes.

The Bush Response: Cut taxes no matter what the problem—fast-growing economy, recession, war, the wealthy, call it tax cuts for everyone.

The "Had Enough" Solution: Get Americans to realize the truth about taxes, simplify the process of paying taxes, and get companies to pay their fair share.

THE PROBLEM IN DEPTH

Here's where we need to start, and Americans aren't going to want to hear this, but our tax code ain't that bad, and we don't pay all that much. After all, there is (or at least, was) a consensus in this country that there is some value in providing for the public good. Without that consensus (and the taxes that support it), we wouldn't have health and retirement programs for the elderly, national parks or an interstate highway system to get to them, or a military. There also is (or at least, was) a consensus that when you make money in a market-oriented, capitalist society, you owe some allegiance to the system that allowed you to earn that money in the first place—the system that establishes the laws and the rules of the game under which you've succeeded. I think department store founder Edward Filene best summed up this philosophy. He's the one who said, "Why shouldn't the American people take half my money from me? I took *all* of it from them." Ironically, he was also the guy who

founded the U.S. Chamber of Commerce in order to encourage businesses to contribute to the welfare of their communities. He quit the organization disappointed that it had become, essentially, a front group
for the right wing and an antitax lobby.

Now, conservatives will have you believe that we pay far too much
for those things, and when you see big chunks of money coming out of
your paycheck, it can sometimes feel that way. So let's look at this objec-
tively: America belongs to a group of thirty countries called the Organization for Economic Cooperation and Development, or OECD. All of
those thirty countries have two things in common: they share a commitment to a democratic government and to a market economy. Some critics
of the group call it a "rich man's club," and though the folks at the OECD
don't like that nickname, it pretty much makes the point. After all, these
thirty countries produce two-thirds of all the world's goods and services. Basically, these are the wealthiest, safest, smartest countries in
the world, and if you didn't have the good fortune to be born an American, you'd probably want to be born in one of these places.

When you put together all of the taxes we pay—federal, state, and
local—and then look at our tax rate compared to our GDP, you see
something interesting. Our tax rate now ranks twenty-ninth out of
those thirty countries. That means we pay less in taxes than twenty-
eight of the top thirty democratic, market-oriented countries in the
world. Only Mexico has a lower rate . . . and given the fact that people
die every day trying to sneak from there over to here, it seems that
plenty of Mexicans would prefer to live in the United States.

Now, let me put my political strategist hat back on for a minute, and
I'll grant you that it may not be a winning tax policy strategy to tell people that, in actuality, their tax burden isn't so heavy. It would, however,

TOTAL 2001 TAXES AS A PERCENTAGE OF GDP

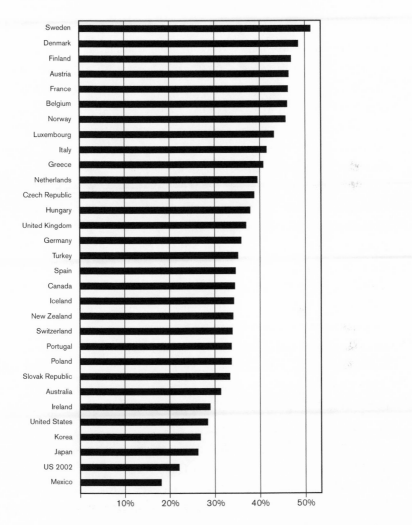

Citizens for Tax Justice, www.ctj.org

be helpful if more Americans realized that we have it pretty good here in these United States. So, since conservatives won't admit it, and sane politicians won't say it, it's up to us to share it. To that end, I urge you to photocopy the chart on the preceding page, and mail it to ten of your most conservative friends. It's a start.

The other problem is one that President Bush would be loath to admit: tax cuts, as a matter of policy, don't cure all that ails ya. If they did, we wouldn't be in the economic fix we're in now.

In fact, for most people, tax cuts usually end up being a negative. Just look at what's happening right now. Bush cut taxes for wealthy people, while average people got a tax cut of a couple hundred dollars. Those tax cuts have hamstrung states, which have been raising things like property and gas taxes. At the same time, those tax cuts are creating greater deficits, which lead to higher interest rates, which cost everyone with a college loan, or home loan, or credit card debt a lot more money. As a result, for millions of families the effects of Bush's tax cuts wipe out the benefits very quickly. And that's just for families—never mind what they do to a society trying to prepare for a retirement tidal wave.

That said, progressives can't simply sit back and say, "Our tax burden is fine, and tax cuts don't work."

But there is something that we can say, and it is this: "There are things in this world more important than tax cuts, and one of them is the overall health of the economy."

A while ago, I had Lincoln Chafee, the Republican senator from Rhode Island, as a guest on *Crossfire*. There are a couple of things I love about Lincoln Chafee. The first is that he's one of the most impressive horse handicappers in the nation. On the show, I asked him for a couple of Kentucky Derby picks. (He gave me Peace Rules as a winner and

FAST FACT

In case you're inclined to believe George W. Bush when he says that the attacks of September 11 threw our economy into a tailspin and that his tax cuts are helping us out, remember that our economy lost five hundred thousand jobs between the time his tax cut was passed and September 11, 2001.

Buddy Gill and Ten Cents a Shine as potential longshots. Only Peace Rules finished in the money, but I won't hold that against him.) The other reason I love the guy is that he's one of the few elected officials who is happy to speak his mind. On the show, Bob Novak thought he was being clever and asked him, "Are Americans being taxed too much, or too little?" Linc didn't miss a beat: "Too little." Watching Bob's jaw drop was priceless. Such is the reaction to honesty in this town. Linc went on, "When I ran [for office] in the fall of 2000, not once, not once did I hear somebody come up to me and say, 'Cut my taxes,' because they like the economy rolling along as it was in the '90s." [25]

Linc—I couldn't have said it better myself.

And that statement points to a powerful truth: whenever a tax cut is proposed, we should look at it through the lens of whether it helps the economy or not. See, in the whole debate about tax cuts—which ones should we have and how big should they be—it sounds like we're talking about shooting a can off a fencepost. By that I mean it's discussed like it's a political game. Will it be higher or will it be lower, and if so, how much? Who will win? The problem is that this isn't like shooting a can off a fencepost, it's like shooting an apple off a kid's head. There are consequences when you miss.

Tax cuts, done incorrectly, can hurt the economy.

Just look at the tax cut that Bush passed in 2001.

At the time, he said, "My overall budget plan funds important priorities like education. It pays down our national debt at a record rate. It sets aside nearly a trillion dollars in a contingency fund for future needs and emergencies. *And we still have surplus money left over for broad, fair, responsible tax relief.*"[26]

That statement should sit as the definition to the word "wrong" in the dictionary. That's if it's not already sitting next to the words "deception," "fraud," or "lie." His budget didn't fund important priorities like education (remember, that's one of the reasons Senator Jeffords left the Republican Party); it didn't pay down the debt (the only "record rate" was how fast the surplus disappeared); and if there's a trillion-dollar contingency fund, they must be keeping it where they hide Dick Cheney, because nobody seems to be able to find it.

But what really chaps my ass is his saying the tax cut would come out of "surplus money left over." Generally when you have money left over, it means that you've done everything else you needed to do first. There is only one thing George Bush did before he started pushing his tax-cut plan, and that was take the oath of office. By jamming through his tax cut first, it meant that anything else he claimed to have wanted to do would have to be done with the money that was left over—which, as we all now know, is none.

Oh, and did he crow about that tax cut. When it passed, he called it a great day for America. He pointed out that it was the first across-the-board tax relief in a generation (a lie). He hailed the fact that his plan was passed in record time. Well, it's a record-breaker all right. It's now responsible for a record fiscal reversal, record job loss, record low level of job creation. Instead of crowing, the guy should be eating crow.

THE MYTH OF THE KENNEDY TAX CUT

A while ago, I had Senator Jim Inhofe (R-OK) on *Crossfire.* Nobody's ever accused Senator Inhofe of being the brightest bulb in the Senate, but when we got to talking about taxes, he started talking about President John F. Kennedy's tax cut as if he were reciting the Bible from memory. He was that sharp. It's an article of faith among Republicans that if you want to defend your tax cuts, you talk about President Kennedy's tax cut. They've been doing it on TV shows, on the radio, and in campaign commercials for years now. It's true, President Kennedy did pass a tax cut. Here's what it did. He reduced the top marginal rate from 91 to 70 percent. It reduced the lowest rate from 20 to 14 percent. So every time someone says that Kennedy cut taxes to raise revenue, get in their face with these facts:

● When the Kennedy-Johnson tax cut was enacted, the nation had a deficit of only $36.5 billion (in today's dollars). Today, the Bush administration faces a $500 billion deficit. Remember, also at that time, the baby boomers were going off to work, not off to retirement.

● Even after the Kennedy-Johnson tax cut, the wealthy still paid a marginal tax rate of 70 percent. Today, the wealthiest taxpayers are paying a top rate of 38.6 percent.

Also, Republicans like to ignore what else Kennedy said about tax cuts, which was that "tax reduction alone, however, is not enough to strengthen our society."

So the next time a Republican embraces the legacy of Camelot by calling for a tax cut, tell them that if they want to truly celebrate the Kennedy legacy, they should double the tax on the wealthiest taxpayers. Of course, they could always support a nuclear test ban treaty or citizen service or something that actually would "strengthen our society."

THE BUSH RESPONSE IN DEPTH

The president argues that tax cuts create jobs, and the bigger the tax cut, the more jobs will be created. "I believe we should enact more tax relief so that we can create more jobs," was how he put it.

First of all, that's just wrong on its face. If tax cuts automatically created jobs—if the math were truly that simple—the fact that Bush passed the largest tax cut in a generation would mean that we should have the largest job creation in a generation. Instead, since that tax cut, America has lost over 3 million private jobs—on track to be the worst job creation under any president in fifty-eight years.[27] In fact, to avoid being the first post–World War II president to lose jobs over his term, President Bush would have to create about 157,000 jobs a month from September 2003 until the end of his first term.

If tax cuts create jobs, it would logically follow that tax increases cost jobs. How, then, do you explain that between 1993 and 2000, President Clinton raised taxes on the richest Americans to reduce the budget deficit, and the economy responded by creating (not losing) 20 million jobs?

Since that simple logic is lost on the current president, let's follow this line of thinking to its inevitable conclusion. If tax cuts create jobs and promote economic growth, then getting rid of all taxes would solve all of our economic problems and lead to full employment. But wait, if we got rid of all taxes, we'd have no government, no military, and no courts. We'd have no police to keep order, no public schools to educate kids, no fire departments to respond to fires. We'd have no laws to protect private property, no one to ensure our drinking water is safe, nobody to make sure our lights stay on and our missiles don't go off. We'd all be fully employed . . . as vigilantes. When you follow Bush's train of thought, you realize that it derails pretty fast.

TRIED AND FAILED

Do me this favor. Every time you hear George W. Bush say that we need more tax cuts, remind yourself that we already had two tax cuts. In fact, we didn't just have little bitty tax cuts, we had massive ones, the biggest in a generation. Now think of the first tax cut. It was nearly three years ago, so it's a little hard to remember. Okay, remember? Now that you've reminded yourself of that tax cut, don't you feel flush from all that tax relief he promised you'd get? Aren't times good? Don't you wish that every two years of your working life was like the last two years? Neither do most people. In fact, if we can't beat the guy in an election, maybe we should have the Better Business Bureau go after him for false advertising.

Back when Bush was pushing that first tax cut, he knew he'd be met with some criticism about it being unfair. Oh, but you've got to give our president credit for being one tough, savvy debater. He said: "If somebody argues with you, just remind them of these facts, that the average family will receive $1,600 in tax relief." [28]

I don't know about any $1,600. Here are the facts I do remember. I remember Mary and me getting a $600 check. I remember almost puking on the thing, because it was sent out from the IRS office in Texas (unnecessary) and stamped on it were the words "tax relief for America's families" (ridiculously unnecessary), and weeks prior to its arrival, we got a letter saying that it was coming (incredibly ridiculously unnecessary use of $72 million of our money and potentially an illegal politicization of the IRS). I remember thinking that this will go down as the most expensive piece of political direct mail in history. Then I remember all my investments going straight into the crapper and half of my nephews asking me to help them find work.

Granted, I stand to do okay by these stupid tax cuts, but that's my recollection. I hope yours is different.

But it probably isn't. When you look at the numbers, you see that a good number of Americans got that $300 or $600 rebate check (by the way, that rebate check happened to be the one Democratic contribution to the plan)—but that was all they got.

In fact, eight out of ten Americans have now gotten just about all they're ever going to get from that 2001 tax cut. The only people who have any real stake in seeing the next stages of this tax cut are the very few people making a million dollars a year. They're waiting on an additional $50,000 in tax cuts to kick in—which is the equivalent of that $300 rebate check every other day, every month of every year, forever. Not bad, huh?

Let's recap. Just about all but the very richest people have gotten just about everything they're going to get from this tax cut. In the meantime, we've lost 3.3 million jobs, and the tax cut is responsible for 45 percent of our fiscal deterioration. When confronted with the hole in which he's put this country, give our president credit—he did not hesitate in asking for a shovel. The man wants to keep digging.

HERE WE GO AGAIN

In fighting the Great Depression, FDR once said, "It is common sense to take a method and try it. If it fails, admit it frankly, and try another. But by all means, try something." He didn't say, "Deny that it failed, try it again, but this time call it something different," but that's apparently what Bush heard, because in response to the monumental failure of his first tax cut, he called for another.

The second tax cut we just passed is almost more of an abomination than the first one. That's because it's based largely on accelerating the one that's already passed (the one where only the millionaires are waiting for their part to kick in) and eliminating the individual tax on dividend income. As far as I'm concerned, speeding up a bad tax cut is like putting a racing stripe on a turd—at the end of the day, it's still a turd.

Once again, he claimed that it's the perfect cure for all that ails us, and once again, he's lying, misinformed, deluded, or all of the above. Let's go through the lies that, because this thing is now law, we're stuck living with:

Bush says, "The tax relief I have proposed and will push for until enacted . . . will create 1.4 million new jobs by the end of 2004." [29]

Ignore for a second that the economy has lost 3.3 million private sector jobs since Bush took office, so this solution, even if it works as advertised, gets us back only about half of the jobs he's lost. Ignore that the White House actually admitted that all that job creation would have happened anyway, just a year later. Ignore that nothing this White House has ever predicted has actually happened. Just because the guy's wrong ninety-nine times in a row doesn't mean he can't be right the hundredth. So, for the purposes of this little game, we'll take him at his word and pretend that this plan is going to create 1.4 million jobs. Now let's think about this for a second. Our president is telling us that $726 billion spent on tax cuts will create 1.4 million jobs. That seems like a lot of money for not a lot of jobs. Luckily, I have my abacus handy. Divide $726,000,000,000 by 1,400,000 and you get $518,571. That's a cost of over $518,000 per job, or about fifteen times the salary of the average American. If job creation was really the goal here, wouldn't it be cheaper for the federal government to give money to the states, which are hurting so bad right now that they're being forced to fire teachers, health workers, and police officers? Of course it would. And so job creation clearly isn't the goal.

Now let's snap out of our best-case-scenario fantasyland and listen to this conclusion reached by the nonpartisan, nonprofit Economic Policy Institute: "Analysis of the Bush plan shows a positive impact over the first two years but an annual GDP decline of .25% thereafter. Consequently, GDP is lower by 1.0% in 2013 than it would be with no Bush package. The result is a loss of 750,000 jobs by 2013." [30] Only this White House could design a "jobs growth package" so bad that it will lose us three-quarters of a million jobs.

Bush says, "The tax relief is for everyone who pays income taxes— and it will help our economy immediately: 92 million Americans will keep, this year, an average of almost $1,000 more of their own money." [31]

This is one of the few cases in the life of George W. Bush where the man is actually above average. Unfortunately—and this is a numerical impossibility that only this White House could achieve—72 percent of taxpayers are below average.[32] That's right, 72 percent of taxpayers will get less than the tax cut the administration is touting, and almost half of all taxpayers would get $100 or less. Forty-two million taxpayers would get nothing at all.[33] I guess it all depends on what your meaning of "everyone" is.

Bush says, "About half of all dividend income goes to America's seniors, and they often rely on those checks for a steady source of income in their retirement. . . . So today, for the good of our senior citizens . . . I'm asking the United States Congress to abolish the double taxation of dividends." [34]

Aw, isn't that sweet? He cares about old people . . . or does he? It turns out that because most seniors make less than $50,000 a year, two-thirds of older Americans would get little or nothing from the dividend cut.[35] You know what most seniors rely on for a "steady source of income in their retirement"? Social Security. And that's where every dime of this tax cut is coming from.

Bush says, "This growth and jobs package is essential in the short run; it's an immediate boost to the economy." [36]

Let's see, here. Eighty-two percent of the costs come after 2003. Doesn't sound immediate. All of the tax cuts are permanent. Doesn't sound short run.

✶　✶　✶

With every argument for this dog of a policy being demonstrably false, George Bush had to do something dramatic to show support for it. So he trotted out to the Rose Garden thirteen economists who support his plan. It was one of the more pathetic things I've seen in recent memory, because the next day Democrats trotted out four hundred economists—including ten Nobel Prize winners—who don't support his plan.

Now this is becoming an increasing problem in the press today. Mark Halperin, the political director of ABC News and one of the sharpest political commentators in town, calls it the "to be sure" paragraph. It goes something like this: "Every American who hasn't been lobotomized believes X. *To be sure,* there are some who disagree, and claim that Y is the case . . ." Right-wingers have cried "liberal media bias" for so long that virtually every media outlet has been cowed into a "to be sure" paragraph. You could have two flat-earth quacks saying one thing, and 2 million people saying something else, and you'll still get your "to be sure" paragraph.

That's exactly how the economist stunt played out. Bush musters up thirteen guys who are probably only supporting the plan because John Ashcroft has pictures of them in compromising positions, and Democrats show up with four hundred economists who actually did their homework in college. The press writes a story with the headline: ECONOMISTS DIVIDED OVER BUSH PLAN.

How to cut through the confusion? Well, we need to find someone whose word cannot be questioned on this, someone who will have total credibility in discussing the Bush plan, someone who has no ax to grind, score to settle, or agenda to pursue. Luckily, we found just the person. His name is Joel Prakken. He is the chairman of a company called Macroeconomic Advisers LLC. I don't know Joel, but he seems to be a pretty impressive guy. He was the senior economist for IBM. Before that, he served with the Federal Reserve Bank of New York. He has held positions on the faculties of New York University's Graduate School of Business, the Economics Department of Washington University, and the Olin School of Business at Washington University. He is the past president and a current director of the National Association for Business Economics, the largest nonacademic association of professional economists in the United States.

His company developed a model of the U.S. economy that is considered to be one of the most sophisticated out there. In fact, it's the computer model the White House used in making all of these glorious claims about their economic plan.

So what did Dr. Prakken conclude about how the plan George Bush put together will affect America's economy? "Surging budget deficits created by the President's proposal would raise interest rates, lower savings rates, and discourage job creation."

That's a pretty blunt assessment of a plan from one of the guys who, literally, wrote the book on it.

This all reminds me of the story of the two brothers from Baton Rouge who went up to the woods of Canada to hunt moose.

They hunted for a week, and each of them bagged a big moose.

At the end of the week, the plane flew in to take them home. The pilot took one look at these two big brothers, the two moose, and all their gear and said, "I can't fly you two out of here. The load will be too heavy."

One of the brothers said: "I don't understand. Last year, each of us had a moose, and the pilot loaded everything."

The pilot said: "Well, if you did it last year, I guess we can do it this year, too."

So they loaded the plane and took off. It climbed over the lake, it climbed over the trees, it climbed toward the mountain, but as the pilot predicted, it was too heavy, and the plane crashed into the mountain.

As they crawled out of the wreckage, one brother asked, "Where are we?"

The other brother looked around and said, "Oh, about where we got to last year."

George Bush walked away from the wreckage in Texas, he walked away from the wreckage of his 2001 tax cut, and now he's giving it another go. We don't need another attempt. We need a new plane, a new flight plan, and a new pilot.

THE "HAD ENOUGH" SOLUTION IN DEPTH

Basically, my view is this: The most brilliant tax code devised by the mind of man is a progressive tax on income, with income broadly defined. Done correctly, it's fair and it's comprehensive. Most people don't resent paying taxes. They resent that it's confusing, complicated, and the fact that it seems like only suckers play by the rules. So here are three ideas that progressives can stand for when it comes to tax policy: fair share, simplify, and verify.

FAIR SHARE

Pop quiz: John Snow is now America's secretary of the Treasury, the man who oversees how much tax is collected from the American people and American companies. Before he became Treasury secretary, he was the CEO of a railway company called CSX. How much money did CSX make between 1998 and 2001?

The answer: It depends who you ask.

If you ask the shareholders of CSX, they can look at their annual reports and see that CSX made $934 million over those four years.

If you ask the IRS, they'll look at CSX's tax returns and tell you that CSX made so little money that it qualified for a $164 million tax rebate.

Shouldn't that massive discrepancy set off alarm bells? Shouldn't John Aschroft turn to John Snow at the next cabinet meeting, read him his rights, and then cuff him? You'd think so, but it turns out what CSX was doing is perfectly legal. They're not even afraid to admit to it in their annual report: Here's what they say to their shareholders on the same pages where they're telling them about all the profits they're raking in: "CSX will pursue all available opportunities to pay the lowest federal, state, and foreign taxes."

If our new Treasury secretary is a champion tax dodger, he's unfortunately one of many.

In reality and in law, corporations are supposed to pay a tax of 35 percent on any profits they make. That's the rule, and that's what John Snow swore to enforce as secretary of the Treasury. In practice, the 250 largest and most profitable companies in America pay only 20.1 percent in taxes. In 1998, twenty-four companies that made a combined $12 billion took home a combined tax *refund* of $1.3 billion. So, while they told their shareholders they were making money hand over fist, they were telling the government that they were making virtually nothing. These aren't shady, fly-by-night companies we're talking about, either, these are companies with names like Chevron, Texaco, PepsiCo, Pfizer, J. P. Morgan, Goodyear, Ryder, Colgate-Palmolive, General Motors, and Northrup Grumman.

In fact, had all 250 of America's biggest companies paid the legal requirement of 35 percent taxes on the $735 billion in profits they told their shareholders they had made between 1996 and 1998, their federal income taxes would have totaled $257 billion—$98 billion more than they actually paid. Just how much money is $98 billion? Well, let's look at the one-year cost of some of the federal government's programs for comparison and see what that $98 billion could buy us, with room to spare:

- Homeland security
  (all necessary funding—port security
  food security, etc.) $30 billion
- Environment protection
  (all programs—clean air, clean water, Superfund) $40 billion
- Head Start $6 billion
- Pell Grants $13 billion
- Title I education $8 billion
- Peace Corps $275 million
- AmeriCorps $65 million

Instead, that money is disappearing into the balance sheet . . . and when it reappears, it tends to find its way into CEO bank accounts. So here's a simple proposal to make taxes more fair and help get us out of debt: If you're a company, when you tell your shareholders how much money you made, you tell the IRS the exact same thing. Fair. Simple. Straightforward.

If you didn't really make that much money in the eyes of the government, you shouldn't be allowed to take credit for it in the eyes of your shareholders. That's the Carville proposal: No more two sets of books—one for the government, one for the shareholders. No more sneaky accounting. Just pay taxes on what you make, like everyone else. Heck, if you want, you can just send the IRS your annual report, and they can do the math. We'll call it the "you say it, you pay it" plan—and it's a winning idea for people who have had enough of corporate tax duplicity.

Another way to get companies to pay their fair share is to make illegal a nasty accounting trick called a "corporate inversion." This is where an American company pretends that it got bought out by some shell company that exists—on paper only—in a place like Bermuda or the Cayman Islands. In the last couple of years, some two dozen companies have done this to avoid U.S. taxes—and some of them have names you recognize, like Tyco, Ingersoll-Rand, and Accenture. Not only are these companies clearly American companies that employ American workers and trade largely on American exchanges, a number of them have American government contracts—a total of $2 billion worth. This leads to some interesting ironies. For example, Ingersoll-Rand, whose tools were used to carve Mount Rushmore, now says that they aren't an American company. Or consider Accenture—they have a contract with the IRS to help them figure out a way to collect more taxes, while they themselves are dodging them.

If these companies that went offshore are brought back to the United States and forced to pay taxes—and Congressman Richard Neal of Massachusetts has a bill to make them do just that—it would bring in an extra $5 billion in revenue. Not chump change at all.

Finally, one other "fair share" approach to the tax code is to end corporate welfare as we know it. In 1998, *Time* magazine estimated that corporate welfare costs taxpayers $125 billion annually. Corporate welfare ranges from things like the $1.1 billion loan guarantee Congress granted to build cruise ships in Trent Lott's hometown to federal subsidies for fossil fuels that cost taxpayers over $5 billion per year. Getting companies to pay their fair share means getting them off the federal dole—and that's something progressives can get behind.

SIMPLIFY

I agree with Republicans. Our tax code should be simpler. And the simplest thing of all would be not having to spend an entire weekend figuring out your taxes in the first place. Well, in thirty-six countries a lot of people don't. Germany, Japan, and England have "no return" systems for at least some of their taxpayers. There's no reason America can't join the club. Right now, about 40 percent of American taxpayers file either a 1040EZ or 1040A. That means for about 40 percent of taxpayers, the IRS already knows all they need to know about your income. There's no reason that the IRS can't simply file for you and then send you a statement that says, "According to our records, this is how much money you made. Therefore you owe us (or we owe you) this amount of money."

Under this system if you think there's a mistake, you can spend that weekend actually doing your taxes. If you made more money than they think you did, you can get your ass audited. But either way, tax time gets a lot easier for a lot more Americans, and, in the fine progressive tradition, the government is doing something for the people.

Also, this is basically how they do it in England—and last I checked we still like England.[37]

VERIFY

As I said before, part of the resentment that comes with paying taxes isn't about the taxes at all, but rather that it's begun to feel like you're a fool if you play by the rules. George Bush has contributed to this in a big way. Thanks to him, the IRS is aggressively going after households claiming the Earned Income Tax Credit (this is about a $2,000 tax credit that goes to households making less than $34,692). In fact, he's asked for $100 million and 650 more IRS workers to help spot erroneous tax-credit claims before any money is paid out.[38] He's also going after waiters' tips—which he says are underreported.[39] True or not, that's a remarkable demonstration of our president's priorities, especially considering that as he's doing those two things, the number of audits and prosecutions of wealthy individuals and businesses has declined[40] while the number of wealthy Americans who pay no taxes anywhere in the world has reached record levels.[41]

The administration claims that the crackdown on poor families has the potential to save U.S. taxpayers between $6.5 billion and $10 billion a year. At the same time, it is estimated that corporate tax shelters cheat the government of about $50 billion a year.

Now, I am not a moral relativist—stealing is stealing, cheating is cheating. Still, say I own a bank and a robber comes in and takes $2 million and runs off with it. As he's running out, he drops $2,000, which some passerby picks up and runs away with. Who am I going to go after first?

If America went after the big cheats the way George W. Bush wants to go after the small fry, it would do a lot to restore some confidence in the system.

A Simplified Salad

I've been giving you a lot of food for thought. At this point, I thought you might want some more thought for food. See, I am a huge salad fan, but I've had enough of the current state of the American salad.

I've had enough of arugula infused with a raspberry vinaigrette. I've had enough of avant-garde chefs thinking that grapefruit and spinach somehow belong together. I've had enough of tasteless or wretched-tasting salads that require an encyclopedia and a map to figure out the ingredients.

You're getting a meal's worth of information, and what would a full meal be without a salad? This is one of my favorite salad recipes. It comes from the late, great Jake Staples, who gave it to my momma to put in her cookbook, *Delicious Heritage.*

People go absolutely crazy for this salad when I serve it out at our farm. The next time someone asks you to bring the salad, this is the one you're going to want to bring.

> **6 ounces Romano cheese**
> **⅓ cup crumbled bleu cheese (no need to get fancy cheeses;**
> **the regular stuff will do)**
> **¾ cup lemon juice**
> **¼ cup white vinegar**
> **2¼ teaspoons salt**
> **½ cup olive oil**
> **1½ cups Wesson oil**

1 teaspoon finely chopped garlic (Mary insists on a lot more garlic, so adjust the garlic upward accordingly, but adjust nothing else)

½ bunch of parsley, broken up (This wasn't in Jake's original recipe, but I find it helps cut the taste of the cheese)

Salad greens

1. Grind Romano cheese in food processor until fine.
2. Add bleu cheese and mix well.
3. Place cheese mixture in an airtight container and refrigerate.
4. Mix remainder of ingredients, except the greens, in a large bowl and whisk well until thoroughly blended. Pour dressing into a 1-quart container. Refrigerate.
5. Prepare greens, using any combination of these: iceberg lettuce, spinach, watercress, endive, romaine, escarole (I like to make sure it's a mix of lighter and darker greens).
6. Mix greens with the oil and vinegar dressing. Toss some of the cheese mixture onto the dressed greens. Serve.

Yield: 10 ounces cheese mixture; 18 ounces dressing

PART THREE

"SECURE THE BLESSINGS OF LIBERTY TO OURSELVES AND OUR POSTERITY"

$\star$ $\star$ $\star$

There are a number of articles of faith in Republican circles when it comes to what helps—or, more frequently, hurts—the economy.

For example, if you raise the minimum wage, you'll hurt the economy.

If you insist on worker safety regulations, you'll hurt the economy.

If you make companies rather than employees pay more for health care, you'll hurt the economy.

If you don't give huge tax breaks to rich people and corporations, you'll hurt the economy.

If you don't let companies foul streams and pump pollutants into the air, you'll hurt the economy.

If you stop American corporations from incorporating overseas to escape U.S. taxes, you're going to hurt the economy.

If you don't let big deficits accumulate today at the expense of children tomorrow, you'll hurt the economy.

My two questions are thus:

First, who are *they* to tell *anybody*, much less the Democrats, about how to build a good economy?

Second, do we want to raise the children of America in an economy or a society?

Republicans claim that the interests of our economy are at odds with the interests of our society and that they hold the morally superior position because they insist on putting the interests of an economy over the interests of a society. (Never mind that it's really not about helping the economy; it's about helping their campaign contributors.)

If we are to truly secure the blessings of liberty to ourselves and our posterity, we need a strong economy *and* a strong society, one that gives people the chance to succeed. In the following chapters, we're going to discuss education, the environment and energy, and health care—three of the big areas where the Bush folks just don't get it and where we need new ideas to demonstrate that we do.

5

EDUCATION

My momma was known to everyone in the town of Carville—and most of the people of Louisiana—as Miss Nippy. Miss Nippy had a rule in life that there were only two acceptable things for someone between the ages of five and sixty-five to be doing: working at a job or developing the skills needed to get a job.

As I see it, the great divide in this country is between people who believe that education, training, work, and opportunity are the essential ingredients to building a stronger and more prosperous nation and people who don't. She sure as hell believed that education was important. She put eight of us through college, and she did it by selling encyclopedias. She was a darn good saleswoman, too. I first shared her sales technique in the book *Buck Up, Suck Up . . . and Come Back When You Foul Up* and I think it's worth telling again. She'd prowl the streets in and around the town of Carville, looking for two things—children's toys and a bass boat.

Being one of the more Catholic states in the Union, and a state that calls itself "the Sportsmen's Paradise," Louisiana had more than its share of both.

She'd find one of these houses—preferably on an evening or on the weekend—and ask to see the man of the house. You'd think that it'd be easier to sell books to women, but Miss Nippy had a strategy. The man would come to the door, and she'd ask, "You the father of these children?" The man would say yes, and she'd start in on him. "Such beautiful children," she'd gush. Then she'd have a word or two with one of the kids and turn to the daddy with awe in her voice, "And so bright!"

One thing I've learned in politics is that adults have a pretty good sense of when you're blowing smoke up their ass. You can flatter them, but they know when you're overdoing it. Parents have no such filter when it comes to hearing things about their children. You can tell them something that runs counter to their entire experience raising that child, and they will eat it up. Every time I run a campaign, and one of the younger campaign workers brings his or her parents by, I make a point of going up to the child, putting an arm around his or her shoulder, looking the parents in the eye, and saying something along the lines of, "Thank you for allowing Jimmy to be part of our campaign. You may not realize it, but this young man that you have raised is the future of the Democratic Party."

It doesn't matter if Jimmy came into the office from Harvard or straight from reform school. No parent has ever doubted me, much less challenged me. And now that I've told you exactly what I say, and someday your child is working for me and I tell you the exact same thing—I'll bet you dollars to donuts that you won't doubt me either. If someone tells me something similar about my daughters, I'll believe 'em, too. That's because all parents believe their child has the potential to do something great in this world—and, in just about every case, they're right.

So, my momma would eyeball these children, declare them bright and full of potential, and the man of the house would flush with pride.

Then she'd say, "You must spend a lot of time with them, reading the encyclopedia. You do have a set of encyclopedias, don't you?"

At that point, the sale was as good as made.

"No? How can that be? Such potential in these children, such God-given talent, and you're going to let it go to waste? Surely not. I am going to personally arrange for you to purchase one of the finest collections of children's educational materials ever published."

If the guy said he didn't want—or couldn't afford—the encyclopedias, Miss Nippy would spring the trap.

"I see you can afford that beautiful bass boat, can't you? You're gonna tell me that chasing a bunch of fish around a bayou is more important than the future of your children? You going to tell me that you're willing to sacrifice your child's future because you and your beer buddies thought it was more important to spend money on fishing than the education of this so clearly gifted child?"

That's when the guy would look down at the half-empty, now warm bottle of beer in his hand, gaze over at the bass boat that was once such a source of pride and had now become an example of paternal negligence, and realize that he was hooked better than any bass ever was.

My momma may have been an expert saleswoman, but she wasn't some sort of con artist. Those encyclopedias were a good investment, and so is an investment in the public education of America's children.

Right now, Republicans are investing a lot of energy in sounding pro-education. It's a shame that that's all they're investing—because while their rhetoric is strong, their education policy is weaker than the public education system they like to bash so much. Let's go through the drill.

The Problem: Less than half of all American students are graduating from high school ready for college, work, and citizenship.

The Bush Response: Institute reform without resources, call for vouchers in all cases.

The "Had Enough" Solution: A student bill of rights—one that allows for parental involvement, a creative approach to high schools, and a federal willingness to pay for our promises.

THE PROBLEM IN DEPTH

Bashing America's public schools is just about the easiest thing you can do in Washington, D.C. Claiming that you're pro-education is the second easiest. A lot of Republicans have developed a certain skill at doing both of those things simultaneously. In Louisiana, we call that having a mouth like a catfish—you can talk out of both sides and still whistle out the middle. The problem is that you simply can't be pro-education if you don't believe in America's public schools. Public schools educate 90 percent of America's kids. No matter what folks choose for their own kids, we all have a stake in the success of America's public schools.

Of course, in the fun-house mirror world of politics, people on both sides actually have an interest in saying how bad things are. Liberals scream that public schools are a failure because that allows them to say, "Look what happens when you don't give us enough money." Conservatives say the schools are a failure because they don't want anything that the government does to work. What nobody is saying is that things aren't that bad, but that there's plenty of room for improvement.

If I were to walk out on the street right now and ask a hundred people what's happening to American students' test scores, I'll bet that ninety-nine of them would tell me that they're going down the crapper. That's because they've heard both liberals and conservatives crying "failure!" for so long—even if they're crying it for different reasons. Well, those ninety-nine people would be wrong. Believe it or not, test scores have actually risen in almost all areas since the 1970s. In math, they've been increasing since 1973.[1] Since that same time, reading scores have gone up for nine-year-olds and thirteen-year-olds. (Scores for seventeen-year-olds have remained unchanged but haven't gone down.) Science is a problem, because while scores for nine-year-olds have improved, scores for thirteen- and seventeen-year-olds haven't.

Still, that's not entirely disastrous when you consider that the number of kids showing up at America's schools coming from broken homes, living in poverty, and speaking English as a second language has skyrocketed. It's kind of like what former Georgia governor Lester Maddox said when he was asked what could be done to reduce the number of riots in Georgia's state prisons. "What we need," Maddox replied, "is a better class of prisoner."

Technically, the "class" of student in America's public schools has been dropping for a while. I don't mean that in the "they're lower class than they ever were" sense—I mean that in the "they are more likely to come from poverty, more likely to be the children of a single parent, and more likely to have English as their second language" way.

And the numbers back that up. In 1972, just over 20 percent of public school students were minorities.[2] In 2000, that number was just under 40 percent. And although the proportion of minority students has increased, minority dropout rates have actually decreased.[3] In addition, the gaps between minority students and white students are closing— even as the proportion of minority students increased.[4] Oh, and by the way, public schools are also serving more students with learning and physical disabilities than ever before.

Just as Governor Maddox didn't get to pick and choose what kind of person ended up in his prisons, the public schools can't pick and choose who shows up at their door. The fact that our public schools are holding their own given what little support they get from Washington is a minor miracle.

I'm not giving you these numbers so you can argue that everything is hunky-dory and we should just be defending the system. We've got problems now and problems ahead. Right now, the children of the baby boom generation have filled our schools, pushing enrollments to the highest they've ever been, and those enrollments are going to keep going up until the end of this decade. As a result, these old schools are literally bursting at the seams. Over 60 percent of public school administrators say that they need to seriously repair or replace a fundamental structural feature of the building—roofs, walls, windows, plumbing, lighting, and basic electrical power. I'm not saying that every public school in America should look like Versailles, but it's no good for achievement when kids are trying to learn while also trying to line up buckets under a leaky roof, or getting sick from faulty ventilation systems, or walking to an entirely different building just to go to the bathroom. And beyond that, what kind of message does it send when kids walk into a school that, clearly, nobody gives a damn about?

Partly as a result, America's students aren't the best in the world. There are a bunch of studies that pit American students against kids from other countries. The one a lot of people pay attention to is called the Trends in International Math and Science Study, or TIMSS. In the latest TIMSS test, American students ranked eighteenth out of thirty-eight nations in science and nineteenth of thirty-eight in math. In each case, that put us in a group with countries like Latvia and Bulgaria[5]— not quite countries we like to think of as America's academic equals. Now, this comparison isn't entirely fair, because a lot of the best-performing countries in this study run their public schools differently. For example, some segregate kids by ability. They test them when they're young, and if they don't show university-track potential, they end up in technical school and never get close to a TIMSS test to begin with. Also, other countries have national curricula, which prepares kids better for this type of test. But even though the comparison isn't clean, there is no denying that we can do better by our kids. And until we do, we shouldn't be in the business of defending the status quo. As Americans, we should settle for nothing less than the best. Our children's future—and America's future strength—depend on it.

That doesn't mean we can't or shouldn't tell people about successes when we see them, but remember my first rule for Democrats to live by: Never just oppose, always propose.

THE BUSH RESPONSE IN DEPTH

The Bush solution isn't a solution so much as it is a cynical scheme to make vouchers the only answer. Basically, it relies on tests designed to demonstrate failure in the hopes that we will say that vouchers are what we need to correct it.

First, a little history and a little explanation—because although everyone seems pretty familiar with the fact that President Bush signed an education bill called No Child Left Behind, most people don't have the first clue about what's in it.

But let's start from the real beginning. Historically, the federal government has never really had too much to do with America's public schools. In fact, it wasn't until 1957 that there was any federal role in education at all. That's the year the Soviets launched Sputnik. Until that time, there had been a bunch of efforts to have the federal government help out with America's public schools, but none passed. That little satellite was America's wake-up call. All of a sudden, everyone started saying that our kids were falling behind in math and science and the Soviets would eat our lunch if we didn't do something. The first bill that passed was called the National Defense Education Act. The point of the title was that our nation's strength and security rested on the type of education we gave our kids. It's something we'd do well to remember today.

The government's role hasn't been expanded much since then. In fact, the government's only real role is to level the playing field, which I'll discuss in a minute. We still leave funding concerns and curriculum decisions largely in the hands of local school boards (which is why they can still teach creationism in places like Kansas). In fact, only about 7 percent of what is spent in America's schools comes from the federal government, and most of that goes into a program called Title I. Title I is aimed largely at schools in low-income areas—that "leveling the field" I mentioned. It's money that goes to schools based on the number of students at that school who are poor enough to be eligible for free and re-duced price lunches. Title I is where most of that 7 percent goes—and it's really the only place where federal reforms have any meaning, be-cause if states and schools don't enact them, they can have that money withheld. So, when we're talking about changes in the federal commit-ment to public education, we're really talking about changes to Title I.

You with me so far? Good.

While he was campaigning for president, George Bush talked a lot about testing, reading, and high standards. When he first proposed his education plan in September 1999, he said that the goal of testing was to determine which schools were failing. Then, if a school was deemed fail-ing for three years, all the kids there would get vouchers to go to a new school. He was a little squirrelly on how much those vouchers would be worth. In fact, the only thing he said was that each child in the school should get "their share" of the money. By that, he meant that they would get "their share" of Title I dollars to go to a private school. Remember, this is all about Title I.

So what would be "their share?" Right now, we are spending about $1,100 a year per Title I eligible kid. (Oh yeah, that's the other thing—some kids in failing schools aren't eligible for Title I because their fami-lies aren't quite poor enough. Under Bush's plan, even if the school was designated as failing, those kids would get nothing.) If the federal gov-ernment fully funded Title I—something it has never done—that "share" would be worth closer to $2,400.

A $2,400 voucher. Not bad? Not quite. Because the average private elementary school will run you about $3,200 a year, the average private high school costs about $7,400 a year.[6] And if you think that your voucher is going to help you afford a swanky place like Andover, where

George W. Bush went, think again. Tuition there is $28,500 a year—although, to be fair, that does include room and board.

By the way, that information on how much a private school costs used to be easy to find. The Department of Education used to have it right there on its Web site. Amazingly, it disappeared recently. Of course, that's not surprising—given the fact that once you compare a $1,100 voucher with a $3,200 tuition, you begin to see that George Bush's voucher proposal is a bridge to nowhere.

Oh, and remember that this whole charade assumes there are private schools that are just waiting to throw their doors open to refugees from the public schools. In 1998, the Department of Education studied the issue and found that there were only about 150,000 unfilled slots for students in America's private schools. That number gets a lot smaller when you take out the private schools that don't want poor kids from the inner city. It gets smaller still when you take out the private schools that don't want to take federal vouchers if it means taking federal regulations.[7]

Still, we'll go with that 150,000 number. Let me get out my old adding machine here for a second: the public schools educate 47 million kids. Just say that 20 percent of the schools are considered failing—even though under the Bush bill, the number will be much, much higher. That still means that 9.4 million kids could be getting vouchers for 150,000 slots. Under this little calculation, you could have sixty-three kids competing for every one available slot. George Bush isn't lying when he says that every child should be given a chance to succeed. He just doesn't mention that chance is less than one in sixty.

Now fast-forward to spring of 2001 and President Bush actually proposing his No Child Left Behind legislation. On a campaign, you get to talk about themes, and ideas, and stuff like that. People don't really pin you to the details. When you're president, and you propose legislation, it usually has some details—and, as the saying goes, that's where the devil is.

The devil was certainly in the details of No Child Left Behind (of course, the devil was in the title a little bit, too, which was outright stolen from legislation being proposed by the Children's Defense Fund—see the sidebar on page 152).

For starters, it tests kids a lot.

Now the idea of testing students to determine how a school is doing is not bad. It's not new, either. Nor is it Republican. Back in 1994, in what was called the Improving America's Schools Act, Democrats actually had to fight Republicans to include something called grade-span testing. Grade-span testing said that schools needed to test their students once in grades three to five, once in grades six to nine, and once in grades ten through twelve. It essentially told schools that they need to test to gauge achievement, but they can decide when is best to do that.

George Bush came into office and said that anything Democrats did was bad, so he decided that grade-span testing wasn't really testing. What we needed to do is what Texas did—we needed to test kids once a year, every year, in grades three through eight.

Now, there's not a shred of evidence that that much more testing gives a better assessment of the quality of the school, but if George Bush wants to use the awesome power of the United States presidency to make America's children fill out little ovals with their number two pencils until their eyes bleed, that's his prerogative.

I have only three problems with all that testing.

First, those tests don't magically get researched, written, printed,

LEAVE NO CHILD BEHIND VS.
NO CHILD LEFT BEHIND

The Children's Defense Fund is one of those organizations that does the Lord's work, day in and day out. Under the leadership of Marian Wright Edelman, it has been steadfast in its mission to ensure every child a Healthy Start, a Head Start, a Fair Start, a Safe Start, and a Moral Start in life—and, in the words of its motto, to "leave no child behind."

But wait, wasn't "leave no child behind" George W. Bush's line? He used it on the campaign trail to talk about his education plan just about every day. He even made "leave no child behind" the official theme of the first night of the Republican Convention. Turns out, he stole that slogan outright, and perhaps even illegally. See, the Children's Defense Fund—an organization that actually cares about leaving no child behind—trademarked "Leave No Child Behind" as its slogan back in 1994.

In fact, the Children's Defense Fund had even put together legislation called "Leave No Child Behind." As a result, George Bush was forced to change the name of his education initiatives and his actual legislation, creatively, to "No Child Left Behind." When you look at the two proposed laws side by side, and realize how limited George Bush's vision is of what it takes to leave no child behind, you start to wish the guy would have ripped off a little more than the name. See for yourself:

Does it . . .	An Act to Leave No Child Behind	Bush No Child Left Behind Act
Reform education?	Yes	Yes
Provide health care for all uninsured children?	Yes	No
Provide Head Start for all eligible preschoolers?	Yes	No
Provide child care for all eligible children?	Yes	No
Provide after-school and youth development programs?	Yes	No
Set a goal of lifting all children out of poverty?	Yes	No
Provide tax relief for low-wage working families?	Yes	No
Provide nutrition and housing assistance for low-income children?	Yes	No
Protect children from abuse and neglect and provide permanent families for vulnerable children and youth?	Yes	No
Protect children from gun violence?	Yes	No
Provide prevention and intervention to reduce juvenile delinquency?	Yes	No
Build supportive communities for children and their families?	Yes	No

So what's in a name? In this case, it's the difference between a real effort to help kids and George W. Bush's crocodile compassion.

and processed. They cost money. And when you test that much, it costs a lot of money. The National Association of State Boards of Education estimated that all this testing will cost $1 billion a year. So George Bush is saying to schools—a lot of which can't afford repairs, or pencils, or chalkboards—that they need to find a way to pay for a billion dollars of tests a year.

Second, all that time taking tests is time that kids aren't learning stuff. I think you should maximize the time spent putting knowledge into kids' heads, not the amount of time getting it out.

My third problem with all that testing is it is absolutely meaningless unless you learn something from the results. And that's where the devil in Bush's bill really lives. See, he put together a formula that looks at all those kids and does something called "disaggregate" them. Disaggregate is a fancy word that means you break them out by race, income, age, disability—all that stuff. Again, disaggregation is good in principle—it allows you to see exactly who is failing so that you can find ways to help them. In fact, that's why some minority groups actually like the Bush plan—because it could help them argue for the people they represent. The problem is how Bush is using disaggregation. Here's what his bill says: schools need to raise the percentage of kids who pass those tests every year. In addition, every one of those subgroups—low income, African American, Hispanic, limited-English-proficient, special needs—has to make progress every year. A school could be labeled as "failing" if even one subgroup didn't make enough progress in any one year. Sounds reasonable, right? Except for one thing. Test scores *never* rise every single year—even at the very best schools in the country. That's because a whole lot of things that have nothing to do with school quality can affect the outcome. In one year, there could be a group of kids that was a lot dumber than the last year's group. On testing week, a bunch of the smart kids could be out sick because they were all hanging out together playing chess and gave one another the same cold. It sounds funny, but it's no joke. Studies suggest that little stuff like that can account for 70 percent of a school's year-to-year score differences. In fact, there was a study done in 2001 by researchers at Stanford University, Dartmouth College, and a think tank in Cambridge, Massachusetts (speaking of smart kids), that looked at the Bush standard and estimated that under this law, 98 percent of elementary schools would be considered failing.[8]

You didn't read that wrong. Under the Bush plan, ninety-eight out of every hundred schools in our great land would be considered to be failing. We know that's not an accurate picture of American public education, so the question is whether this is an honest policy blunder or a cynical ploy. I'm willing to hear someone make the "honest blunder" argument, but I happen to believe that their true goal is to set up this scenario: If, by the gold standard of testing, every school is failing, we're in crisis. If we're in crisis, we need to do something dramatic. What would be something dramatic we could do? You got it: vouchers.

THE MYTH OF VOUCHERS

Now, up until this point, I've been withholding judgment on the wisdom of vouchers—despite the fact that at best those vouchers would pay for half a year of private school and despite the fact that no private school is going to take the kids anyway.

I'm done withholding judgment now. Vouchers don't work. They are a myth. They are a fraud. They distract us from the real issues we should be dealing with. The only reason they continue to be discussed as a viable policy is because of conservative orthodoxy and liberal guilt. The only reason vouchers have currency among Republicans is that Republicans never much liked the idea of the government being involved in America's schools to begin with. The only reason they have any currency among liberals is that there are a number of elites who feel that vouchers allow them to square their support for public education with their feelings of guilt that they send their own kids to really nice private schools.

Regardless of how folks feel, though, it now turns out that conservative arguments in favor of vouchers, like so much else you hear from conservatives, are a pile of stinking, steaming you-know-what.

First, let me be totally clear. I have nothing against private or parochial schools. I happened to graduate, if just barely, from a Catholic school. And while I graduated with genuine fear of—and a hearty respect for—the type of discipline that would get most public school teachers fired, I happen to think I got a pretty good education. That's why I'm quite comfortable in the knowledge that a fair number of my twenty nieces and nephews got their education from nuns in Louisiana. However, I think that parents who send their kids to private school still have a responsibility to support public education—and not the other way around.

That's my first beef with vouchers: they drain money away from the public schools that everybody has a stake in.

My second beef with vouchers is that they take public money but aren't accountable to the public. Wondering what's being taught at the

Eric Robert Rudolph Militant Survivalist School? Or how about the American al Qaeda Prep? You can stop wondering—because with vouchers it may be your money supporting those schools, but it's no longer your business what goes on there.

But again, my biggest beef with vouchers is purely utilitarian: they just don't work.

There is one study that conservatives just love to cite when it comes to vouchers. It came out in August 2000, in the middle of the presidential campaign, and it said that school vouchers significantly improved test scores of black children. It was done by a Harvard professor named Paul E. Peterson. Back in 1997, 20,000 New York City students each applied for a $1,400 voucher to private school. What Peterson did was look at the 1,300 kids who did get vouchers and went to private school and compared their performance to 1,300 of the other kids who *wanted* a voucher but didn't get selected. When the results came back, it was clear that the vouchers made no difference in test scores for the 2,600 students as a whole. So the researchers broke the group down by ethnicity and race, and that's when they noted that there was a 6 percent increase in sixth-grade test gains for the black voucher group.

Well, you throw that sort of information into a heated presidential campaign and it's like throwing chum into a shark tank. Everybody ate it up. "The facts are clear and persuasive: school vouchers work," the *Boston Herald* editorialized on August 30, 2000. "If candidates looked at facts, this one would be a no-brainer for Gore."

That same day, the *Atlanta Journal* editorialized, "The ground is shifting under the feet of any voucher opponent who continues to cling to a philosophy that no tax dollars should be used to educate students in a private setting. With this evidence emerging about improvement in student learning, politicians and community leaders can no longer stand in the door of the neighborhood private or parochial school."

William Safire in his *New York Times* column added, "The improved test performance of African-American students who were able to take advantage of vouchers suggests a stunning reversal of their fortunes. . . . Bush is on the right side of this. He should embrace the successful voucher students and joyfully join the controversy in states where children's futures are now at stake."

Then, three weeks later, Professor Peterson's partner in the study, a research firm called Mathematica, felt compelled to come out publicly and note that the only people who showed gains in Professor Peterson's experiment were black students in sixth grade—despite the fact that five grades had been studied, and nowhere else did black students, Latinos, or whites who received vouchers show any gains. Of course, if the initial report was met like chum in a shark tank, the second report made less noise than a mouse peeing on cotton.

But a couple of researchers including a Princeton economist named Alan Kreuger did take advantage of the fact that Mathematica went and made the entire database for the New York voucher study available to people who wanted to take a closer look. And what he saw was pretty amazing. The study had never meant to break out kids by race at all, so it just counted race by the race of the mother. A child of a black mother and a white father was considered black. A child of a black father and a white mother was considered white. Making those definitions consistent added a bunch more black kids to the sample. Then Kreuger added another 292 black kids who had been mysteriously left out, and reran the numbers. Turns out that those vouchers made no difference in the educational success of the kids that used them. None at all.[9]

Now that the Bible on which they swear their allegiance to vouchers has been shown to be a fraud, it's time for all of those folks who had been crowing about vouchers to shut their mouths and stop trying to dismantle America's public schools.

THE "HAD ENOUGH" SOLUTION

I've always thought it funny that just about every governor calls him- or herself the "education governor," just about every senator calls him- or herself the "education senator," and just about every president calls himself the "education president."

If these people were all telling the truth, that would make America the "education nation." Of course, when we spend forty times more on a tax cut than we do on education, our claim on being the education nation becomes a little less plausible. And until our students are the best in the world, we aren't the education nation. But we should be. Here are some ideas that can help get us there.

Now I'll be the first to admit that some of these ideas aren't particularly novel or fresh sounding. That's because when it comes to education, there isn't going to be some easily affordable, quickly obtainable silver bullet. Nobody's going to come up with some idea that nobody ever thought of before that is going to be our salvation. It's time to stop reinventing the wheel and just start rolling—because the truth is we already know what works.

Parental involvement matters. I'm always amazed when I go to my daughters' school for parent/teacher conferences, or back-to-school night, or something like that, because the traffic jam starts about four blocks from the school and the parking lot is as packed as an LSU football game. Those parents care about what's going on at their children's school, and the children do better as a result. And it's not just at schools where the traffic jams involve fancy cars, either. In 1969, I worked as a teacher at a middle school for boys in South Vacherie, Louisiana. I was fresh out of the Marine Corps, and I taught science the way my sergeant had run our platoon. I learned a lot of things that year. I learned that if you expect a lot from kids, they'll rise to the challenge. I learned that if you care about the work you do, they'll care about the work they do. And I learned that, almost universally, the kids whose parents supervised their homework, set limits on their television, showed up for back-to-school night—those were the kids who were doing the best.

So I saw with my own eyes that dedicated teachers and parental commitment are necessary. And, again, the statistics back that up. Students whose parents are involved in their schools are more likely to get higher grades, be in advanced programs, attend school more often, have fewer behavioral problems, and go on beyond high school. And those results cut across all types of kids—rich or poor, black or white, urban or rural. Now I know that we can't write the "Give a Damn About Your Children's Education" bill—but we can call for things like learning contracts and mandated parent/teacher conferences. And I realize that getting involved in your kid's school is harder if you have two jobs, no car, and no time. That's why we should expand family and medical leave to allow parents to take time off for parent/teacher conferences.

Let me give you just one example of what a difference that involvement makes: In Indianapolis, Indiana, there's a school called Arlington High School. It's a high school of about 1,800 kids, and by 1989, disorder and violence in the hallways had reached such a point that kids were skipping classes and activities just to avoid the halls. The school shut down and locked the doors at 3:30 P.M. because it just wasn't safe when the teachers left. Then the school hired a new principal, who asked parents to get involved. As a result, a group of ten fathers set up a program called "Security Dads." They wear uniform shirts and jackets and go to the school whenever they have time (for some, it's just for lunch, others spend a half day a week, some just attend sporting events) and monitor the halls and public spaces. Just as a result of their presence, the number of fights has gone down, attendance has gone up, and after-school programs have been added (because it's now safe and orderly in the school). As a result, achievement is on the rise. Today, "Security Dads" has been replicated in twenty schools, and the dads are beginning to do more than just walk the halls—they're providing counseling about drugs, violence, and gang-related activity. That's the power of parental involvement. We need more of it.

High schools matter. I'll give it to President Bush, he's right when he says that reading is the foundation of all learning. But what's interesting is that the place where our kids are starting to falter isn't in elementary school so much as it is in high school. High schools—though you don't hear about them a lot—are the weak link in American public education. Our kids do pretty well against their international counterparts when they're in grade school. It's when they hit high school that they start falling off.

I was one of the people who, for a long time, thought that big high schools were the answer—especially in rural areas. They'd give kids a chance to take better classes, have better equipment, all that stuff. Most of America agreed with me. In fact, for a century, America's high schools have been based on the "comprehensive" high school model. As a result, 60 percent of American high school students now attend schools of at least a thousand students. However, it's becoming increasingly clear that smaller high schools that foster a sense of community that is good for both teachers and students might be the way to go.

The most telling example of this is at a school that was called Julia Richman High School, on the Upper East Side of Manhattan.* Until recently, Julia Richman was a typical example of a bad inner-city school. There was graffiti in the hallways, there were metal cages in the vice principal's office to separate students who had been fighting, and local cops had taken to calling the place "Julia Riker's."

Today, Richman is clean and safe. Attendance is up, dropout rates are down. That's because Julia Richman High is now the Julia Richman Educational Complex—home to six smaller, separate schools that share the old space. The smaller schools allow teachers to really know their students and come to have a stake in their success, and students to really know their classmates, which reduces theft and fighting. Of course, the story isn't that simple, and the transition isn't that easy—but the principle is one worth looking at.

Now, opponents will immediately say that small schools cost more than large ones. As someone who has had enough, your first reaction when someone says that we shouldn't do something that will improve the education of our children because it's too expensive should be to tell

---

*The story of Julia Richman is told by Thomas Toch in "Divide and Conquer," *The Washington Monthly* (May 2003).

HOUSTON, WE HAVE A PROBLEM

Houston, Texas, was the home of George W. Bush's education miracle. Now it turns out that, upon closer inspection, Houston's education miracle was a fraud. It seems that a number of Houston schools simply made up numbers to show that attendance was rising, dropout rates were falling, and more students were heading to college.

Some high schools reported absolutely zero—zero—dropouts. Even at a wealthy school, zero dropouts would be seen as either a lie or a miracle. Amazingly, George Bush—and the complicit media—saw a miracle. Of course, it wasn't. It was just that Houston decided not to count thousands of dropouts. Unfortunately, George Bush didn't leave the mess in Texas. Houston's superintendent—the architect of this made-up miracle—is now *America's* secretary of education.[10]

those people to screw themselves, because an ignorant society is always, ultimately, the most costly option.

But this is a case where you don't even need to go that far. Sure, it makes sense that big high schools are cheaper because they spread their costs over a lot of students. But when you look closely at them, you notice something interesting: big high schools often employ a lot more nonteaching staff than small ones. Because they don't know the students, they need more security guards, guidance counselors, and administrators. In small schools, there are fewer nonteaching staff because in a smaller school, administrators have time to teach, teachers who know their students can also be counselors, and more resources go directly into the classroom. A study conducted by New York University's Graduate School of Education examined the finances of large and small high schools nationwide and found that small schools are only about 5 percent more expensive than large ones—a small price to pay for a high school that works. The same study also looked at the cost per graduate—and when you add the fact that fewer kids drop out of smaller schools, you see that educating students at a small school is actually cheaper.[11]

Money matters. Plain and simple, money matters. The wealthiest 10 percent of school districts in the United States spend nearly ten times more than the poorest 10 percent—and that difference is ultimately reflected in things like test scores and college admissions.

We shouldn't be afraid to defend an investment in education. In 1992, Jonathan Kozol came out with a book called *Savage Inequalities*. It made the argument (in much more detail than I'm going to make it here) that money matters.

Again, there will be detractors who say that we shouldn't spend money until we know what works—that the problem isn't investment, or equity, but excellence. Rather than parrot another rant from me, listen to what Kozol said when asked to respond to that claim:

> *The problem is not that we don't know what works. The problem is that we are not willing to pay the bill to provide the things that work for the poorest children in America. And we have not been willing for many, many years. After all, if poor black parents on the South Side of Chicago want to know what works, they really don't need a $2 million grant from Exxon to set up another network of essential schools. All they need to do is to take a bus trip out to a high school in Wilmette and see what money pays for. All they need to do is go out and see schools where there are 16 children in a class with one very experienced teacher. All they need to do is visit a school with 200 IBMs; a school where the roof doesn't leak; a school that is surrounded by green lawns, where the architecture and atmosphere of the school entice people to*

feel welcome; a school in which the prosperity of the school creates the re-
laxed atmosphere in which the teachers feel free to innovate, which they sel-
dom do under the conditions of filth and desperation.[12]

What's a "had enough" solution? Simple. The federal government
should simply pay for its promises. For example, in the mid-1970s, the
federal government created the Individuals with Disabilities Education
Act (IDEA). This landmark legislation said that students with disabilities must get the public education and other educational accommoda-
tions and support they need in order to achieve. IDEA was designed to
help states and school districts meet their legal obligations to educate
children with disabilities, and to pay part of the extra expenses of doing
so. Congress set a goal of providing 40 percent of the cost of the program. They've never come close to meeting that goal. In fact, the federal
government currently provides only about 20 percent of the cost. If the
federal government simply paid for its promise, it would free up about
$10 billion of local money that could then be used freely throughout the
schools. Same goes for Title I—if we fully funded that, it would save
states and towns another $6 billion. So, if the federal government simply
paid for the things it had promised in those two programs, we would increase federal aid to education by one-third—by far the largest increase
in history.

To suggest that we can't afford to pay for promises already made
while saying that we can afford a trillion dollars in new tax cuts is a dramatic demonstration of misplaced priorities. It's time for Democrats
who have had enough to set those priorities straight.

Sum it up—"The Student Bill of Rights." I said before that none of
those ideas are particularly new or novel. Put them all together, though,

and you do have something new and visionary. You have, in essence, a "Student Bill of Rights." And that's what we should be out there talking about—a bill of rights for our kids that says that every child deserves access to the things they need to succeed in school and beyond. It would say that kids have the right to good, trained teachers, up-to-date books, materials, and technology, safe school buildings, and small classes. It would say that every parent has the right to be involved in the education of his or her child, and that child has the right to a fair share of the resources. After all, if George W. Bush really cares about leaving no child behind, he should agree that every child has the right to get ahead.

In sum, saying that our education system is failing because some schools are failing is like saying the NFL is failing because the Detroit Lions are failing. That's screwy logic. And certainly the solution to that problem isn't revamping the NFL—it's improving the Detroit Lions. We should go at education the same way.

6

ENVIRONMENT
AND ENERGY

Here's a quiz.

Is global warming . . .
A. Real and serious?
B. An academic, made-up, BS issue cooked up by raving, kumbaya-singing leftists?

If you answered "A," keep reading. If you answered "B," go argue with someone about the shape of the earth or something.

Still with me? Good. Because I'm not sure what conservatives are trying to conserve—but it's not the air, land, and soil God gave us.

I've been in politics a long time, and one of the most heartening developments I've seen over time is the fact that it is no longer politically acceptable to express open contempt for the environment. In fact, voters, by and large, actually like the environment. They think it's worth protecting, even if doing so requires a little sacrifice. That's not too surprising—after all, it doesn't take some sandal-clad tree-hugger to realize that clean air and clean water and protected open spaces are important. You also don't need to drive a solar-powered moped to realize that we are not nearly as energy-independent as we should be.

That's why, as a candidate, President Bush pretended to be a friend of the environment. He spoke lovingly of God's creation. He even surprised voters with a pledge to regulate power plant emissions of carbon dioxide, a key contributor to global warming. Two months into his term, he broke that promise—and told senators that regulating carbon dioxide emissions would have led to "significantly higher electricity prices," which, as we all know, were far too high already, thanks in large part to Enron's efforts to create a shortage.

And then he got into office and had to either make good on his rhetoric or walk away from it. It's no secret what he chose. I could tell you that he withdrew from the Kyoto treaty, put forward an energy plan disdainful of environmental health, came out in favor of weaker arsenic standards for drinking water, made it easier for developers to eliminate wetlands, opposed the cleanup of hazardous waste sites, and brought back mountaintop mining, which is where mining companies literally cut off the top of a mountain to get to what's inside and then dump the mountaintop in valleys and streams.

I could tell you that he's made it easier to cut down trees and build roads in the wilderness places that Bill Clinton and Al Gore worked so hard to protect. And that's different from his "healthy forest initiative"—which should really be called "Leave No Tree Behind" because it allows loggers to go chop-happy in our national forests. If that's a healthy forest, then I've got a healthy head of hair.

I could tell you that this administration has also opened protected areas to new oil exploration. Bush and Cheney say it's the highest act of patriotism to decrease our dependence on foreign oil, but they also say that conservation is nothing more than a personal virtue. Using that logic, we need to decrease our dependence on foreign oil by ripping up our environment so that we can keep guzzling domestic oil. Of course, they conveniently ignore the fact that we hold only 3 percent of the known world oil reserves (not counting our quasi-ownership of Iraq) but consume 25 percent of the world's supply. So, even if we drilled in everybody's backyard, we could never meet our own demand with our own supply.

I could tell you that the best way to reduce dependence on foreign oil is to reduce dependence on oil, period. Then again, I'm biased: unlike Cheney and Bush, I didn't make millions selling oil. My oil buddies didn't bail me out of failed business deals, grant me sweetheart loans, make me the most prolific fund-raiser in political history, or lend me their private planes so I could ship in armies of lawyers to win the election in Florida. So I guess I don't really feel I owe them anything.

I could tell you all of these things, but I'll spare you the details, because it can all be summed up by one shining, towering example of their cynical approach to the environment.

In 2001, the administrator of the Environmental Protection Agency, Christie Whitman, commissioned a comprehensive report on the state of the environment. It was actually a pretty decent idea—she wanted to have a comprehensive review of what we know about various environmental problems, what we don't know, and how to go about studying what we don't know.

That report was just about ready to come out at the end of June 2003. But before she released it (and stepped down as EPA administrator, apparently because she wasn't quite as contemptuous of environmental regulations as Bush wanted her to be), she gave it to the White House so they could take a look at it. Well, they didn't just take a look—they took out a big red pen.

Of particular concern to the Bush folks was the section on climate, specifically global warming. Remember, this is an administration that withdrew from the Kyoto Protocol on climate change. In fact, at an international conference in Bonn after Bush made that decision for all of us, the leader of our delegation got up to insist that the United States was committed to taking measures on climate change. She was booed loudly, and the rest of our delegation snuck out.[13]

The reason we were booed is that, with the exception of a few quacks, the science on the existence of global warming, its causes and its impacts, is overwhelming, unequivocal, and accepted. Also accepted is the fact that the United States, which represents 4 percent of the world's population, produces about 25 percent of the planet's greenhouse gases.

So it made sense that the EPA report said what we all know to be true, that the vast majority of studies have found that global warming is caused, at least in part, by rising concentrations of smokestack and tailpipe emissions, and that it threatens to have an impact on our health and our environment. That was not what George Bush wanted to see. So, as happens with every truth this administration doesn't want to see—they simply denied its existence.

For example, the White House took the sentence "Climate change has global consequences for human health and the environment" and replaced it with a paragraph starting, "The complexity of the Earth system and the interconnections among its components make it a scientific challenge to document change, diagnose its causes, and develop useful projections of how natural variability and human actions may affect the global environment in the future." Basically, that's a whole lot of words saying, "Global warming? What global warming?"

But the cuts didn't stop there. The draft EPA report cited another report—one that Bush had *endorsed* in 2001—about the fact that humans are contributing to global warming. The White House cut it out. They also deleted a reference to a 1999 study showing that global temperatures had risen sharply in the previous decade compared with the last thousand years. In its place, administration officials substituted a reference to a study that was financed by the American Petroleum Institute, which basically said the opposite. Yup, when I want honest information on the impact of tailpipe emissions, I always go straight to the good people of the American Petroleum Institute.

A memo circulated among staff members at the EPA said that after the changes by White House officials, the section on climate "no longer accurately represents scientific consensus on climate change."[14]

They're being generous. The administration didn't just make the part on climate change inaccurate, they cut it out entirely. Last I checked, this wasn't Stalin's Russia, where you could solve a problem by just airbrushing it out of an official photo. But now we apparently don't need to remember or worry about global warming—because it ain't there anymore.

This whole charade reminds me of a story about the Boston Pilgrims and their most famous fan. Before Boston's American League baseball team was the Red Sox, they were called the Pilgrims. The Pilgrims had a lot of great players; Cy Young was one of their pitchers. They also had some great personalities. One of those was Michael T. "Nuff Ced"

McGreevy, a local bar owner and the leader of a group that called themselves the Royal Rooters. Nuff Ced owned the Third Base Saloon. It
was called that because, like third base, it was the last stop before home.
Because the bar was a big hangout for fans after games, and there were
a lot of debates between fans of the Beaneaters—Boston's National
League team—and the Pilgrims, it tended to get a little rowdy. Nuff Ced
McGreevy earned his name because any time a dispute got too heated,
he was able to end it quickly and completely by bellowing, "Nuff Ced!"

Sometimes, I think those two words are exactly what we need to
end a bunch of heated debates in Washington. So let me just say this and
let it serve to summarize this administration's approach to all things environmental: they literally erased global warming. Nuff Ced.

The Problem: Americans want water safe to drink, air clean to
breathe, and land that is protected. America also has to be able to produce all the energy we need. Otherwise we'll always be stuck kissing up
to countries we have no business kissing up to—like Saudi Arabia.

The Bush Response: Use everything as an excuse to dig, drill, and
burn. When protecting the environment comes into conflict with promoting the interests of your industry friends, choose the latter every
time—but announce big, bad changes on Fridays so people won't notice.

The "Had Enough" Solution: Nothing less than energy independence
is acceptable. That's what progressives should be for, and we should be
willing to make the small trade-offs that may be required in order to
achieve that larger goal.

THE BUSH RESPONSE IN DEPTH

Basically the Bush approach to environmental issues is to govern against the environment and the will of the people, but to do it mostly in secret, preferably when nobody is watching.

I'm convinced you could not get one-quarter of the American people to vote for their agenda if you actually wrote down their record and had people read it. In fact, I have written down their agenda in a number of polls. When people do read it, they're disgusted. When you tell them that's exactly what the Bush-Cheney folks are doing, they don't believe it. And they don't say it in that surprised infomercial sort of way, like "I can't believe an angled grill drains the fat from my hamburger." They say it in a "I don't believe that anyone elected to serve the American people would do this to us" way.

The Bush folks know that people feel that way, too, so they're very careful about how they go about selling out the environment. Here's their MO: They load the administration with former industry lobbyists. The lobbyists—now policy makers—are the ones who have to decide whether to file or defend against lawsuits by the industries they used to (and still seem to) serve. In almost every case, they respond to litigation by reaching a settlement that is generous for industry, but they invariably call it a reasonable compromise. In that way, they can help their friends, hurt the environment, and look like they're being balanced and fair in the process.

Now, there are some occasions when they have to take action or make a clear decision. In those cases, they try to do it when no one is watching.

It's your basic political rule of thumb that if you've got news you're not proud of, you push it out in a release just before a weekend or a holiday, when few people see it, and those who do see it don't have the time or the chance to organize against it. If you judge the Bush administration environmental record by how many announcements are made Friday afternoon, you just know they know they're doing wrong.

In the space of two months at the end of 2002 and the beginning of 2003, a proposal to open 9 million acres of wilderness on Alaska's North Slope for oil exploration was announced on a Friday. New guidelines that would cause 20 million acres of wetlands to lose federal protection from industrial pollution was announced on a Friday. A decision to cancel federal oversight on cleanup of 300,000 miles of rivers and 5 million acres of lakes was announced on a Friday—the Friday before Christmas. Rules that would allow aging coal-fired power plants to upgrade their facilities without installing anti-pollution equipment was announced on a Friday—the Friday before Thanksgiving—and the rules were published on New Year's Eve. (By the way, when nine attorneys general filed suit against these rules, New York's attorney general said, "This action will bring more acid rain, more smog, more asthma, and more respiratory disease to millions of Americans." The EPA spokesman said: "These rules will be positive for the environment." When they're doing bad, they say they're doing good. If Karl Rove really believed it would be positive for the environment to let old coal-fired plants avoid putting in anti-pollution devices, he would have had the president make the announcement next to a smokestack—that is, if the Secret Service didn't stop it for the health risk.) On the Friday after New Year's, they fast-tracked a bunch of logging projects, saying that environmental reviews weren't necessary. And the Friday after that, they announced that they were removing Clean Water Act protections from 20 million acres of wetlands.[15] Seven major environmental announcements all on a Friday.

If you ask the administration about it, they probably won't say, "We know the American people are against what we're doing, so we're trying to announce this when no one's paying attention." What they'll probably say is, "We announce new policies and initiatives when they're ready to be announced, and they just happen to be ready on Fridays."

There are five weekdays, so, assuming that nobody's making new policy on the weekends, the chance that any given announcement is ready to go on a Friday is one in five. Therefore, the chance that two announcements both coincidentally happen to be ready to go on consecutive Fridays is 1 in 5 multiplied by 1 in 5—1 in 25. The chance that three announcements are all ready to go on Fridays is 1 in 125. The odds of four anti-environmental announcements all being ready on a Friday are 1 in 625. Five in a row? One in 3,125. How about six Fridays? One in 15,625. And, put it this way, if the White House says those seven Friday announcements are just a result of random scheduling, the chances that they are telling the truth is 1 in 78,125. As a point of reference, you have better odds of being dealt a straight flush in poker.

So, you can look at this in one of two ways. Either the chances are 1 in 78,125 that they're telling the truth. Or, the odds are more than 99.999 percent that they know they're governing against the wishes of the vast majority of Americans, and they're hoping that in the midst of war on terrorism and war in Iraq, and the sagging economy, and the busy pace of people's lives, no one will notice they're poisoning America.

You tell me which is more likely.

Then again, you tell me if you'd do anything differently if your vice president put together an energy task force that met with energy industry officials 714 times yet had contact with nonindustry groups (environmental, conservation, public interest) only 29 times and then came out with an energy "plan" that was essentially $30 billion in tax breaks for the oil and gas industries.

THE "HAD ENOUGH" SOLUTION

Everyone's always whining to me that we don't have any ideas, anything big and new to stand for. Energy independence is a big idea, and we ought to own it.

To do that requires the ability, as I've said before, and forgive my language, to avoid letting little crap get in the way of the big s—t. Total and complete energy independence is a big deal. Drilling for oil in the Arctic Refuge is a big deal, but only symbolically. In the grand scheme of things, it's little crap. I would sacrifice oil drilling in the Arctic Refuge if, in so doing, we were able to achieve total energy independence.

Don't get me wrong; opening up the Arctic Refuge to drilling is stupid. It will hurt wildlife, and people estimate that there's maybe 3.2 billion barrels of oil there. Just as a point of comparison, if we all put replacement tires on our cars that were as good as the ones that came with the cars when they were new, we would save 5.4 billion gallons of oil—close to double what's in the reserve to begin with.

But if Republicans are so hell-bent on a symbolic thing that isn't a real solution, we should be able to sacrifice that symbolic thing *in favor of* a real solution. We should be willing to say, "If you want to go kill caribou to drill for a couple of tablespoons of oil in one of the few untouched natural gems this country has, you're going to have to give us something big, and that something big is . . ." And here's where you hit them with a serious fuel standard, a true commitment to conservation, renewable energy, advanced energy research—all the stuff that's going to make us truly, fully energy-independent.

Now, you talk to energy people, and they'll tell you that we can never truly be energy-independent. I refuse to believe that. I refuse to believe that the smartest, most successful, richest nation in the world can't figure out how to meet its energy demand with its energy supply. Here are some ideas to help us get there. Like our economic plan, we need ideas for the short term and for the long term, because we're not going to get there in one step, but that doesn't mean not presenting Americans with a vision for how we get there, period.

CONSERVATION:
NOT JUST A PERSONAL VIRTUE

Nothing represented this administration's attitude toward the environment and energy better than when Dick Cheney called conservation "a sign of personal virtue, but not a sufficient basis for a sound comprehensive energy policy." That statement isn't just stupid, it's wrong. Conservation helps us be more efficient, save money, clean our air, keep our kids healthy. It has the potential to dramatically reduce our dependence on foreign oil and to release us from our marriage of convenience with Saudi Arabia. Doing those things isn't personal, it's patriotic—and that's how we should frame it.

Consider this: If you replaced just four 100-watt incandescent bulbs that burn four or more hours a day in your home with four 23-watt fluorescent bulbs, you'd get the same amount of light, but, over three years, you'd also save at least 452 kilowatt-hours of electricity and $82. That's a personal virtue, yes. But if every household in America did the same, we'd save as much energy as is consumed by 7 million cars in one year.[16] That's a policy.

Or consider this: A refrigerator sold today uses 70 percent less energy than one built in the 1970s. Are you giving up anything by not using your orange refrigerator from 1970? Is your nice new fridge a personal virtue?

Or consider this: Simple standards to improve the efficiency of air conditioners, to reduce energy consumption in new buildings and houses, and to improve the efficiency of existing buildings would keep us from having to build 473 new power plants.[17]

The only people who don't benefit from this so-called personal virtue are the energy companies at whose altar Dick Cheney and George Bush prostrate themselves. Apparently, conservation isn't a personal virtue, but sucking up to oil companies for campaign contributions in return for sweetheart energy deals is. A true, commonsense conservation initiative doesn't mean turning off all your lights or wearing sweaters at home; it means doing the little things that can make a big difference, and that's what we need to encourage.

CALL AN SUV AN SUV

We import roughly 10 million barrels of oil a day. Half of that is used in transportation. And more than half of all new vehicles sold are SUVs.

Something's got to give. Now, I love SUVs as much as the next guy. In fact, until mine got stolen (rising crime—another effect of the Bush economy), it was my favorite thing to drive. But I'll be the first to admit, SUVs for urbanites and suburbanites make about as much sense for the people who drive them as putting a sweater on a dog. Seriously, how many SUV drivers do you know who need to ford a river and scale a mountain on the way home?

Fuel economy today is at a twenty-two-year low, and the reason is vehicles known as "light trucks" (SUVs, vans, and pickups). In 2001, sales of these "light trucks" surpassed car sales for the first time. In addition to being notorious gas-guzzlers, federal law allows vehicles in the "light truck" category to emit 75 percent more smog-forming emissions than cars. So SUVs don't just make us dependent . . . they make us sick.

Now I'm not going to say that nobody's allowed to have an SUV, but I think it's time for SUV drivers to pay the costs that the luxury of sitting three feet above traffic and getting six miles to the gallon incur. That means we impose a nice fat "fuel or freedom" tax on every SUV sold in America. If you want an SUV, fine. You just have to pay the tax. And here's how we're going to calculate the tax. Back in 1962, a gallon of gas cost 34 cents. If you adjust for inflation, it would be over $2 today. Basically, gas right now is about as cheap as it's ever been since World War II. But if you passed on to consumers the true cost of gas—the tax credits we give for oil and gas exploration, the military costs of keeping supply safe and steady—it would be about $4 a gallon. You figure out how many gallons the average SUV uses in a year and pay a tax of $2 a gallon (the difference between the pump cost and the true cost), and that's your Carville SUV "fuel or freedom" tax.

Of course, the auto industry will cry to holy heaven on this one.

They'll say (as they've said before when people have said that SUVs should be subject to the same safety, emissions, and fuel standards as cars) that you can't differentiate between an SUV and a light truck. Now, taxing the ever-loving crap out of that whole category isn't really fair—because a lot of folks make their livelihoods on their pickups. I would argue that not a single person does the same with their SUV. That's why I've created the Carville guide to identifying an SUV. It's this simple.

If your car . . .

● Has four-wheel drive as well as a built-in DVD player, a six-CD changer, or a satellite navigation system—it's an SUV.

● Has a roof rack that in the catalog appears to be used for carrying bikes, kayaks, or lumber, but that you've never used—it's an SUV.

● Has a name that is a verb turned into a noun (explore, escape, navigate) or is also the name of a bucolic or rugged region (Dakota, Yukon, Tahoe, Tundra)—it's an SUV.

● Is a Hummer but has never carried troops—it's an SUV.

● Appears in commercials circumnavigating the globe, driving through rivers, and scaling cliffs, yet you mostly see them in the parking lot of Pottery Barn—you bet your sweet ass it's an SUV.

If any of these things apply to you or your car, you are subject to Carville's "fuel or freedom" tax. If you feel you are being subjected to this tax in error, you should be allowed to go to the DMV, where they will test you by showing you a bass boat, horse carrier, or some other trailer and asking you to demonstrate how to attach it to your vehicle. (Hint: that shiny silver knob is called a trailer hitch.)

Seriously, the fuel efficiency of our cars and SUVs is a joke. Detroit can do better, and they will . . . if we require it. Federal fuel efficiency standards (known as Corporate Average Fuel Economy, or CAFE standards) increased new car and truck fuel economy by 70 percent between 1975 and 1988. Those standards saved American consumers $92 billion, kept 720 million tons of global-warming pollution out of our atmosphere, and reduced oil use by 60 billion gallons of gasoline.[18]

If we just raised fuel economy standards to forty miles per gallon by 2012, something the automakers say they can do without sacrificing safety or performance, we'd save 1.9 million barrels per day—more oil than we currently import from Saudi Arabia.[19] It can be done. It takes progressive leadership to say, "Go do it."

INCREASE DOMESTIC SUPPLY

Those things—conservation and fuel economy—reduce demand. We need to be honest with ourselves that we also need to increase supply, as well. Over the next twenty years, demand for natural gas consumption will increase by more than 50 percent. Natural gas is the cleanest fossil fuel, and it's something America has a lot of. Until recently, we just haven't had a lot of ways of getting it.

Right now, there's 35 trillion cubic feet of known natural gas reserves on the North Slope of Alaska that we're literally pumping back into the ground because we can't get it to the people who need it. There's a proposal for a pipeline to bring it to the lower forty-eight. This gas pipeline would create an estimated four hundred thousand jobs, use a huge amount of U.S. steel, and ensure that we do not become dependent on imported liquefied natural gas from the Middle East. Energy for

BUSH–KEEPING AMERICA IN THE DARK

Speaking to the New Jersey business community in June 2003, George Bush famously said, "There are some who would like to rewrite history—revisionist historians is what I like to call them." He would know a thing or two about revisionist history. On August 14, 2003, the day after an epic blackout shut down power from New York to Detroit, President Bush said, "We'll have time to look at it and determine whether or not our grid needs to be modernized. I happen to think it does, and have said so all along."

There's only one problem with that bit of history—it's a lie. In June 2001, Bush opposed and congressional Republicans rejected legislation that would have provided $350 million of loans to address the known reliability and capacity problems with America's power grid. Because of the Bush administration's lobbying, House Republicans voted down this idea three separate times. [Roll Call Vote #169, June 20, 2001] Unfortunately, because of Bush's obstinacy, he's no longer the only one in the dark.

America, jobs and opportunity for steelworkers, and no damage to sensitive environmental areas—if anything, *this* is the type of pro-development, pro-jobs energy project we should be encouraging.

We need to do more than just get at fossil fuels, though. We need to encourage new ones—like wind, solar, and biomass, which is a fancy term for things we grow and things animals expel. For example, in his campaign for president, Senator John Kerry has called for getting 20 percent of our electricity from renewable sources by 2020. He calls his plan 20/20—"a clear vision for America." I agree.

✷ ✷ ✷

All of these supply-and-demand things are near-term solutions. Progressives also need to give America a vision for the long term of what an energy-independent America can look like—and what that means for jobs, the economy, the environment, and our national security.

INVEST IN THE FUTURE

Each and every year, we spend $20 billion to import oil from the Persian Gulf. This isn't bad just for our economy (it'd be better to keep money and jobs here), it's bad for energy security. Instead of sending all that money to all those people who hate us, we should launch an energy strategy to invest in America, one that will create new technologies and new jobs here at home. I've heard it called a Manhattan Project for energy independence—and that's the right idea. Americans have always been able to do amazing things if they gave those things focus and resources.

For example—and I'm not going to pretend I understand the science behind this—hydrogen has the potential to power cars that emit not pollution but water vapors. If we become the leaders in building these cars . . . and more energy-efficient light bulbs . . . and all that stuff, it doesn't just mean independence, it means jobs, and that's something worth pursuing.

If it sounds like telling companies to make air conditioners that are more energy-efficient . . . or telling Detroit to make cars that get better gas mileage . . . or telling our scientists to develop hydrogen as a fuel sounds like a ridiculous thing to ask, remember the story of the catalytic converter. In the Clean Air Act, Congress mandated a 90 percent reduction for auto emissions. Period. Automakers were apoplectic. They had no idea how they'd ever comply. So they put their heads together and

184 ■ JAMES CARVILLE

came up with a new invention, the catalytic converter.[20] That one invention managed not only to meet that goal, but also to create a huge new industry in the United States.

Energy independence can be achieved—America needs and deserves nothing less. And Democrats need to demonstrate that we're the party to get us there.

7

HEALTH CARE

In the chapter on education, I told you that everybody called my momma Miss Nippy. Her real name was Lucille, but to this day, if you asked me what her first name was, I'd need to think about it for a second.

How she came to be called Miss Nippy is an old family story—and one that has helped shape the way I think about the issue we're going to discuss in this chapter: health care.

She grew up in Avoyelles Parish during the Great Depression, and from very early on it was clear to everyone that she had a generous spirit and a taste for adventure. Every day, when she was done with her chores, she'd go out exploring. One day, as she was out wandering around, an enormous thunderstorm came up on her, and as the rain pounded down, she became increasingly soaked and disoriented. While trying to get home, she came across a tent that someone had pitched and ran into it for cover. She wasn't in the tent but a couple of minutes when someone else popped into it—a hobo.

He looked so surprised to see Lucille that his mouth just dropped open. She was surprised to see him, too, but she didn't want to forget the manners her grandma-mère had taught her, so she took a deep breath and said: "I'm Lucille, what's your name . . . and how do you do?"

The way I've heard the story is that this wanderer stood there, confused, a little scared, and completely slack-jawed.

So my momma just kept on talking, asking him if he lived in the tent.

The man finally got his composure and answered, "I didn't use to, but right now I do. I can't find work. But I'm lookin' hard."

It was the height of the Great Depression, so my momma had heard her daddy and uncles talking about how hard it was to find work quite a bit.

In the tent, she saw that the hobo had some playing cards, so they played bouré (the only way to describe it is as kind of a cross between poker and spades) until the storm broke. When she left, the hobo finally told her his name. It was Nip.

The next day, there was a big family gathering, so Momma sneaked a whole bunch of extra food, hid it in the cistern behind her house, and brought it to Nip's tent that evening. Nip was appreciative but told her that times were tough for everyone and not to bring any more of her family's food. Momma, being clever and wanting to help, figured out a loophole. She decided it wouldn't be wrong if she brought him food that was *hers*. And that's what she did—except that the next day, on getting to Nip's tent, she found her father (my grandfather). He had gone out to tell Nip about some farmhand work he heard was available.

At first, my grandfather was shocked to realize that Lucille knew Nip and had been visiting him—those may have been more innocent times, but a father still didn't want his daughter hanging out with drifters. When Nip explained that she had been bringing him food, my granddaddy's anger turned to pride. Then it grew to amusement—Little

Lucille taking care of ol' Nip. That's how she came to be called Miss Nippy.

Now, what does this have to do with health care?

Well, for Republicans, it's individual this, individual that. And my momma was an example of the power of individual compassion and responsibility. But that went only so far. Sure, individuals could help other individuals (essentially Hoover's approach to the Depression), but individual charity is about as much of a solution to society's systemic challenges as my momma's charity was an answer to the Depression—it's important, it's meaningful, and, taken alone, it's just not enough to get the job done. After all, back then—as it is today—people needed jobs, and while a meal could help them get through a day, a job was the only thing that could help them get through life.

Health care's kinda the same way. It's not something we can handle as individuals (though George W. Bush would have us try). It's something that requires us doing collectively what we really can't do alone. And the fact is that today, in the richest nation on earth, our trillion-dollar-plus investment in health care doesn't get the best care or the most affordable insurance, and it has left 43.6 million people without any coverage whatsoever.[21] That should be enough to make us all sick.

✫ ✫ ✫

When you sit down and really think about it, we are willing to stomach a staggering amount of inequality in our society. Someone can show up for a $100 dinner in a Mercedes and not worry about the fact that the person filling their water glass is going home in some old beater to feed his family a dinner of macaroni and cheese.

We're okay with the fact that some people spend thousands of dollars a year on preschool—preschool—so that their kids can earn the opportunity to get into a $15,000-a-year elementary school, while other people have kids who go to schools where the most sophisticated technology is the metal detector at the door. Again, we probably shouldn't be okay with these things, and progressives need to keep working to make sure they change, but people are largely accepting of them.

But as a people, and to our credit, we are not okay with the idea that a poor child with cancer should get worse medical treatment than a rich child with cancer. Americans believe that other Americans should have health care. You know the old saying, "Your health is everything." It's literally true. You can be poor and happy, but—theological discourse on the afterlife notwithstanding—I find it very difficult to believe that you can be dead and happy.

As Americans, we believe that health is everything. Or some of us do, at least. In one of the more telling moments way back in the 2000 campaign, George W. Bush was in South Carolina when a woman came up to him and told him about a disease her son had and how medical insurance wasn't covering everything he needed. After hemming and hawing for a minute, he said, "I'm sorry, I wish I could wave a magic wand." [22]

What's that? Faith-based health care? The irony is that when George W. Bush got elected, he conveniently forgot that a $5.6 trillion surplus is nothing if not the political equivalent of a magic wand. Actually, he didn't forget that it was a magic wand, it's just that he used it to perform one trick only—he magically made rich people richer while simultaneously making the surplus disappear.

And how about health care? In his time in office, George W. Bush has done nothing to increase the number of people with health care, virtually nothing to bring down the cost of health care, and little to improve the quality of health care. By comparison—as of this writing—at least seven of the Democratic candidates running for president have offered major plans to improve America's health care and make sure tens of millions more people are covered. That's seven declared candidates for president who, as of day one in the White House, would be doing a heck of a lot more than this president to make health care in America more affordable, more available, and better.

That's good, because America is facing a health care crisis.

You used to hear the number 41 million a lot. Forty-one million Americans go without health insurance: 41 million Americans for whom getting sick or hurt can mean going broke. Today that number would be an improvement because 43.6 million Americans now lack health insurance. And in truth, the number is even higher than that. A recent report released by the Robert Wood Johnson Foundation found that over a two-year period, nearly one in three nonelderly Americans—nearly 75 million people under the age of sixty-five—went without health insurance for at least part of the year.

Now you'll hear conservatives say a lot of stupid things about the uninsured—that they don't work, that they're largely young and healthy or older and wealthy, that they go without health insurance by choice, or that they're simply undeserving. Just so you can hit those right out of the box, here are the facts: about 7 million of the uninsured are poor children, and eight out of every ten uninsured people work—many of them at jobs that don't offer health benefits or that make it difficult to get them.[23]

I've even heard some folks have the temerity to suggest that when the number of uninsured people goes up, health insurance gets cheaper because we're taking the costs out of the system. The truth is, we all pay for the uninsured.

The other thing conservatives argue is that hospitals don't turn away people, so if you don't have insurance and you get hit by a bus, you'll get care. In one sense, they're right. Someone will call an ambulance and it will pick you up and will eventually find an emergency room that will take you in and patch you up. But don't think that's free. We all pay for it. It gets built into the cost of our own health insurance. It gets built into the cost of the procedures the hospital uses. It gets built into everything. When people are uninsured, it isn't bad just for them, it's bad for all of us.

Here are the five key reasons insurance matters.

1. **When you're uninsured, you don't get preventive care.** Uninsured adults are 30 percent less likely to have had a regular checkup, where a lot of health problems can be caught early. Uninsured men are 40 percent less likely to have had a prostate exam, and uninsured women are 60 percent less likely to have had a mammogram. That means that when uninsured folks are diagnosed with a disease, it's at a later stage where treating it costs more money but offers less hope. As a result, uninsured Americans are sicker and die earlier than those with insurance. And again, that makes health care more expensive for everybody.

2. **When you don't have insurance, you put off getting the care you need until you end up in the hospital unnecessarily.** Uninsured people who know they are sick still go to the doctor less. For example, uninsured people with heart disease go to the doctor's of-

fice 28 percent less than insured people. It's about the same for people with hypertension, diabetes, and other diseases. As a result, the rate of unnecessary hospital stays for uninsured adults has more than doubled. More than 10 percent of hospital stays for uninsured people could have been avoided if that person got treatment earlier—and those unnecessary hospitalizations cost, on average, $3,300. Again, bad for them, more expensive for all of us.

3. **When you're uninsured, you're more likely to die.** A recent study by the National Academy's Institute of Medicine found that every year, eighteen thousand deaths are associated with people not having health insurance. It doesn't get more simple than that.[24]

4. **Medical care costs more for the uninsured than for the insured.** That's because, for starters, major insurers negotiate big discounts with hospitals and doctors. Uninsured people can't do that. The other reason is that uninsured people often have to pay big medical bills on credit cards, which can take a long time to pay off. In fact, paying for health care is the second leading cause of personal bankruptcy.[25] And when someone files for bankruptcy, those costs—you guessed it—get passed on to all of us.

5. **When you're uninsured, going to the doctor means going to the emergency room.** Uninsured Americans are four times more likely to go to the emergency room as a regular place of care. For children, it's five times more likely. That makes health care more expensive for everybody. In fact, a recent study by the Kaiser Family Foundation found that every year hospitals provide $35 billion in uncompensated care.

So even if you're a cold, callous, heartless human being, doing the selfish thing means doing the compassionate thing—it means making sure all Americans have access to health care. Let's go through our drill.

The Problem: Health care costs are rising at the rate of 9 percent a year, and even for people who don't use much health care but have health insurance, premiums are going up by about 13 percent a year. The number of uninsured Americans is at 43.6 million and rising. Businesses say they can't afford health care for their workers because it drives up their costs and makes them less competitive, and workers can't afford to go without it.

The Bush Response: First, he wishes he could wave a magic wand. That failing, Bush wants to use his other magical solution. By this point, you've realized that George W. Bush never met a problem that couldn't be solved with tax cuts, vouchers, or less regulation. George Bush's approach to health care is to combine all three.

The "Had Enough" Solution: Increase coverage, constrain costs, increase quality. Let's let Americans get the health care Congress gets—a nondiscriminatory group policy, predictably priced, that has a meaningful benefit—and give new meaning to the expression "good enough for government work."

THE PROBLEM IN DEPTH

Health care is an area where George Bush doesn't get it and doesn't even try to get it. I think he thinks that if we all just lived his lifestyle, there wouldn't be a health care crisis. After all, why don't we all just go for a jog in the morning, lift weights in the afternoon, and take a nap after lunch? We'd be a healthier nation. Then again, if everyone operated on the same work schedule as GWB, our GDP would probably drop by about 50 percent.

The truth is, what's happening in American health care is simply not sustainable. As I said before, the cost of health care is going up by 9 percent, premiums are going up by 13 percent—more than three times faster than wages—and both deductibles and co-payments are increasing. At the same time, the cost of prescription drugs is going up by double digits every year.

This is also hitting business. Businesses simply can't afford health care for their workers—and for one of the few times recently, they're not lying.

Consider this: more than $1,000 of the price of every car or truck that rolls off a General Motors assembly line is health care for the workers who built it. There's more money's worth of health care costs in those cars than steel.[26] That makes us a lot less competitive against competitors abroad who get those costs covered by national health care systems.

Real health expenditures in the United States per person are about twice that of any other major industrial nation—and more than twice the average of the other OECD countries. The only country that comes close to shelling out what we do for health care is Switzerland, and, as we all know, the government of Switzerland will just about pay to have a masseuse come over to your house if your back hurts. The bottom line is that skyrocketing health care costs are about as bad for business as they are for families.

THE BUSH RESPONSE IN DEPTH

As I said before, George W. Bush never saw a problem that couldn't be solved with a tax cut, a voucher, or less regulation. In this case, he's managed to combine all three. He basically wants to give people a tax credit so that they can go buy health care in the individual market. Sounds reasonable, right? Wrong. This proposal has bigger problems than a crawfish in a stockpot.

The first problem is that the individual market is the most unregulated, expensive, and discriminatory health care market we have in this country. It also has the worst benefits. Even if you get people into this market, there's no guarantee that they're going to get health care out of it.

The second problem is that providing tax credits for people to buy their own health care creates an incentive for employers to drop the health care coverage they do offer. The truism in this whole debate is that payment for health care comes from only three places: individuals, employers, or the government. When President Bush talks about "reform," he's talking about the government getting rid of its own burden, helping "bidness" get rid of its burden, and passing on more costs to individuals. That's what would happen here. If you give people a tax credit to pay for health care (ignoring the fact that the tax credit won't come close to actually covering the cost and that you basically need to prove that you've never been sick and don't plan on getting sick to get health insurance in the individual market), businesses are going to say, "Hey, employee, now that you get this tax credit, we're going to stop providing health care, so why don't you take your tax credit and go buy health care for yourself?"

Some folks will, some folks can't, and many folks won't. Meanwhile, the government and businesses will have washed their hands of the moral obligation to provide for the health of their people. Congratulations, George W. Bush. Only you would come up with a health care plan that could leave more people without insurance.

The other thing George W. Bush wants to do is to have the federal government wash its hands of the responsibility to take care of poor people, too. He wants to do this by using his fourth favorite governing tool (behind tax cuts, vouchers, and deregulation): block grants. Medicaid is the state-federal partnership that provides health care to poor people. George Bush wants to take the federal part out, giving states a set amount of money to take care of their own poor people. The problem is that with the economy tanking and health care costs rising, the states can't handle it all themselves. States will be forced to cut care or cut services, and George Bush will plausibly be able to say, "I didn't do it."

Block grants, tax credits—those are all spoonfuls of sugar to help a whole lot of vinegar go down. George Bush said he wouldn't pass on America's problems, yet that's exactly what all of his health care proposals do.

THE "HAD ENOUGH" SOLUTION

For starters, neglecting the problem doesn't solve it. The number of uninsured has gone up by about 3.8 million since George W. Bush took office (reversing the progress we made during the Clinton administration) and, if the current pace continues, could go up by 30 percent over the next decade.[27]

Basically, when it comes to health care, progressives should have three goals. Increase coverage; decrease cost; and improve quality. Believe it or not, those goals are not necessarily at odds with one another—in fact, each can reinforce the other. Here are some ideas that sound pretty sensible to me.

Increase Coverage. Tom DeLay is forever flapping his gums about how the private sector does everything right and the government couldn't effectively run a two-car parade. So here's my proposal for Mr. DeLay. He can go get his health care coverage in the private individual insurance market, and the rest of America can have the health plan he has.

See, Tom DeLay and every member of Congress get to enroll in something called the FEHBP—the Federal Employees Health Benefit Program. With 9 million federal employees and their families now getting health care through the FEHBP, it is the largest employer-sponsored group health care plan in the world. It's made up of a lot of plans (about 180) that offer all kinds of different health care packages. The government gets to say which plans participate and then negotiates prices, covered services, and other standards for care. Because health care companies want access to those 9 million people, they go along with these requirements. As a result, it's a good system. Here's where the health care that America gets should truly be "good enough for government work"—we should let small businesses and individuals buy into this program with tax credits that will make it affordable. This isn't a new idea—but it's a damn good one.

The other thing I think is a moral imperative is to make sure every child gets health care coverage. It is shameful in our society that there are some kids who don't get the immunizations and basic care they need.

Senator John Edwards of North Carolina has said, rightly, that universal coverage of children is possible only if both the government and parents honor their responsibilities. Somewhere around 7 million children nationally are eligible for Medicaid and the Children's Health Insurance Program but aren't enrolled. We should not recommend that they get enrolled, we should require it. And for those who aren't eligible for these programs because they make a little too much money, we should help them buy into it.

Those two ideas alone could help us cover the two largest groups that go without coverage—children and employees of small businesses. Not bad for a day's work.

Constrain Costs. First of all, just by increasing coverage, you decrease cost *growth* for all the reasons I listed above—more preventive care, more diseases caught early, all that good stuff. When you stop and look at what is really making the cost of health care increase, you see that it's really three big things—prescription drugs, doctors, and hospitals. We're going to talk about prescription drugs in chapter 11, but for now, let me just say this: Prescription drug companies do a lot of good in this world. They come up with some amazing things—a lot of it underwritten by federal grants and research money. They've now reached the point, though, where they are spending more money on advertising than they do on research. When you hear a commercial for Viagra, or Prilosec, or Allegra, or some other pill that promises to have you running happily in a field/hiking through a canyon/strutting through a restaurant for no apparent reason, and that commercial asks you to "tell your doctor about Bullshitium," something has gone horribly wrong. "Tell your doctor"? Shouldn't you be trusting your doctor—the person who presumably went to school for an extra seven years so that he or she could come to understand the inner workings of the human body—to be the one telling *you*? After all, the minute you're telling your doctor what you want prescribed, doesn't that make him or her not a doctor but actually a drug dealer? I digress, but my point is that big drug companies are so hell-bent on making money that they're not only content to turn your doctor into a drug dealer, they're trying to keep cheaper generic drugs from coming to market by cajoling, conspiring, and outright bribing congressmen and competitors in an effort to keep their patents and keep generic versions of the same drug from coming to market, intro-ducing competition, and reducing price.

We should have a zero-tolerance attitude toward this behavior. Drug companies who invest in research should be able to keep their patents until they've made back the amount they spent on research plus a reasonable profit; then it's open season. Senator Chuck Schumer of New York came up with a bill that would keep drug companies from gaming the patent system, and Democrats—while they were in control—actually managed to pass it. Republicans, of course, love the concept of competition right until the moment it comes into conflict with the concept of rewarding your powerful contributors. So they blocked the bill from passing in the House. Here's where all you progres-sives who are fed up need to remember the basic difference between a Democrat and a Republican. A Republican is willing to take on people in the interest of power. A Democrat should never be afraid to take on power in the interest of people. This is one case where taking on that power promotes competition and would save all Americans—rich and poor alike—an estimated $60 billion over ten years.

We also need to reduce hospital and doctor costs. A while ago, I was on a panel with Newt Gingrich, and we were talking to health care executives. Newt was positively giddy about the role technology could play in reducing health care costs. He talked about how all these car Web sites reduced the price of cars and how all these travel Web sites reduced the price of travel. Now, most of the folks I grew up with wouldn't know what carfax.com or orbitz.com was if it bit them in the ass, and given the choice between using a computer and using an abacus, I'll take the abacus. But Newt was so hyped up I finally had to ask, "Newt, this is all well and good—e-mailing prescriptions and all that— is this something Democrats are against?"

And he said, "No, not really."

So I did a little looking into this, and the more I looked into it, the more I realized that this isn't some mumbo-jumbo, pie-in-the-sky, futurist dream. As much as one-quarter of all the money America spends on health care doesn't go to health care at all—it goes to nonmedical costs like paperwork, advertising, and paying bills. No other industry in our country is this inefficient. Here's what Senator John Kerry had to say about this shocking statistic: "While banks have cut their costs to less than a penny per transaction using computers and technology, a single transaction in health care can cost as much as twelve to twenty-five dollars—and not a penny of that goes to care. Eliminating this inefficiency in our health system is . . . the only way to bring America's health care into the twenty-first century." [28]

So why aren't we—the party of change and progress—the ones championing the use of technology for something other than nudie pictures? Let's get behind the power of technology and the Internet to bring down the cost of health care—heck, according to some, we invented the damn thing to begin with.

The other thing about health care is that nobody thinks there's such a thing as getting too much of it. Your doctor says you should have an X ray, good. An MRI? Even better. A CAT scan—great, just give me a shot of that barium. It's all good. Except that it's not. We are spending the largest amount of money in the world on our health care system, but we aren't getting the best health care results in the world. Medicine is about science, and sometimes you have to follow the science. Which means sometimes all that stuff isn't necessary. We should take all that information that we get from all the patients (keeping their privacy, of course) and really figure out what technologies are most effective; then we should use those standards for the government to do creative things like rewarding hospitals that achieve good outcomes, empowering businesses and consumers to "ask their doctor" about more than just the new drug Bullshitium, and to encourage prevention. Researchers say that reducing unnecessary excessive health care could save Medicare alone 30 percent—that's about $70 billion.[29]

Improve Quality. A lot of times we hear about the really, really bad medical errors—the wrong leg gets amputated, the wrong organ gets transplanted, really egregious stuff. What you don't often hear is that medical errors in hospitals across America are estimated to cost about ninety-eight thousand lives per year, according to a report by the Institute of Medicine. This is a place where things like electronic medical records aren't just money savers, they also improve quality for a silly but very real reason—it's impossible to read a doctor's handwriting. The other thing we should do is require health plans and providers to report performance data on quality and staffing levels—so we can see, truly, what works best. There's the saying that when students enter medical school, they're told by the dean or someone that "half of what we will teach you is wrong. Unfortunately, we don't know which half." With medical knowledge increasing so rapidly, doesn't it make sense for us to take some time and energy, and maybe even spend some money, to figure out what works so that we can make it work better?

More people getting better care. It's something we should be for, it's something we should feel proud to talk about, it's something Bush's lack of attention to is damnable. Heck, it even fits on a bumper sticker.

★ PART FOUR ★

"ESTABLISH JUSTICE"

✷ ✷ ✷

In 1985, I was living in Baton Rouge working for Mayor Pat Screen. That year, Baton Rouge had been selected to host the National Sports Festival, which is part of the Olympic movement. Hosting the National Sports Festival involved holding a series of competitions in a bunch of different Olympic sports and sprinkling a lot of fund-raisers and receptions in between.

To Baton Rouge and Mayor Screen, this was a big deal, because one of the perks is that when you host the National Sports Festival, you also get to keep the Olympic torch around and use it for those ceremonial events.

Up until that point, I had been under the impression that there was only one Olympic torch and that it was kindled from a flame at Mount Olympus in Greece and had been burning eternally since then, sheltered lovingly over its journey of many thousand miles. I was a little disappointed when we got a whole box full of torches sent to our office—so I decided not to share that fact with everyone else.

The first night of the festival, we had planned a big reception out on the levee by the Mississippi River. We had gotten Rodney "Hot Rod" Milburn, who won the gold medal in the 110-meter hurdles at the 1972 Olympics, to be the person who would run the torch into the reception, thereby kicking off the festival. Rodney was a big hero in Louisiana—having been born in Opelousas and later coaching track at Southern University in Baton Rouge.

Again, I was under the impression that the torch would be arriving in some ceremonial fashion but soon learned that it was up to us to have Rodney stand about a half mile away from the reception, where we then lit the torch with some cop's Zippo lighter and told him we'd give him a call when we were ready for him to come trotting in with the thing.

At that point I went back to the reception and was busy mingling with all the muckety-mucks, getting kind of bored. Looking to cause a little trouble, I asked a police officer who was there to come up to me, looking very grave, and whisper something in my ear. So, couple of minutes later, he came up to me and tapped me on the shoulder. "Mr. Carville," he said, "we have a situation." At that point, he whispered some nonsense in my ear, and I turned to the folks I'd been talking to and said, "We've got a terrible problem, I've got to go deal with this."

So I hustled out of the cocktail party, waited a couple of minutes outside the party—watching everyone nervously preparing for the arrival of the torch—and then came back in. At that point, the society matrons come up to me, saying, "What is it, what went wrong?"

"Well," I told them. "Hot Rod was running the torch over here, and apparently he's lost a step or two over the years, because I'll be damned if the fool didn't just trip off the levee into the river. The torch went in with him. They're trying to dry the thing off right now with a blow-dryer, but it doesn't look too good. I hate to be the one to tell you this, but the eternal Olympic flame got extinguished in Louisiana."

Man, you should have seen these ladies' jaws drop. They turned so white, so fast, that I didn't have the heart to string them along much longer, and I didn't. But before I could tell them I was just yanking their chains, one of them gasped, "My God, this is going to be *just terrible* for Baton Rouge."

✷   ✷   ✷

If there is an "eternal flame" in America, it is what we often refer to as "the system." Our system of government is a beacon of light and hope to nations around the world. The vote of the richest American can be canceled out by the vote of the poorest. Our system of capitalism is free, open, and transparent. It rewards innovation and allows but sees no great shame in failure. Our courts protect individuals who often don't have either means or power from being wronged by the powerful. That is our system. That is our torch. And, under Republicans, it's really been dropped in the river.

In this section, we're going to look at campaign finance reform, corporate governance, and tort reform—three areas where "the system" has been hurt or is being hurt by Republicans—and what proud progressives can do to strengthen each one.

8

CARVILLE'S CAMPAIGN FINANCE REFORM PROPOSAL

You simply can't have as much power and as much money as you have in Washington and not see it have a damaging effect. It's just human nature. All of the corrosion we see in the current system—from "statesmen" constantly groveling for cash to quid pro quo bargains for special interests—is predictable from human experience. Water will always find its level, and so will money. Unfortunately, the fact that it's predictable doesn't make it any less harmful.

All of the magnificent accomplishments of our federal government—indeed, our political system itself—are put in danger by this constant undermining of people's trust. The more folks hear about their representatives serving the highest bidder over the public interest, the more voter turnout and trust in government will continue to plummet.

This graph was constructed from a number of questions about people's trust in government. Here are some of the questions:

TRUST IN GOVERNMENT INDEX, 1958–2000

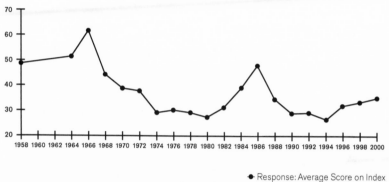

Response: Average Score on Index
Source: The National Election Studies, August 27, 2001.

● How much of the time do you think you can trust the government in Washington to do what is right—just about always, most of the time, or only some of the time?

● Would you say that the government is pretty much run by a few big interests looking out for themselves or that it is run for the benefit of all the people?

● Do you think that quite a few of the people running the government are crooked, not very many are, or do you think that hardly any of them are crooked?

The answers are then weighted to create an index. Total trust would be 100. Total distrust would be zero. We're at 36.[1] That ain't good, and a lot of it has to do with who people think is pulling the strings.

Despite the gravity of this threat to our democratic system, debate in Washington on campaign finance reform has pretty much been confined to the McCain-Feingold bill, which right now is being challenged in court by the likes of Senator Mitch McConnell from Kentucky and a lawyer by the name of Kenneth Starr. I'm not going to waste too much breath on Mitch McConnell, but y'all know how I feel about Ken Starr. If you don't, here's a hint. I wrote an entire book about the guy, in which I elaborated upon my contention that he is an abusive, privacy-invading, sex-obsessed, right-wing, constitutionally insensitive, boring, obsequious, and miserable little man who has risen further in this life by his willingness to suck up to power than his meager talents and pitiful judgment ever would have gotten him.*

If the law survives—and I expect it will because most things that Ken Starr tangles with end up damaged but not destroyed—it will ban political action committees' (PACs') unlimited so-called soft money.

But that gets at only part of the problem. Of the $3 billion that was spent in the 2000 congressional and presidential elections, only (and I use the term "only" loosely) one-fifth of that was soft money.[2]

So, although this is a step in the right direction, nobody but a congressman will tell you that it's going to rid politics of the stench of money. In fact, all this fuss about McCain-Feingold reminds me of one of these westerns where the sheriff's posse mount up to catch a killer and end up riding around in a circle all day shooting their guns in the air.

Simply put, McCain-Feingold is not enough. What we have to do is completely separate the money from the power. Until this is done, politics will remain a tool for those who take on people in the in-

---

* . . . *And the Horse He Rode In On: The People v. Kenneth Starr* is still available at a bookstore near you.

DOES MONEY BUY INFLUENCE?

Poor Saxby Chambliss—he carries the double burden of being an idiot and a jerk. And it didn't take him long in the Senate to make himself an example—of the corrupting power of money. See, ol' Saxby thought he was having a nice, private chat with his boss, Senate majority leader Bill Frist. Turns out that Bill was trying to show a reporter from *The New York Times* what a big swinging dick he was, and so—unbeknownst to Saxby—Bill put him on speakerphone. Before hanging up, Chambliss asked for Frist's support in appointing a friend and Republican donor to be the ambassador to an economic development organization. (A little-known secret in Washington is that there are a bunch of ambassadors who don't even have to leave the country.)

"He has lots of dollar figures down there?" Frist asks.

"That's exactly right," Chambliss said. "And he did raise a chunk of money for me."

"All right," Frist said. "You're a good man."

When Democrats started asking some tough questions, Chambliss sent his mouthpiece out to say that "someone's political activities may or may not be one of several factors for these positions."

Funny, it seems to me that the only factor I heard discussed was money.[3]

terest of power, rather than those who take on power in the interest of people.

The Problem: Money is replacing ideas as the currency of politics.

The Bush Response: Call it free speech, begrudgingly sign soft money legislation, support a court challenge of said legislation.

The "Had Enough" Solution: Get politicians out of the money business—period.

THE PROBLEM IN DEPTH

It seems to me there are only two justifiable reasons for a company to spend its money. The first is to acquire a product or service. That can mean hiring and paying an employee or buying a piece of equipment that will help it run better. The second reason a company should spend money is to increase the company's value by improving its position. That can mean investing in research and development or buying advertising to sell more products. Any other expenditure of money, you'd think, would not only be a waste, it would be corporate mismanagement. So how do you explain that companies spent over $400 million in 2002 in soft money campaign contributions?[4] There can be only two explanations. The first is that they were simply being good Americans and supporting the democratic process. If that were the case, though, they would be giving away money for free, they would expect no return on their investment, and that would be a waste of shareholder money.

The second and more likely reason is that they are behaving rationally, and they seek to influence legislation. If that's the case, they are spending money in a way that a company is right to spend money, to improve its position. There's only one problem: There's another word for spending money on an elected official with the hope of some tangible return. That word is bribery.

Who gets hurt? You guessed it—those citizens who can't afford to purchase their very own congressperson or to run their very own trade group.

As an illustration, let's take the example of the pharmaceutical companies. Between 1991 and 1997, the companies that belong to the Pharmaceutical Research and Manufacturers of America (PhRMA), the trade group for brand-name drugmakers, gave $18.6 million in political contributions. Between 2001 and 2002, they gave over $3 million in soft money to Republicans alone. That's small change in a $90 billion drug industry. Here's what they got for their money: patent extensions.

Basically, when a drug company invents a new drug, a patent says, "You invested a lot of time and energy and money creating this cholesterol-lowering pill/ulcer medication/erection enhancer. You should be able to have exclusive rights to it for a while so that you can be free of competition, sell it at a high price, and make back the money you spent creating this cholesterol-lowering pill/ulcer medication/erection enhancer." Fair enough.

Where it gets unfair is once the drug company has made back all that money and then some, and generic drugmakers want to get in on the action by making a lower-priced version of the same drug, thereby introducing competition and lowering prices. This would be the vaunted market that Republicans love, so you'd think they would like this competition. Turns out that when it comes to monopolies, money can make the heart grow fonder.

Back in 1994, Congress passed a law that put in place a General Agreement on Tariffs and Trade (GATT). That law had an unintentional loophole: it allowed a lot of companies to keep those patents for an extra year or two. Consumer groups and the generic-drug industry asked Congress to eliminate this windfall for brand-name drugmakers. But drugmakers and their toadies in Congress were able to stop that effort, so the generic versions of more than one hundred prescription drugs were delayed. All of this cost average consumers—mostly old people—dearly.

For example, Glaxo Smith Kline's patent on Zantac was supposed to expire in December 1995. Because of its victory in Congress, the company was able to hold on to that patent for an extra nineteen months. If you are an average person who had been prescribed Zantac for your heartburn, you were paying $180 for a two-month supply. A generic—had it been on the market—would have cost you $90, so that nineteen-month extension cost you $855—more than any Bush tax cut will likely save you. During that time, Glaxo earned an additional $1 billion.

Glaxo has given more than $2 million in political contributions since 1991. Think about that return: a billion dollars in extra profits for $2 million in campaign contributions. That's a pretty good deal, unless you're the consumer.[5]

And that's basically what happens for just about every industry that buys its way into legislation—mining, oil and gas, financial services, you name it. They get the best policies their money can buy, not the best policies for America.

THE BUSH RESPONSE IN DEPTH

What's the Bush solution to this problem? Well, you can't really have a solution if you don't think what's going on is a problem. During the presidential campaign, George Bush adamantly opposed campaign finance reform, saying that it was "unilateral disarmament" that would harm the GOP. Let's think about that for a moment. Unilateral means "of, on, relating to, involving, or affecting only one side." So if the president says that taking money out of politics is unilateral disarmament, he's admitting something pretty big. He's saying that if you take the

THE BUSH WHITE HOUSE: OPEN FOR BUSINESS

INDUSTRY	WHAT THEY GAVE	WHAT THEY GOT
COAL	Over $100,000 in industry contributions—the most given to any federal candidate. Coal executives "Buck" Harless and Irl Engelhardt gave another $550,000 to the Republican National Committee, the Bush campaign, and the Bush-Cheney Inaugural Fund. [Center for Responsive Politics, www.opensecrets.org; *Washington Post*, March 25, 2001]	A new policy exempting factories from air pollution regulations [*New York Times* and *Washington Post*, both Nov. 23, 2002] Fewer requirements that old coal plants upgrade air pollution controls [Associated Press, Aug. 28, 2003] Justice Department settlements with the energy companies sued during the Clinton administration for pollution violations [Associated Press, Aug. 28, 2003]
OIL & GAS	$1.8 million in contributions in 2000, $447,000—so far—in 2004 [Center for Responsive Politics, www.crp.org; *USA Today*, March 1, 2001]	Bush support of opening Arctic Refuge to oil companies. Open door access to Cheney energy task force meetings [*Bloomberg News*, March 3, 2002]
INSURANCE	Over $500,000 to Bush 2004 campaign (opponents of Patients' Bill of Rights donated over $50 Million to Bush and GOP) [Center for Responsive Politics, www.crp.org; www.tray.com; www.opensecrets.org; FEC Data]	Opposition to and obstruction of a Patients' Bill of Rights
FINANCIAL SERVICES	Commercial banks have given over $500,000 to the Bush 2004 campaign. MBNA alone gave Bush over $300,000 in 2000 [Center for Responsive Politics, www.crp.org]	Support for bills to make it harder for individuals to file for bankruptcy and erase their debts

money out, only the GOP is disadvantaged, which means that money is the only "weapon" they have. Of course, nobody called him on that statement.

Then again, what incentive does George Bush have to support campaign finance reform? The man raised $100 million for his 2000 presidential campaign . . . and that was just in the primaries. If he wasn't goaded by John McCain during the presidential campaign and later from Capitol Hill, and if the Enron scandal didn't break as Democrats and Republicans were debating campaign finance reform (remember, Enron was not only President Bush's largest corporate donor, it was nice enough to lend its corporate jet to get his staff to Florida to contest the recount), Bush would have actively opposed the thing. Instead, he held his nose and signed it. In fact, he signed it in his office at 8:00 A.M. with no cameras present, he didn't tell John McCain, Russ Feingold, Chris Shays, or Marty Meehan that he was doing it until after the fact, and then he left Washington to raise nearly $4 million for Republican candidates on a two-day southern swing, telling reporters, "I'm not going to lay down my arms."

This is not a man who is hell-bent on getting money out of politics.

THE "HAD ENOUGH" SOLUTION

The American people aren't stupid. They understand that special interest money too often influences who runs, who wins, and how they govern.

Believe it or not, there is a way, a constitutional way, to fix our campaign finance system and start changing this perception. Forget all the spending caps and loopholes and assorted gobbledygook—here's how it works. We make a law that says, "No member of Congress can take or solicit anything of value from any person." It's that simple. Nothing of value. Not a lunch. Not a flight. Not an American flag lapel pin. They can't even solicit money for the March of Dimes. (Trust me, the March of Dimes will do just fine without those 537 volunteers.) Good causes, bad causes, Sisters of Mercy, Nazi Youth—it doesn't matter. As soon as you're chosen by the people to be a member of Congress, you're out of the money business. You don't go near it, you don't ask for it, you don't raise it. You just do your job. Think how nice it would be if, instead of spending hours a day raising money, our elected officials spent a little more time studying legislation or seeing those families of theirs they claim to want to spend more time with. You could look at what politicians were doing and how they were voting, and you could say they were doing something because they wanted to get reelected. Okay. Or that they're doing it because they're egomaniacs. Okay. Or that they're doing it because they lack courage. Fine. But the one thing you could finally say is that they didn't do it for a campaign contribution. I don't think that's asking too much.

Well, then, James, one might ask, how do you intend to fund political campaigns? That, too, is simple.

All *nonmembers* of Congress who want to be members of Congress can solicit money from whomever they please, provided the minute they receive a contribution that contribution is fully disclosed. Got it? A challenger can raise all the money he or she wants. Here's the trick. The moment that money is deposited into the challenger's account, the incumbent is credited with 85 percent of that amount from a publicly guaranteed fund. That's it. Why does the incumbent get 15 percent less than the challenger? Because he or she didn't have to pay the fund-raising costs—such as direct mail leaflets, phone solicitations, and other items, like those little hot dogs and the cocktail napkins with the candidate's name on them.

What about when there are two challengers for an open seat? Spend all you want, spend till you drop. But once someone is elected, he or she is out of the money business. Done.

How about when someone in the House wants to run for the Senate? You'd have to get out of one before running for the other.

What happens if soft money is still legal after the courts get through with McCain-Feingold? First, as someone who has run campaigns, I can tell you that a hard dollar is worth four soft dollars. Trust me. You can use hard dollars any way you want, but there are restrictions on how you can use the soft dollars. But say someone is using independent expenditures to run television commercials. I think there should be a disclaimer under federal law that says: "The incumbent named in this advertisement doesn't have the resources to respond. The viewer and/or listener should take this into account when assessing the validity of the charges contained herein." I'd hope that would at least limit that crap substantially.

So, what happens if you do raise funds? If you're in the Congress, and you break the law in any way, you're out. Congress has always had the right to determine the qualifications of its own members. There'd be no independent counsel, no six-year, drawn-out investigation. If you're a congressperson and you're caught grubbing for money, you're outta there faster than Bob Dornan at a mariachi festival.

GOOD ENOUGH FOR WAL*MART, GOOD ENOUGH FOR WASHINGTON

Republicans are always railing about how the government can't do anything right and the private sector can do no wrong. I'll be the first to admit that there are some cases where the private sector can do it better, and we should use those as a lesson. For example, Sam Walton knew a thing or two about building a business. His vision of big stores, low prices, and good service turned Wal*Mart into America's largest retailer. Today, Wal*Mart is number one on the Fortune 500. In fact, Wal*Mart is so big that the day after Thanksgiving 2002, Wal*Mart stores did $1.4 billion of business. One point four billion dollars, in *one day.*

It's no surprise, then, that a lot of folks want to be suppliers for Wal*Mart. With the volume of merchandise moving through the stores, Wal*Mart's buyers are pretty powerful people. One big deal can make a supplier a millionaire. And the suppliers know it. In fact, throughout American industry, suppliers have been known to lavish some pretty nice gifts on buyers in the hopes of getting preferential treatment. Of course, this would corrupt the process. It could lead to a store buying an inferior product. Well, I called Mona Williams, the vice president of communications for Wal*Mart (she happens to be an old acquaintance from Baton Rouge; we even went on a date once), and I asked her if Wal*Mart has a policy to prevent this from happening. It turns out they do. Here's what Wal*Mart says to anyone who wants to be a supplier: "No gifts or gratuities, which have monetary value, are to be given, offered, or encouraged in any way to any Wal*Mart Associate or potential Wal*Mart Associate." Period.[6]

And here's what Wal*Mart says to its associates: "You cannot accept anything from a supplier—nothing. Not a can of Coke, not a Christmas ham."

It's simple. There are no gray areas. It works.

Here's what I say: If it's good enough for a $30,000-a-year associate at Wal*Mart, it should be good enough for a congressperson.

Simple to understand, simple to administer, and totally constitutional.

Unlike other reform proposals, this plan in no way infringes on anyone's First Amendment rights, as defined by *Buckley* v. *Valeo*. People can still throw their money around as much as they want (although incumbents can't accept donations). They can make contributions to a challenger's campaign, they can buy TV time, they can do whatever they please. But, no matter where the money comes from, 85 percent of all funds spent on a challenger will be credited to the incumbent, with one notable exception: If any candidate chooses to put his or her own cash into a campaign, 100 percent of those funds are matched for the other candidates in the race.

As I see it, this plan will have a chilling effect on fat cats and corporations attempting to influence Congress with cash. It will open elected office to those citizens out there who don't have a few million dollars handy. It's not going to do the oil companies any good to buy a few pet politicians if 85 percent of their dollars are credited to the accounts of their stooges' opponents.

It'll keep high-profile elected officials who don't draw legitimate challengers from amassing huge campaign chests and then spreading the money around to curry favor with their colleagues.

Similarly, it will discourage the Michael Huffingtons of this world from spending ridiculous amounts of their own cash to get elected. If rich folks want to use their money to effect change, they can help charities of their choice rather than lining the pockets—and then pulling the strings—of our nation's representatives.

Folks, the only way to clean up our system is to get rid of all the money. Unlike the piecemeal approaches currently offered by Congress, this plan is the only one I've heard that's both constitutional and eliminates all the fund-raising shenanigans infecting our body politic. I'm not naive. I know that this will be harder to pass than a golf ball through a garden hose, but if we don't do something bold to restore the ideal of one person, one vote soon, this endless congressional gold digging is going to result in a permanently dysfunctional dime-ocracy.

9

CORPORATE GOVERNANCE

Republicans used to say that "if a CEO did what Clinton did, he'd be fired."

Did Bill Clinton manipulate energy markets, causing an energy crisis in California in an attempt to profit from it, or cash out on his stock options while prodding others to buy? (Like Ken Lay of Enron.)

Did Bill Clinton use a $19 million, no-interest loan to buy a fifteen-thousand-square-foot waterfront mansion in Florida, or use $25 million of company money to furnish his apartment with things like a $6,000 shower curtain and a $15,000 umbrella stand, all while trying to avoid paying taxes on millions of dollars of artwork? (Like Dennis Kozlowski of Tyco.)

Did he accept $3.1 billion in off-balance-sheet loans so that—among other things—he could build his own private golf course? (Like the Rigas family of Adelphia Communications.)

Did he borrow over $400 million from his company to cover personal stock losses? (Like Bernie Ebbers of WorldCom.)

If a CEO did what Clinton did, he'd be fired. Spare me. By the way, none of these people was fired. Not one. Ultimately, they all resigned in disgrace or got led away in handcuffs—but not one was fired.

After the wave of corporate scandals this country has seen, I wish more CEOs were busy doing what Clinton did. And I mean that in every possible sense of "doing what Clinton did." I mean, if they were innovating, creating more jobs, leading their organizations to unprecedented prosperity based on real numbers, and along the way they were engaging in a little hanky-panky in the office, so be it. I'd much rather have a CEO who screwed his assistant instead of what we got—a bunch of CEOs who screwed all of us.

Consider this: From 1999 to 2002, the CEOs at firms now being investigated for accounting fraud pocketed $1.4 billion. (That works out to an average of about $20 million per year per lying, cheating, stealing CEO. By contrast, the "honest" leading CEOs earned an average of $12 million a year.[7] How those "honest" CEOs dealt with such hardship, deprivation, and want, we may never know.)

At the same time the dirty CEOs were pocketing their millions, the value of the firms they were leading plunged by $530 billion. That's billion, with a "b."

Oh, and while the CEOs were taking all this money, what was happening to their employees? Well, it seems that rewards need to be balanced out by sacrifices. From January 2001 to August 2002, executives at firms under investigation laid off 162,000 workers.[8]

Think about that: Around sixty people walked away with over a billion dollars, while costing 162,000 workers (and counting) their jobs and costing all of us $530 billion in lost investments, savings, and retirement money. Talk about evildoers. These guys shouldn't be sitting on their yachts living off the wages of sin. They should be in jail. And they shouldn't be in those nice, cushy, federal minimum security deals where the only hardship is getting a tee time on the penitentiary golf course. They should be in a "don't drop the soap" jail where the only conjugal visits they get are from big men from neighboring cellblocks.

Failing that, you'd think when millions of Americans are essentially robbed, the president would step in to catch the criminals and keep it from happening again. Maybe some other president would, but not this one. Let's go through our drill.

The Problem: Corporate chiefs have been robbing their employees, their shareholders, and the American people. The crisis of confidence brought on by their behavior has undermined markets, and the power they exert through lobbyists and congressional toadies has put them largely above the law.

The Bush Response: Talk about slapping them with handcuffs, but actually slap them on the wrists. I guess that makes sense—you don't really want to send your buddies and contributors to jail.

The "Had Enough" Solution: Get tough on corporate wrongdoers, keep them from hiding money (overseas, off the books, wherever), and protect America's pensions.

THE PROBLEM IN DEPTH

Markets run on confidence. Confidence that the numbers are accurate. Confidence that CEOs are telling the truth. Confidence that strong performance is rewarded and weak performance is remedied or punished. At the same time, we know that humans are not angels—that with so much money at stake, there's going to be the temptation to bend the rules. So we've got to make sure people are playing by the rules, not breaking them or, in the case of our government, paying off Congress to rewrite them.

When CEOs lie, cheat, and steal, it undermines that confidence and leads to a cloud of uncertainty. There's nothing markets and economies hate more than uncertainty. In the last couple of years, it's also led to billions in lost savings and hundreds of thousands of lost jobs.

As long as we have loopholes in our laws, shoddy enforcement, and overstretched enforcers, that cloud of uncertainty will still be there. And as long as people can't tell a blue chip from a Ponzi scheme, all businesses will suffer, our economy will suffer, and Americans will suffer as a result.

We need a real response.

THE BUSH RESPONSE IN DEPTH

From the very outset, George W. Bush embraced the attitude so nicely summed up in the campaign slogan of Warren G. Harding: "Less government in business, and more business in government."

And boy, did he ever follow through on that one. Let's just use as an example one of Bush's favorite companies: Enron.

Ken Lay, Enron's CEO, has personally contributed over $550,000 to George W. Bush over the course of Bush's career—making him Bush's single largest career patron. During the 2000 campaign, Enron gave over $1.3 million to Bush and the GOP.

But say what you will about George Bush, he's an honorable man. He made sure he gave something back. For example, he gave Ken Lay veto power over Bush's nominees to the Federal Energy Regulatory Commission, the government body that would oversee Enron's activity. Enron was given access to Dick Cheney's White House Energy Task Force, meeting with them six times. Ken Lay met with Dick Cheney twice. And the White House led an effort to help Enron settle a $2.3 billion dispute with the government of India. And Enron didn't just have its hands in Bush's pockets; it had its people in Bush's government. Ken Lay served on Bush's transition advisory team for the Department of Energy. Cynthia Sandherr, one of Lay's employees, served on Bush's transition team for the Department of Commerce. Basically, "transition teams" help staff cabinet departments with political appointees when a new president comes into office—and they made sure they got their friends in some pretty high places. Bush's economic adviser, Lawrence Lindsey, worked as an economic adviser to Enron. The former secretary of the army, Thomas White, was a vice president at Enron. (White has since redeemed himself in my book by admitting that not nearly enough planning was done for postwar Iraq.) U.S. trade representative Robert Zoellick was on an Enron advisory board. Alberto Gonzales, the White House counsel (and possible Supreme Court nominee), worked for a law firm representing Enron and received over $34,000 directly from Enron when he was running for the Texas Supreme Court. Marc Racicot, the former RNC chairman, was a lobbyist for Enron.

I feel your pain, Dubya. When a corrupt company has its hooks so deep into you, pushing them away hurts.

Now let's go back to the original Republican claim. If Bill Clinton was a CEO, he'd have been fired. What if Bill Clinton, before he was president, *was* a CEO who did all of this? Republicans would be apoplectic.

Well, my progressive friends, meet George W. Bush.

George W. Bush was an Enron-style CEO before it was cool. In one of his jobs before being selected president by the Supreme Court, George W. Bush was the chairman of a company called Harken Energy Corp. During his time there, Bush watched as Harken used shady accounting to fool investors into thinking that the company was financially sound when, in reality, it was failing. Luckily for Bush, he got out before the house of cards collapsed—and managed to turn himself a tidy little profit in the process. For example, Harken hid its 1989 losses through a transaction with an off-book partnership that was actually run by Harken executives. Here's what happened: Harken's annual report for 1989 showed a profit of $8 million on the sale of its subsidiary, Aloha Petroleum. Aloha was sold to a partnership of Harken insiders called International Marketing & Resources for $12 million—$11 million of which was financed through a note held by Harken. When Securities and Exchange Commission (SEC) accountants eventually discovered that Harken had concealed its 1989 losses by claiming a profit on the sale (despite the fact that Harken held the note on the sale), the commission objected, saying that the income could be recognized only when the principal on the loan was paid. What type of accounting firm would let this shady deal take place in the first place? Arthur Andersen.[9]

Of course, all of that stuff is too complicated for a cracker like me to understand, but the next year George W. Bush went and did something pretty much everyone can understand quite well. He sold his stock based on inside information. In the spring of 1990, Bush, as a member of the company's audit committee, was informed that Harken was suffering a cash "crisis."[10] Banks were demanding the company pay down its debts. What did our fearless leader do with this troubling news? He got off that sinking ship without a thought for the women and children. On

June 22, 1990, Bush unloaded 212,140 shares of Harken stock at $4 per share. Two months later, Harken announced that bad news Bush had been warned about. The value of Harken's stock fell to $2.37 per share immediately following the announcement of losses and was trading at only $1 by the end of that year.[11] Bush walked away with nearly $850,000.

Before he got canned, Bush administration Treasury secretary Paul O'Neill had this to say about deceptive CEOs: "What they really ought to wear around their neck would transport them to a branch on the highest tree, not the mantle of leadership."[12] If I ever said that we should string up George Bush, Mary would have me sleeping on the couch until the end of time. Luckily, Paul O'Neill said it, not me. He didn't lose his wife for speaking the truth, just his job.

✳   ✳   ✳

Unfortunately, when it came time to take Wall Street to the woodshed, Bush talked tough but pulled his policy punches. He said, "We must usher in a new era of integrity in corporate America,"[13] but then he went and proposed just about nothing. He said nothing about a regulatory body to audit the auditors. He said nothing about protection for whistle-blowers. He said nothing about enhancing the power of the SEC (remember, it's about power for your friends, not the government). He said nothing about criminal penalties for corporate fraud. Maybe he was afraid that if he did, he'd be giving the end of his speech in hand-cuffs.

As a result, the more the markets heard from him, the more they realized they weren't getting the bold leadership they needed. The lasting image of that speech on Wall Street is Bush opening his mouth and the

Dow Jones tanking to the tune of around four hundred points (it rallied to be down only two hundred by the end of the day). I guess the moral of that story is that there's never a bull market for bullshit.

THE "HAD ENOUGH" SOLUTION

First, let me say that this is one area where Democrats did a darn good job. While Bush was out there proposing business as usual, Paul Sarbanes of Maryland was working away, putting together a series of really, really good changes to the accounting industry—changes that make up the largest reform to America's accounting industry since the creation of the SEC back in 1934.

The problem is that we did a darn good job in just about utter stealth.

For example, because of Democrats, and Democrats alone, there is now an independent oversight board that audits the auditors.

Because of Democrats, and Democrats alone, there are now restrictions on the nonaudit services that an accounting firm can provide to the public companies it audits. Put another way, it keeps auditors from conflicts of interest.

Because of Democrats, and Democrats alone, CEOs and CFOs and their boards are now responsible for the accuracy of operation and financial reports—and there are now actual criminal penalties for corporate fraud.

Because of Democrats, and Democrats alone, when corporate insiders sell stock, those sales must now be reported to the SEC within two days.

Because of Democrats, and Democrats alone, there's now a wall between the stock analysis side and the investment banking side of the big
investment houses. That keeps the analysts from being pressured to give
good ratings for stock dogs that the investment banking folks are supporting.

Did you know all this? I didn't.

And that's part of the problem for progressives. This is an issue
where Bush is in the wrong, we're in the right, and we have a policy to
back it up. We look for solutions to problems, not political weapons—
and that's to our credit. But as a political consultant, I need to tell you
that good policy is good politics only if you make something out of it.

HARVEY, THE PITTS

You'd think that Bush and Cheney—or at least Karen and Karl—knowing that they had zero
credibility on corporate governance issues, would appoint someone to run the Securities
and Exchange Commission who had a shred of credibility on the issue. Again, you'd be
wrong. Enter Harvey Pitt, accounting industry lawyer, friend, and apologist. As a lawyer, Pitt
represented individuals like insider trader Ivan Boesky against charges brought by the SEC.
He pushed for auditor independence from federal oversight and opposed tough insider-
trading regulation. When he came to the Securities and Exchange Commission, he called
for a "kinder, gentler" SEC and backed that up by abandoning a report that criticized the
accounting industry and opposing new accounting standards legislation. So what was Harvey doing as revelation of corporate fraud was sending the markets to hell in a handbas-
ket? He was asking for a pay raise and for his position to be elevated to cabinet level. A
man worth between $4 and $8 million asking for a pay raise as Americans are seeing their
savings disappear—that's a man after George W. Bush's compassionate heart.

For example, when Dick Cheney crows in a video that Arthur Andersen provided him with "over and above just sort of the normal by-the-books auditing arrangement" (see the sidebar on page 233 for more), we should be going absolutely crazy. He's not going to explain himself and his shady arrangements unless someone makes him—and we've got to stop looking around hoping that someone else is gonna be that someone. We're it.

When Mike Oxley tries to water down Paul Sarbanes's Accounting Reform bill (which he did), or George Bush won't commit to supporting it (which he didn't do until it finally passed 97–0 in the Senate and he saw the writing on the wall), they need to pay a political price. They will act with impunity until they realize that the next time they're going to actually get punished. Stop it once, you'll stop it forever. Get rolled over now, get used to getting rolled over.

Today, about 84 million Americans own stock. That means there are 84 million Americans who care about having a strong, truthful stock market. Which means that there are 84 million voters or potential voters who should have reason to feel really good about Democrats and really bad about Republicans.

Our job is to get them there. And that means getting behind the next wave of corporate responsibility legislation and establishing ourselves as the protectors of a shareholder nation. There are a lot of ideas about what that should include. I want to name just a few.

Break Up the Crony Capitalism of Corporate Boards. Corporate directors and executives are supposed to look out for a company's shareholders, not themselves. These days, though, lot of boards are hand-picked by CEOs and it's often their friends or cronies (even if you're one of those people who sends back your proxy statement, you're still picking among the handpicked). A lot of times, the executives of one company will get put on the board of another company and give someone from that other company a seat on their board in return. It's become a way for a select group of people to play insider games, pick up a fat salary, and get a couple of nice corporate retreats a year. Instead of real shareholder representatives, you get a bunch of directors who rubber-stamp audits, budgets, and CEO pay. The only people missing from the equation are the shareholders. It's no surprise that these were the boards that were either woefully incompetent or willfully blind as corporate scandals unfolded around them. That's why we should make it easier for shareholder picks to be on corporate boards to compete with the CEO cronies.

Clamp Down on Corporate Tax Abuse. What do Stanley Works, Ingersoll-Rand, Tyco, and Accenture have in common? The answer is that these icons of the American economy are no longer American companies. They renounced their citizenship in order to reduce their taxes. That's a disgrace. When these companies rely on the protection of the American armed forces, rely on the largesse of American contracts, thrive in an environment of American intellectual property protection, they seem to believe in a different Declaration of Independence—independence from doing their patriotic duty by paying taxes. One thing we ought to do is say that if you incorporate offshore, you never get a U.S. government contract again. Democrats have tried to pass such a bill—Republicans have blocked it. Let's make them pay and make it pass. Then let's cut down on the other corporate tax fraud that's out there—like when companies tell Wall Street that they're making a lot more money than they tell the IRS. (See the chapter on taxes for more on this.)

CAUGHT ON TAPE

A lot of times if politicians can't attend an event but want to do something nice for the people there, they'll record a short videotape to be played at the event. Or sometimes they go to an event not realizing that someone is taping it. The problem is when something they think is going to be played behind closed doors becomes public. That's when you've got politicians caught on tape.

For example, a tape unearthed by the *Houston Chronicle* shows President Bush at an Enron party in 1997 calling former Enron president Rich Kinder "too good a man." It also shows former President Bush telling the Enron brass, "I don't think anybody did more than you did to support George." Later in the tape, it shows Jeff Skilling joking that his accounting practices could "add a kazillion dollars to the bottom line."

In a promotional video for Arthur Andersen, Dick Cheney is caught on tape saying, "I get good advice, if you will, from their people based upon how we're doing business and how we're operating—over and above just sort of the normal by-the-books auditing arrangement." Arthur Andersen was later convicted of impeding a federal investigation into the Enron collapse and is now under scrutiny for approving Halliburton's questionable accounting practices. Over and above the normal by-the-books auditing arrangement indeed.[14]

Protect Pensions. Mutual funds have diversification requirements; why should pensions be any different? Enron workers lost everything because their entire pensions were in Enron stock. There's a reason the saying "Don't put all your eggs in one basket" is considered wise. It should be considered a requirement, too. Senator Edward M. Kennedy has put forward a plan where we require 401(k) plans with assets that are overconcentrated in company stock to insure against corporate wrongdoing and require those plans to give workers quarterly benefit statements with a special "overconcentration notice" when company stock exceeds 20 percent of total investments.

The other problem at Enron was that workers were "locked in" to their stock. Many couldn't sell, even as it plummeted. We should give pension holders real investment choice by allowing them to sell all their shares of company stock as soon as they have worked for the company three years.

End the Practice of Pump and Dump. Stock options have played an important role in giving people an ownership stake in the company. But I have to agree with Warren Buffett on this one: stock options are not free. They shouldn't be treated as such. When executives and directors award themselves millions of shares and the shareholders never see it on a balance sheet, there's a perverse incentive to manipulate balance sheets and inflate stock prices so they can cash out on top.

☆ ☆ ☆

Basically, the problem with President Bush is that he brought the worst business practices to government—putting the worst offenders in positions of power, condoning corporate misconduct through his own example, refusing to get tough with bad companies, and running the government as if it is a bad company. Under President Bush the government is protecting corporate tax shelters instead of eliminating them. And it writes bill after bill behind closed doors with industry lobbyists. To strengthen our markets and promote economic growth, we've got to make it clear that we've had enough.

10

THE MYTH OF TORT
REFORM

George W. Bush has introduced a lot of words and phrases into the American lexicon. Things like "misunderestimate," "subliminable," "federal cufflink," "full analyzation," "revengeful person"—the list goes on and on. In fact, Jacob Weisberg put them all together in a book called *George W. Bushisms*. Though the book is a lot of fun, I wouldn't call it one of your more confidence-inspiring reads.

Then again, I've been known to mangle a word or two, so I tend not to give George a hard time about it. In fact, most of the phrases he's introduced are like farts—sometimes they're disgusting, sometimes they make you laugh, but ultimately they're pretty harmless.

But there is one phrase he's brought to the public consciousness that is serious—and seriously flawed—and that phrase is "tort reform." Tort reform means reforming (restricting) people's access to the civil justice system. This is a movement bought and paid for by companies and individuals who stand to gain a lot of dough if you can't sue them

when their tires fail, their medicine is toxic, or their machines are unsafe. Recently, it's been hailed by Republicans as a solution to the specific problem of skyrocketing malpractice insurance rates. After all, if all
those pesky lawyers weren't filing all those pesky lawsuits, we wouldn't
need things like malpractice insurance to begin with. Of course, if we
could guarantee that no doctor would ever cut off the wrong part of
somebody's body or make some other mistake, we wouldn't need malpractice insurance, either. And if nobody ever hit anybody else's car, we
wouldn't need auto insurance. And if we could somehow "undiscover"
fire, we wouldn't need fire insurance. And if men were angels, we
wouldn't need laws. The bottom line is that people ain't perfect and neither is the world—so we've created mechanisms to deal with it.

But back to malpractice insurance reform, which is basically a very
targeted kind of tort reform. Republicans maintain that if doctors didn't
get sued by lawyers, they wouldn't pay so much in malpractice insurance. If they didn't pay so much in insurance, they wouldn't charge so
much. If they didn't charge so much, the cost of health care wouldn't
skyrocket. And if the cost of health care wasn't so high, maybe there
wouldn't be 43.6 million Americans without it. O glorious tort reform,
how could we have failed to see that you are our salvation! Of course, like
many of their proposals, the truth behind tort reform is a far cry from
what they say about tort reform.

After all, if tort reform is the cure for rising malpractice insurance
rates, why were right-wingers pushing for it when rates were low? The
truth is that "tort reform" is just a newer term for a Republican policy
goal that's been around for a long, long, time. And reducing rates isn't
the goal we're talking about, either. The goal is to cut off the one avenue

the little guy often has when he's been wronged by some of the biggest guys in America—the courts.

Now this book is about big ideas, and some of you might be thinking that tort reform is my "transgender amendment"—a little side issue that gets in the way of some big stuff. The reason I think it's worth talking about is not that I love lawsuits (I've been subject to more than my share of them), it's that access to the courts is one of the avenues open to people in our society who don't have power but get wronged by the powerful. If we are to stand up to power in the interest of people, we need to keep right-wingers from closing the doors of the one branch of government that should be open to those without power, regardless of what party is in power—the courts.

If you've ever talked to a business executive for more than five minutes, you'll learn that it is absolute gospel among these guys that lawsuits and lawyers are the source of every problem they've ever had. In the name of full disclosure, I feel the need to tell you that I, James Carville, am a lawyer. Most people are surprised to learn that I achieved an advanced degree in anything other than mixology, but for a time I was actually bar-certified in the state of Louisiana. Although I am eternally grateful to my uncle Lloyd for helping to pay my way through law school at LSU, I'll be the first to tell you that my career in the law was brief and inglorious. It ended one day in 1980 when I looked up from my desk and said, "If I had to hire a lawyer, I wouldn't hire me." And I quit.

With that now admitted, I'll grant that some lawyers are slimy, some lawsuits are stupid, and some cases should be tossed out of court straightaway. But I'll tell you that I've never once heard a business executive say, "Maybe we shouldn't have made a swimming pool drain that sucked out half of a child's internal organs," or, "Maybe we should have told people that if you happen to have a beer while using our product, your liver will fail." No, tort reform is to business executives what tax cuts are to Republicans—the answer to everything. Over the years, it's gone by a bunch of different names: product liability reform, common-sense legal reform (that's what they called it in the Contract with America), and now tort reform. Presumably, each of those things sounds better than "a proposal to tilt the playing field even further in favor of big business," which is what tort reform would do. The name has changed, the basic idea hasn't. As far as I'm concerned, they can call it whatever they want, because I call tort reform the biggest, dumbest fake issue Republicans could have ever invented.

Are there real steps we can take that will lower malpractice insurance rates? Yes, but tort reform ain't one of them. Let's go through our drill.

The Problem: Malpractice insurance rates are skyrocketing, forcing some docs out of business. Businesses feel beleaguered by lawsuits.

The Bush Response: Preach the gospel of tort reform.

The "Had Enough" Solution: Take two key steps that will actually reduce malpractice insurance rates without closing the door to the courts: police the physicians and end insurance company monopolies.

THE PROBLEM IN DEPTH

In January 2003, twenty surgeons in the Northern Panhandle of West Virginia began taking leaves of absence to protest their insurance rates.

Essentially, they went on strike. They weren't being all that melodramatic, either. Each of them had seen their malpractice premiums jump by over $10,000.

A similar walkout was narrowly averted in Pennsylvania. President Bush even went there to visit with the docs and used a hospital in Scranton as a backdrop to call for tort reform. On average, doctors across America saw their malpractice insurance premiums increase by 11.3 percent in 2002—the largest increase in a decade (although lower than the average annual increase of 11.6 percent since 1975).[15] In places like Miami, Dallas, and New York, doctors in high-risk specialties can end up paying over $200,000 a year in malpractice premiums. A number of insurance companies have stopped providing coverage altogether, and the skyrocketing rates are forcing a number of doctors to close up shop or retire early—and leaving their patients scrambling to find care. It's a real problem. That's why it demands a real solution.

THE BUSH RESPONSE IN DEPTH

President Bush went to Pennsylvania to call for tort reform. Standing at the University of Scranton, he talked about the patients and doctors he had met, and then he said, ". . . unnecessary costs don't start in the waiting room or the operating room. They're in the courtroom."[16]

In his State of the Union address, he said, "Everybody pays more for health care because of excessive litigation." (As we've learned, just because he said it in a State of the Union address doesn't mean it's true.)

In a speech to the American Medical Association, he said, "There are too many frivolous lawsuits against good doctors. If lawsuits are running up the cost of medicine and are driving docs out of business because practicing medicine is too expensive, we've got to do something."

The man is quite confident he's got his finger on the problem. And he's pretty sure he knows the solution—a federal law that would set a $250,000 limit on damage awards for pain and suffering. Caps.

Here's what's wrong with that solution. First, caps don't work. I can't put it any more clearly than that. California is the perfect example of this. California put in place some of the strictest medical malpractice reform way back in 1976. Since then, malpractice premiums have increased by 190 percent—and insurance companies have been petitioning to push them up another 40 percent. Basically, the cap didn't do a thing, and the only thing that helped wasn't tort reform—it was *insurance* reform.[17]

Same thing in Nevada. The state legislature there passed a new tort reform bill, and doctors were happy because it meant that insurers would reduce malpractice insurance rates. Those reductions never happened.[18] In fact, of the five states that have the highest premiums in the nation—Florida, Michigan, Nevada, Ohio, and West Virginia—all of them cap lawsuit awards.

Caps don't work because premiums have never corresponded to increases or decreases in lawsuit payouts. Even though President Bush likes to conjure up images of waiting lines in front of courtrooms where people go, make a ridiculous claim, and are handed a big brown bag of cash, malpractice payouts have been steady for thirty years.[19]

Caps also happen to be deeply unfair to parents of young children and those who care for their elderly parents. That's because when a child dies, or a senior citizen suffers some horrible harm, the loss they suffer isn't economic—they weren't making any money to begin with. That loss is noneconomic, exactly what George Bush wants to cap.

More important, lawsuits, payouts, damage awards—all those things—account for about one-half of 1 percent of health care costs. Don't believe me? Listen to the nonpartisan Congressional Budget Office: They said, "Malpractice costs account for a very small fraction of total health care spending; even a very large reduction in malpractice costs would have a relatively small effect on total health plan premiums." [20]

Think about that for a second: if, as of today, lawsuits became illegal and no lawsuit was ever filed again, the growth of health care costs in America would slow by less than 1 percent.

All of a sudden, tort reform isn't quite the silver bullet.

The real factors that are responsible for rising insurance rates are stupid companies that get protection from competition and, to a much lesser extent, bad docs.

No joke, if you want to point your finger at the single largest cause of rising insurance rates, point to the Bush economy. That's right. One of the reasons that insurance companies are sending their rates through the roof is that—just like you and me—they got absolutely creamed when the market plunged. As USA Today put it: "Insurance companies are boosting rates partly to make up for price wars in the 1990s, when competition kept premiums low, and to counter recent declines in their investment incomes." [21]

Here's how this works. If you're one of the people in this country who is lucky enough to have a job and health care, you pay your health insurance company a certain amount of money a month. So does your employer. When you go to the doctor, you probably pay a small

"A LAWSUIT NEVER HELPED ANYONE"

George Bush likes saying that "no one has ever been healed by a frivolous lawsuit." In fact he likes saying it so much that he said it in his State of the Union speech.

Of course, by "frivolous lawsuit" he means "any lawsuit." So let me share with you what some "frivolous lawsuits" have accomplished over the years. Did they heal the people in whose name they were filed? No, because in most cases those people were dead. What they did do is prevent more people from dying and make companies think twice when they were deciding what would be more costly—fixing a problem or forgetting about it.

Flammable pajamas: A company called Riegel Textile sold highly flammable fabric for use in baby and children's pajamas. The company knew for years that the fabric was flammable but refused to treat it with flame-retardant chemicals. They also refused to warn consumers. As a result, a bunch of kids were severely burned. One girl was hospitalized for two months when her pajamas caught fire while she was leaning over an electric stove. It was a jury award that forced that unsafe product off the market.

Toxic shock syndrome: In the 1980s, a number of women in this country got sick and died from toxic shock syndrome after using superabsorbent tampons. It turns out that Playtex had disregarded studies and medical reports that linked their product to toxic shock. It took a lawsuit to get the most dangerous products off the market—and get a warning put on others.

Faulty football helmets: Young athletes were dying from head and spinal injuries due to poorly designed football helmets. It was liability claims that spurred improved football helmet design and led to no football-related deaths for the first time in sixty years.

Lilly-liver danger drug: A while ago, Eli Lilly came up with a new arthritis pain-relief drug. The only problem was that the drug also caused a fatal kidney-liver ailment. Eli Lilly knew of the hazard, but didn't tell doctors, patients, or the FDA. It took a lawsuit to make that information public and get the drug off the market.

Famous Ford Pinto: People sometimes forget that the Ford Pinto wasn't always a joke. There was a time in the early 1970s when it was a car that a lot of people bought because it was affordable. Unfortunately, it also had a tendency to burst into flames when hit from behind. Ford had made a conscious decision before the car's 1972 release not to fix what they knew back then was a design flaw, and did so only after a punitive damage award.

Death cribs: A company called Bassett Furniture made a line of cribs that were designed in such a way that babies were being hanged to death on the headboard. They were smart enough to stop making the crib but decided it wasn't worth notifying everyone who had already bought the crib of the risk. Only after a lawsuit did they recall the faulty—and deadly—product.

Chrysler minivan latch: Chrysler put a defective door latch on one of its minivans. The fact that the door would fly open in an accident ended up being responsible for 37 deaths, 98 injuries, and 134 ejections. Even though Chrysler knew the latch was unsafe, it wasn't until a class-action lawsuit that they redesigned the latches and replaced the faulty ones.

Asbestos: As early as 1918, manufacturers knew that people who inhale asbestos get asbestosis, which causes lung cancer. In fact, that was the year insurance companies stopped covering asbestos workers. But for seven decades, the asbestos industry hid the risk from the public and had Congress try to shield them from liability. It was lawsuits and a 1989 EPA ruling that finally banned most uses of asbestos. By the way, when President Bush says a lawsuit never helped anyone, think of this: Asbestos killed 171,500 people in the United States between 1967 and 1997 and, due to its lingering effects, is expected to kill another 118,700 by 2027.

Without those frivolous lawsuits, we wouldn't even know about the problems—much less have actually fixed them.

co-payment, and your insurance company pays the rest. So you pay your insurance company, they pay the doctor, they pay their underwriters and workers and the people who put you on hold when you have a question, and what they've got left over is their profit. What do they do with that? You'll be surprised to learn that they invest it, just as you or I would if we found we had some extra cash. Unlike you and me, they're not allowed to invest all of it, but they can invest a pretty good chunk.

In the early 1990s, those investments were doing so well that the insurance companies were actually able to charge people less than they paid out to doctors and hospitals. They just let all that investment income cover the difference—another invisible benefit of a strong economy. Over the past couple of years, however, the economy tanked, those investments dried up, and they had to get the money from somewhere. There's only one place they could get it: from you and me and that doctor behind the tree.

Now I said that there were two causes of skyrocketing insurance rates—dumb companies and bad docs. So let's talk a little bit about the bad docs, because if tort reform is the biggest, dumbest fake issue Republicans could have ever invented, they've got some help from doctors, the smartest, best-educated, most talented dumb people in our society.

RICK SANTORUM, TORT REFORM
HYPOCRITE

Rick Santorum has recently gained fame for his comments in which he equated homosexuality with bestiality and child molestation. But Rick Santorum is much more than a world-class homophobe, he's also a world-class hypocrite.

Rick Santorum, the Republican senator from Pennsylvania, has been one of the fiercest proponents of so-called tort reform in Congress. He has sponsored and co-sponsored a bunch of bills that would cap damages in lawsuits, limit attorney fees, and make claimants go through a bunch of hurdles before they could file suit.

In 1993, he co-sponsored a bill that would have prohibited a medical malpractice liability action from being brought in any state court unless the claim had previously gone through some other dispute-resolution process, and then limited damages if it made it to court.

In 1994, he introduced the Comprehensive Family Health Access and Savings bill, which would have also limited the total amount of noneconomic damages a claimant and his or her family members could receive to $250,000.

He's consistently voted against Patients' Bill of Rights legislation that would have granted patients the right to sue their HMOs and supported versions of another bill that would have capped malpractice verdicts.

In fact, in 1995, Rick Santorum went to the Senate floor to lament a "too costly legal system" and blasted those who "hit the jackpot and win the lottery in some cases."

It turns out, Rick may decry the jackpot, but he had no problem going for it himself.

You see, Rick's wife, Karen, went to a chiropractor for a spine manipulation and claimed to have sustained a herniated disk in her back as a result. Luckily, none of Rick's laws passed, because otherwise she wouldn't have been able to go right to court and sue for $500,000—which is exactly what she did.

During the trial, Senator Santorum testified on behalf of his wife and talked about the impact her injury had on him. For example, he said that her back problems have limited her abilities to participate in his campaign. A jury found the testimony so convincing that it awarded Karen Santorum $350,000.

Let's summarize: Here's a guy who's run races vilifying trial lawyers, has repeatedly tried to impose $250,000 caps on damages for pain and suffering, supports the rights of HMOs over patients, and then uses a trial lawyer to secure hundreds of thousands of dollars in pain and suffering damages in a malpractice suit. To modify something I once said: "It's the hypocrisy, stupid."[22]

Don't get me wrong; I've got nothing but respect for doctors. A good, conscientious doctor who insisted that I get a colonoscopy may have saved my life. Lord knows, they wouldn't let me mop the floor at a medical school, much less attend one.

But right now, the 95 percent of doctors who are great are covering for the 5 percent of doctors who aren't. That's literally true. Five out of every hundred doctors are responsible for more than half of all malpractice payouts—that includes both jury awards and out-of-court settlements.[23]

Why is it so tough for those doctors in West Virginia? Well, they are home to a disproportionate number of doctors who have had five or more malpractice payouts—and virtually none of those bad docs was disciplined. In fact, West Virginia has the second highest percentage of doctors who have been successfully sued five or more times.

If West Virginia is number two, what state do you think is number one? You got it, Pennsylvania—George W. Bush's poster state for tort reform. In fact, Pennsylvania has about 5 percent of the doctors in the United States, but those doctors make up close to 20 percent of all doctors with five or more malpractice payments.[24]

You don't need tort reform to fix that, you need doctors who are willing to police their own and state medical boards that aren't afraid to discipline bad doctors.

Now before I get to our solution, I just need to say something as someone who's been in the political consulting business for a little while. I watched George Bush show up at that hospital in Pennsylvania and talk to those doctors about tort reform. If George Bush wants to show up at every hospital in every state in the Union and talk about tort reform, we should let him. Heck, we should encourage him. Because if he thinks that when people see the president of the United States standing in front of a hospital they want to hear him talk about caps and lawsuits and liability and malpractice—he's even more out of touch than I thought.

Every time he stands in front of a hospital and doesn't say a word about the 43.6 million Americans who don't have health care, he is being negligent as a leader. Every time he puts his arm around a doctor but doesn't say a word about how millions of seniors can't afford the drugs that doctor can prescribe, he demonstrates for the entire country just how little he actually gets it. Every time he does one of those things, we need to be tough in reminding him that hospitals are a place to talk about health care.

Of course, he's got another goal in calling for tort reform, and that is to get doctors back on his side. That's because by standing so strongly against a Patients' Bill of Rights, he actually managed to be a uniter, not a divider—he united doctors and lawyers against him. Doctors didn't like the Bush position that insurance companies should be able to override the decisions that they make for their patients, and lawyers didn't like the fact that when these insurance company decisions led to patient suffering, Bush wanted to limit their recourse in the courts. Come to think of it, when he's standing in front of a hospital, we should remind him that he's the reason we don't have a national Patients' Bill of Rights in this country, too.

Now let's get serious. Instead of using this crisis to justify a political goal Republicans have had for a long time—beating up on trial lawyers—let's be the folks who come up with a real solution to this real problem.

THE "HAD ENOUGH" SOLUTION

End the insurance company monopoly. There are only two entities in this country that are now exempt from antitrust law—Major League Baseball and insurance companies. Major League Baseball is exempt because it claims that the antitrust exemption keeps teams from jumping from city to city, and that baseball—without an antitrust exemption—would cease to exist. (I'll let somebody else write the book about whether that's true or not.) The insurance industry is exempt because they spread around a ton of campaign contributions (nearly $50 million to Republicans alone in 2000 and 2002) and because they employ an army of lobbyists on Capitol Hill.

As a result, big insurance companies decide whether patients get the tests and treatment they need, how doctors practice medicine, how much doctors are paid for their services, and how much doctors pay for medical malpractice insurance—and they can all collude with one another, fix prices, and then impose their collective will on the American health care system.

We're not proposing to limit their power with some big government Soviet-style solution. We're going to propose a solution Republicans claim to love: competition. No more colluding; start competing. In 1998, that's exactly what the state of California did. They said that their state's insurance industry shouldn't be exempt from antitrust law. What happened? Insurance reform—not tort reform—forced a 20 percent rollback in premiums.

That's a solution a doctor can love, a lawyer can love, and the American people can love.

American Medical Association—Heal thy physicians. I said before that a very small number of bad doctors are responsible for a huge percentage of malpractice claims. The problem is that the public doesn't know which doctors are the bad ones. That's because while hospital and medical boards can see the records of individual doctors, Congress (under pressure from the AMA) has forbidden that information to be released to the public. My guess is most people, if they knew, would avoid the bad docs. After all, when you're sick or hurt, you just want a doctor to help you get well. Nobody I know wants their doctor to screw up in the hopes that they'll be able to take them to court.

Here's what I say—let's adopt another Republican solution; let's use the power of the market. We do that by just making the damn thing public and letting people choose for themselves. I understand there are times when a doctor is successfully sued but it's not really his or her fault. (The example I keep hearing is an obstetrician who delivers a baby to a mother who had no neonatal care. Because she didn't take care of herself during her pregnancy, something is wrong with the baby and she sues.) That's why we're going to be fair and do this in a reasonable way—if a doctor has one claim against them, they get a pass. Presumably they learned from their mistake. If they have more than one, we let a panel of experts review the case. If they're found negligent there—and every time thereafter—it's public knowledge. They can explain their side of the story, but people get to know there is a story.

The market will then weed out the doctors who aren't qualified, which reduces the number of lawsuits, which (moderately) lowers costs. Maybe I'm missing something, but as far as I can tell, this is a democratic, market-driven solution.

If all else fails, a tax credit for rich people. Now, I don't necessarily love this idea, but I know that Republicans have never seen a tax credit for rich people that they didn't like—so here's mine: We say to doctors that if you're in a high-risk specialty, and your premiums go up by a certain percentage in any given tax year, you get a credit to offset that rise.

✷ ✷ ✷

It seems to me that rather than creating some big fake issue of tort reform as George Bush seems intent on doing, we just do what it takes to fix the problem. So there you have it—three real solutions for one real problem.

★ PART FIVE ★

"INSURE DOMESTIC TRANQUILITY"

★ ★ ★

In Louisiana, we have a thing called a *boucherie*. When someone has a pig to slaughter, they invite all their friends and neighbors over, and it becomes a big communal dinner. Besides the person supplying the pig, everybody brings something—contributing whatever they contribute. Maybe someone brings an étouffée, and someone else brings an oyster loaf. Maybe all someone else can afford to bring is a potato salad. But everyone gets together, and everyone eats better.

Now, that may sound like communism to some people. But when you go to some of these things, you realize it's not communism—it's community.

That's what I learned growing up—community and respect for your elders. At these *boucheries*, you'll see every momma tells her child to go kiss Grandma . . . or go kiss Aunt Fanny. And the kids'll complain that they're going to get their cheeks pinched, or get lipstick on their foreheads, or get slobbered on. But they do it—and from an early age, they learn respect. And I think that respect and that sense of community we learned have something to do with the fact that Louisiana has the lowest number of nursing homes per capita—of any state in the nation.

So, in this section, we're going to talk a little about respecting our elders, among other things.

Now any constitutional scholar out there is going to tell you that I'm totally misinterpreting what "insure domestic tranquility" means.

That's because when the framers wrote the Constitution, they were worried that some states might go to war with each other over territory (as almost happened between Pennsylvania and Connecticut over Wilkes-Barre). Therefore, they wanted to make sure the federal government had powers to squash rebellion and to smooth tensions between states—thus ensuring domestic tranquility.

Because I'm not too worried that anyone's going to battle over Wilkes-Barre anymore, I'm interpreting that phrase a little differently. I think ensuring domestic tranquility means not pitting elements of our society against one another—like young versus old. That's why, in the following chapters, we're going to talk about entitlements and then have a few short conversations on lying, religion, and friendship.

11

"THOSE DAMN ENTITLEMENTS"

There is no social event in the world quite like the A-list Washington gathering. I wouldn't have been allowed to park the cars at one of these things until I helped Bill Clinton win the presidency and married Mary.

These parties are the biggest group masturbatory affairs ever invented—and fun as hell. Take a book party, for example. Some publisher lays out a lot of cash for top-shelf drinks, great appetizers, and all the guests feel good because they are celebrating the act that represents the pinnacle of civilization—the transmittal of the written word.

Now, what's funny is that in Washington, very few people actually read. Those who do read, read news digest publications like *The Hotline* or *The Note*, which essentially do your reading for you and summarize it.

The only problem with the Washington cocktail party is that you can never leave. You try to leave, but you keep getting sucked into conversation after conversation. I'm pretty strict about my bedtime; it's probably the one thing George W. Bush and I have in common. I like to be in bed by 11:00 P.M.

Mary and I were at one party and it was getting late. I made a beeline for the door and was standing outside when I realized that Mary was stopping every ten feet to have another conversation. It wouldn't have been so bad if I was just tired, but I had had a drink or two, and I had to piss something awful. I wasn't about to walk back inside and have ten more conversations just to get to the bathroom, and I wasn't going to make it home, so I shuffled off behind a tree and relieved myself.

Now I know what all my siblings are thinking: James, you country-ass cracker. You did *not* go to some fancy party and then take a leak outside.

Well, I soon learned that the other thing every Washington cocktail party has in common is that everyone is just waiting to call a reporter and tell them the delicious goings-on. This is *The Washington Times* story I woke up to the next morning. (Actually, I didn't wake up to that story— the only time I hold in my hands *The Washington Times* is when I'm using it to clean up after one of my dogs. Mary woke up to it and she was mortified. She thought I had committed the Beltway equivalent of backing an SUV over the patrons of a Hamptons nightclub.)

CALL OF THE WILD
The Washington Times
September 23, 1999
Inside the Beltway [p. A5]

. . . as for the Democratic strategist who brought "zippergate" to the Oval Office, James Carville is another story.

"He has no couth," says a limousine chauffeur who idled directly behind Mr. Carville's carriage at a Tuesday night reception for radio host Diane Rehm at the Corcoran Gallery of Art. "He could have gone back inside."

Mr. Carville, the chauffeur says, was waiting for his wife to emerge from the gala at around 10:30 p.m., when he strolled to the corner of 17th and E streets NW, glanced around him, and then crossed into the Ellipse behind the White House.

There, says the chauffeur, the outspoken Democrat irrigated a tree. "He comes back, pulls out some money, hands it to his chauffeur, Mary comes out, they climb in, and speed off into the night."

Mr. Carville was unavailable for comment.

If I had given him a comment, it would have been this: "That's the difference between a Republican and a Democrat—we'll pee behind a tree, but we'll tip the driver. Republicans would never do either."

It didn't take long for the phone to start ringing, and the irony is that most people thought I had actually planted the story myself, because it looked "too good."

Only in Washington can a Cajun boy become the toast of the town for whipping it out while a president can get impeached for it.

But I don't like these parties for their news potential. For me, they're great for picking up the buzz in Washington (which is why candidates near election shouldn't be allowed to attend—the buzz in Washington is distinctly *not* the buzz in America). They're a one-stop shop where you can find out what the purveyors of power are thinking about the issues of the day. I basically walk around, busting in on conversations.

There's Tim Russert, buttonholing anyone who has uttered the words "save Social Security" until they admit that saving Social Security might require raising the retirement age or raising taxes. Russert's prey usually tries desperately to find a way to turn the conversation to the Buffalo Bills.

Bill Kristol is over in another corner, starting another war. I overhear the words "As a matter of fact, I do have a problem with Syria."

Henry Kissinger is holding court, saying to Mexico's ambassador to the United States, "If only we had a leader like Carlos Salinas." I wonder—silently—if his consulting firms got any of the billions that Salinas stole from the Mexican people.

Bob Barr and Dick Armey are standing with their new liberal friends, extolling the virtues of the ACLU.

Tom Daschle and his wife, Linda, are being fawned over by Thomas Donohue of the Chamber of Commerce, whose organization just authorized a front group to spend $100,000 in ads to air in South Dakota, accusing Daschle of being an unpatriotic obstructionist.

Bill Bennett is on his third martini, thirteenth cigarette, and thirtieth little hot dog, inveighing against the lack of self-discipline and willpower among our nation's youth. Newt Gingrich and his third wife nod sagely in agreement. (Meanwhile, Bill's limo is waiting to take him to Atlantic City later that night.)

There's Colin Powell and his wife, Alma.

There's Andrea Mitchell and Alan Greenspan.

And there's one thing you hear, over and over, in conversation after conversation—"We've got to do something about those damn entitlements."

✯ ✯ ✯

It's a constant refrain in Washington. We've got to do something about those damn entitlements. When you hear this so often, it becomes gospel.

What too many Washingtonians forget is that "those damn entitlements"—Social Security and Medicare—are two of the most dramatic and successful examples of the power of the federal government to effect huge, positive societal change.

Too often, we forget what this country looked like before Social Security and Medicare. Here's what it looked like: If you were old, you were poor. If you weren't poor, but you got sick and paid for health care, you got poor. If you were poor, and you got sick, you didn't get health care. Basically, there was no safety net. It was like Thomas Hobbes's vision of life, "poor, nasty, brutish, and short."

And Social Security and Medicare did nothing short of cut elderly poverty by two-thirds, increase life expectancy by three years—from seventy-nine to eighty-two—and provide virtually every senior citizen with health insurance at the time in their lives when their need for health care is greatest. Sixty-four percent of retirees rely on Social Security for more than half of their retirement income. One-third of them rely on it for 90 percent or more of their retirement income. With Social Security, 9 percent of America's elderly live in poverty. If Social Security checks stopped going out today, 48 percent of elderly Americans would immediately be thrown into poverty.

And what about Medicare? Consider this: There is only one positive health statistic in which the United States is a world leader—life expectancy after age 65. In 1960, before the creation of Medicare, the average life expectancy after age 65 was 17.4 years for women and 13.2 years for men. In 2000, the average life expectancy after age 65 was nearly 20 years for women, and 16.2 years for men. Access to health care for seniors is hugely responsible for that.

When people say that the government squanders our money, remember that over the past forty years, the federal government has spent half of its money on three things: defense; Social Security; and Medicare. As a result, we won the Cold War and have the most powerful military force the world has ever seen; we cut the rate of elderly poverty by two-thirds; and we gave our seniors the best health care in the world. Not too shabby.

The problem now is that with the baby boomers nearing retirement, the programs that have been icons of American progressivism face both political and demographic challenges. Progressives need to do more than defend them, we need to improve them. Let's go through our drill.

The Problem: Social Security and Medicare aren't prepared to handle the retirement of the baby boomers, and Medicare doesn't reflect changes in American medicine, like the rise of prescription drugs.

The Bush Response: Privatize 'em all, let the market sort it out.

The "Had Enough" Solution: Explain, expand, and solidify Social Security. Modernize Medicare. Stop sounding like the defenders of dinosaurs—make these programs matter again.

THE PROBLEM IN DEPTH

Social Security is a deceptively simple program. It's basically money that workers pay in, and that money is then paid out to retirees, widows, surviving children, and some people who have work-related disabilities. As of today, it pays retirement benefits to 29 million workers, disability benefits to nearly 6 million workers, family benefits to 3 million spouses and over 2 million children of retired and disabled workers, and survivor benefits to nearly 7 million survivors of deceased workers, including more than 2 million children.[1] Of course, this pay in/take out system would work perfectly in perpetuity if in every generation there was a consistent ratio of workers paying in to retirees taking out. Now, for the last couple of decades, baby boomers have been paying in, while their parents have been taking out. Because there are more baby boomers paying in than people taking out, the surplus is held in what is called a trust fund, which sits and gains interest. (By the way, administrative costs are less than 1 percent of total trust fund outlays—find any other form of insurance with administrative costs of less than 1 percent.)

Of course, because there are more baby boomers than their kids, the system is going to face a real crunch. In 1960, there were 5.1 workers paying in for every worker taking out. By 2010, there will be about 3.2 workers paying in for every worker taking out. You don't need to be a math genius to figure out what this all means. Here are the key dates when it starts hitting the fan.

- 2018, the first year that payouts exceed the amount of tax income that comes in (the first time interest from the trust fund is needed to pay benefits).

- 2028, first year that payouts are more than tax plus interest income (the first time trust fund assets are needed to pay benefits).
- 2042, the year that the trust fund assets are exhausted (trust fund income will be able to pay 73 percent of the benefits).

Notice that none of those dates is 2004 or 2006—which is why so few elected officials want to tackle the real steps necessary to fix this thing now. Actually, that's not entirely true. Some people do want to make major changes now, President Bush among them. The problem is that people who do want to do something now don't really want to fix the system, they want to use the looming problems as an excuse to dismantle it—but we'll get to that in a second.

If Social Security is simple, Medicare is confusing as hell. But there are some basic structural similarities. Whereas Social Security takes money out of your paycheck to pay retirement income to your parents, Medicare takes money out of your paycheck to do the same thing for health care. Medicare then guarantees a basic set of health benefits—like doctor visits, hospital stays, and medical equipment such as oxygen and wheelchairs.

Medicare pays hospitals a set amount for these things based on a complex formula and pays doctors a set amount based on a slightly less complex formula. It was modeled after your basic 1965 health plan, which makes sense, because that's when it was invented. But that's also a problem, because there have been a lot of advances in medicine since then. For example, we've learned that preventive care (which it doesn't cover) is good, and that prescription drugs (which it also doesn't cover) are the best, most cost-effective treatment for some diseases. Let me give you just a couple of examples—examples that George Bush himself cites:

Medicare will pay for all the costs associated with treating a stroke—hospital bills, rehab costs, doctors, outpatient care, all of that stuff. Those things can add up to $100,000, and Medicare will pay that—but it won't pay $1,000 a year for the blood-thinning drugs that prevent a stroke in the first place. Medicare today will pay up to $28,000 per patient for a hospital stay for ulcer surgery, but it won't pay for the drugs that get rid of most ulcers by eliminating their causes—drugs that run about $500 a year.

So that stuff isn't covered, and, after a deductible, everything else is covered 80/20. (Sometimes, to cover the 20 percent that the government doesn't pick up, people buy medigap insurance from the private sector.)

Because Medicare is structured like Social Security, it has a similar problem to Social Security—a trust fund has been built up because there are so many more baby boomers than retirees, but it's going to get spent down real fast when the boomers start retiring. Add to that the fact that health care costs are skyrocketing, and you get a real problem.

THE BUSH RESPONSE IN DEPTH

It makes sense that Republicans love the insurance industry. Between 1995 and 2002, the insurance industry gave over $40 million in soft money to Republicans, about three times what it gave to Democrats.[2] The irony is that Republicans don't care much for the *concept* of insurance. They don't like sharing risk over a large group of people. Maybe to them that sounds like socialism or something, because from health care to Social Security, their attitude is basically, "Let the rich people opt out of it, provide incentives for young and healthy people to get out of it, and let the poor and the sick fend for themselves."

Add to that the fact that if you don't believe in government, you sure as hell aren't going to believe in what are arguably the federal government's greatest success and flagship programs—Social Security and Medicare.

Combine those two things, and you understand the way Republicans approach Social Security and Medicare.

If you don't want to deal with a problem, or don't want to look responsible for what you say needs to be done, there's one surefire thing to do: You appoint a commission. That's what President Bush did with Social Security. Now, commissions can be a good thing when they genuinely and openly explore ideas and don't have to worry about politics. Of course, a commission can also be appointed to reach a foreordained conclusion—and that's when they're worthless and cynical. Just look at a couple of the folks Bush appointed to his Social Security Commission and see if you can figure out what type of commission this was:

- **Co-Chair: Richard Parsons, AOL Time Warner co–chief operating officer.** At Time Warner, Parsons managed a "permatemps" system under which a whole bunch of full-time employees were classified as contract workers so that the company didn't have to pay them the same benefits—or make the same Social Security contributions—as they did for other workers. In 2000, a settlement forced them to pay $5.5 million in back compensation.[3] How can you trust a guy who doesn't want to pay in to Social Security to strengthen it?
- **Robert Pozen, former vice chairman, Fidelity Investments.** I've got no problem with Robert Pozen, the only problem I have is that he used to run a $450 billion financial services company that could

stand to make billions in profits from any privatization system he recommends. Where does his loyalty lie?

● **Robert Johnson, who used to own Black Entertainment Television.** Again, I think he's a heck of an entrepreneur and a brilliant businessman. The problem is that he's been trying to create a new airline, DC Air, which requires regulatory approval from the Bush administration. This administration seems willing to "out" covert agents who are *related* to people who anger them. If I were him, I wouldn't want to piss them off.

In fact, not one person on the sixteen-member commission was there to represent the 45 million Americans who actually depend on Social Security today. Given this membership, it wasn't a surprise what the commission came up with: three different ways to privatize Social Security. Instead of going through each of the plans they came up with, I'll just tell you what they all have in common.

Each of the jury-rigged plans the Social Security Commission came up with allows people to set up individual accounts. You'd think that watching the market lose over $5 trillion in capitalization would have gotten Republicans to relinquish their privatization ideas. But since the sheer, hard facts can't get them to let go of the pantleg of a bad idea, it's up to us. The problem is that if people start putting money in Social Security for themselves, they're not putting it in for their parents—the way the program was designed to work. That leaves a big hole—a $1 trillion hole, to be exact—that none of the proposals says how they intend to fill.

Which means one of three things.

First, that trillion-dollar hole will be filled by cutting benefits for current or future retirees—by anywhere from 24 to 43 percent.

Second, that trillion-dollar hole will be filled by a stealth increase in the retirement age (by adjusting the formula for life expectancy).

Third, that trillion-dollar hole will be filled by taking money from other government programs, which would be fine if we happened to have an extra trillion lying around, but which we don't because of those tax cuts.[4]

When you look at the small print, those proposals look even less sexy. But why would we expect that a fake commission would come up with anything other than a fake solution?

✵ ✵ ✵

When it comes to Medicare, they're trying something even more cynical. They really want to hand all those Medicare responsibilities over to the private market, which isn't what seniors want, so they use prescription drug coverage as the bait in the privatization trap. That's the big secret—of course, when you've got a conspiracy, you can count on the dumb member of the team to slip up and let the cat out of the bag. In this case, that someone was Rick Santorum. Here's what he said: "The traditional Medicare program has to be phased out." And that "a higher drug benefit [could be used] as an incentive" for recipients to move into private plans.[5]

This is bad for two reasons: The first is that the prescription drug benefit they're talking about ain't all that good—it doesn't meet George W. Bush's commitment, as he said, to "making sure our seniors have got a guarantee of a prescription drug coverage in Medicare."[6] It doesn't meet that promise because the bill he supports doesn't cover nearly the

MYTHS ABOUT MEDICARE

Talk to any Republican about Medicare and I guarantee you'll hear the words "obsolete" or "antiquated." Well, that obsolete, antiquated system is now serving 88 percent of seniors in America. If there's one lesson the Bush administration has taught us, it's that if you repeat a lie often enough, people begin to believe it—and the two biggest lies you'll hear about Medicare are that when it's compared to private plans, it costs more and is less efficient. Let's shine the light of truth.

Myth 1: Medicare costs more than private plans. Actually, a report in 2000 by the federal General Accounting Office (GAO) found that when people used the private Medicare+Choice plans, it cost the government more than if its members had been treated through traditional Medicare. (And a lot of those Medicare+Choice plans went bankrupt, leaving seniors in the lurch.) So Medicare is actually cheaper and more stable than private plans.

Myth 2: The vaunted private sector is more efficient than that big government, bureaucratic Medicare. Actually, Medicare's overhead runs at 2 percent while Medicare HMOs spend around 15 percent. Look at it this way—for the same dollars spent, private plans use up more for salaries, paperwork, and profits, while traditional Medicare spends more on caring for patients.

Sure, those Republican lies may be halfway round the world, but it's time for those of us who now know the truth to get our boots on.[7]

costs many seniors need to have covered to make a drug benefit meaningful. It is estimated that over the next ten years, prescription drug costs for folks on Medicare will cost $1.8 trillion. That's a lot of money—but if you're going to make a commitment, you gotta make a commitment. The president is in support of a bill that costs $400 billion—also a lot of money, but decidedly not $1.8 trillion.[8] Now, I didn't do so well in advanced math in college, but even I could tell you that this isn't a half-assed solution, it's actually less than a quarter-assed. And the difference gets made up by big coverage gaps and out-of-pocket expenses for seniors—the same problems that the program is supposed to deal with in the first place.

At the same time, it makes seniors move to private insurance to get that insufficient benefit in the first place. So, when George W. Bush says, "drug coverage *in* Medicare," that little preposition—*in*—is another lie. Instead of using Medicare's well-tested, effective, and inexpensive system to deliver prescription drugs, he's using the issue of prescription drugs as a Trojan horse to get folks out of Medicare, so that Medicare, as Idiot Santorum said, can be "phased out."

The problem with private insurance—the private insurance seniors would have to get in order to get that drug coverage—is that the exact reason Medicare was invented was that private insurance failed to reach nearly half of the elderly population. In the years since Medicare was enacted, that private insurance system has only gotten worse for seniors. For example, Medicare has tried an experiment with private insurers called Medicare+Choice. Here's what we saw. Private health plans cost more than Medicare. So, to make money they cherry-picked the healthy populations and avoided sicker populations; they bypassed rural communities and stuck to the places that gave them the highest rates and profits.

In the places they couldn't make money they just left a lot of seniors in the lurch. I need to stop and make a political consultant note here—the people who get hurt the worst by being forced from Medicare into private plans are *rural* seniors, people living in places where there just aren't enough people to make it profitable to run a private health plan. A lot of those rural seniors live in "red" states. A lot of those "red" states could become "blue" states if a small percentage of the people there decided that the Republican Party wasn't looking out for them. This is a case where the Republican Party is actively screwing them. If we're a political party worth our salt, we've got to make them understand this.

Basically, a reliance on a private system that we know will cost more, work worse, and leave a lot of folks in the cold is George W. Bush's vision for the whole Medicare system, and it ain't pretty.

Once again, the most antigovernment solution isn't the best one.

THE "HAD ENOUGH" SOLUTION

Let's be honest with people about what Social Security is. It's not going to make you rich, but it's not going to leave you poor. That's the point. That's why it's called a "safety net." Republicans want people to treat it like a 401(k). So here's a little job for you. Call a financial services company and ask them if they provide a 401(k) that provides disability insurance to you and your family . . . that provides life insurance for you and your family . . . that provides a guaranteed benefit regardless of what happens in the economy and the market . . . and that reduces poverty across society. You won't find one. And if a company could actually put together such a plan, you would need just about everybody in America to participate. Does that sound familiar? It should; it's called Social Security.

We've got to defend that basic principle—while at the same time fixing the problems that Social Security does have. Here's the thing Republicans won't admit: it can be done without undermining Social Security's guaranteed benefit—the one thing that none of those private plans can offer. Here are three ideas that, taken together, actually fix Social Security for the long term:

1. **Invest the Trust Fund Like a Pension Plan.** "Now, hold on a second, Carville," you're saying. "With one breath you say that we *shouldn't* have private investment accounts, and with the next you're saying that we *should* invest Social Security in the markets." Yes, that's what I'm saying, and here's why and how. The law requires that the Social Security Administration purchase government bonds with the Social Security surplus—an investment that is heavy on security but low on return. This rule makes Social Security the only pension plan in the world that doesn't invest in equities. If we let the trust fund managers invest the trust fund like a pension plan and earn a higher rate of return, it would solve a lot of the funding problems, while letting younger generations get a better return on their contributions (better than privatized accounts with their administrative fees and risks). Because the trust fund is so big, it could weather volatility over many years (unlike private accounts) while still providing guaranteed, lifetime benefits defined by law and backed by the full faith and credit of the U.S. government (unlike private accounts). Republicans should like this solution because it puts more in the markets, and Democrats should like it because it maintains Social Security's same benefits and basic structure. By the way, when you run the numbers, it solves about half of Social Security's long-term problem.

2. **Drop the Tax but Up the Cap.** When Social Security was designed, the goal was to have people contribute (that FICA tax you see on your pay stub) so that 90 percent of all national earnings would be subject to contributions. Right now, people pay Social Security tax (FICA) on their salary up to $87,000—which means that someone making $86,000 pays the same into Social Security as someone making $860,000. Because wages have grown so much for people at the top, rather than collecting Social Security tax on 90 percent of all wages, it's actually only being collected on 84 percent of all wages. Here's my proposal: We tax everything over $87,000—but we do it at only 2 percent (everything up to that is 12.4 percent). That would keep us from taking a big bite out of middle- to upper-middle-class taxpayers, but it would get rid of about 15 percent of the long-term deficit.

3. **Make the Cost of Living Adjustment Reflect the Change in the Cost of Living.** Every year Social Security benefits are increased to reflect an increase in the cost of living (as measured by a thing called the Consumer Price Index, or CPI). A lot of experts believe that the CPI overstates inflation by about a percentage point. Therefore, the Cost of Living Adjustment, or COLA, is actually going up a little too fast. If we simply set the COLA at half a percentage point lower than the CPI, it would solve about 40 percent of Social Security's long-term deficit.

Think about it. Those three things, taken together, pretty much solve (and may actually *over*solve) Social Security's long-term problem. Is there some pain involved? Sure. Are people going to scream bloody murder about the "tax hike" and the COLAs? You bet. But our options are limited. I happen to believe that we shouldn't raise the retirement age anymore. Sure a sixty-seven-year-old news reporter may have his best years left in him, but a lot of the folks I grew up with are beat up and beat down by age sixty-seven, and they *need* to retire. There's no surplus left to solve the problems with magic money that comes from somewhere else, so you make the tough choice. At least if you're talking about ways of making sure Social Security lasts a lot longer, you're doing more than defending the status quo.

☆　☆　☆

As for Medicare, consider this: In 1995, Newt Gingrich said that Medicare should be allowed to wither on the vine. In 2003, Rick Santorum said that "the traditional Medicare program has to be phased out." Two Republican Party leaders, two different centuries, one consistent position. People like Medicare. The view of the Republican Party, as expressed by its leaders, is that it has got to go. Progressives need to pound this point home as hard as possible.

That's the politics—here's the policy.

First, remember that there's only one difference between Medicare and Social Security. The structure is the same, it's just that Medicare's added problem is health care's added problem—health care costs are going up. Therefore, everything we said in the chapter on health care about lowering costs helps Medicare, too. That said, here are some other ideas. They aren't sexy, but they're something—and advancing something is better than sounding like you're defending doing nothing.

● **Manage the Chronically Ill.** One percent of Medicare beneficiaries account for between 15 and 18 percent of all Medicare costs. The thing that costs Medicare the most money is when people are actually staying in the hospital. So if you take that 1 percent of people and find ways of reducing how much they're in the hospital, you can save Medicare a boatload of money—some folks think it could be as much as 25–30 percent of those costs. A lot of folks think that you'll get people better care, too.

- **Get More People the Right Care.** Speaking of better care, I was shown a study in the *New England Journal of Medicine* that said 46 percent of the health care people get is wrong.[9] That's stunning. And it tells us that if we actually invested a little money in what medical folks call "outcomes research"—research that tells us which things work the best—we could use it to set standards, reduce costs, and get people better results. For example, three times more prostate surgeries are performed in Monroe, Louisiana, than in Olympia, Washington.[10] But there's no evidence that the cancer death rate is any different—which means that a lot of those surgeries might be unnecessary. That's what an investment in "outcomes research" will tell us—and, by some estimates, it could save Medicare $70 billion.

- **Competitive Bidding for Medical Equipment.** Today Medicare pays the suppliers of things like wheelchairs, canes, and walkers from a set payment schedule, and even the suppliers admit that Medicare is paying them way too much. For example, in 1997 Medicare was paying 38 percent more for home oxygen than the Veterans Administration was.[11] If Medicare suppliers simply had to bid for their Medicare contracts the same way they presumably have to bid for every other contract they get, Medicare would save between $7.5 and $9 billion over ten years. To do this right you would put protections in place to assure that people in rural and underserved areas can always get what they need, but in the end it's a free-market solution (which conservatives should like) and it strengthens Medicare (which liberals should like).

None of these are sexy ideas. And Social Security and Medicare aren't sexy programs. But I'll take massively effective over sexy any day. And we all need to take anyone to task who tries to weaken—rather than strengthen—these two core pillars on which our party—and our nation's compassion—rest.

12

A NOTE ON LYING

There's a joke going around about the senator who died and went to heaven. As he stood in front of St. Peter at the Pearly Gates, he saw a huge wall of clocks behind him. He asked, "What are all those clocks?"

St. Peter answered, "Those are Lie-Clocks. Everyone on Earth has a Lie-Clock. Every time you lie, the hands on your clock will move."

"Oh," said the senator. "Whose clock is that?"

"That's Mother Teresa's. She's never told a lie, and therefore the hands have never moved."

"Whose clock is that?"

"That's Abraham Lincoln's clock. The hands have moved only twice, telling us that Honest Abe told only two lies in his entire life."

The senator then asked, "Where's George W. Bush's clock?"

St. Peter replied, "It's in Jesus' office. He's using it as a ceiling fan."

★ ★ ★

Now, I've made no secret of the fact that I think the mendacity of the Bush administration is beyond compare. The folks in this administration remind me of this guy I used to know who lied so much that he would lie when the truth served him better. I once asked him why. He said that he didn't want to get confused.

Of course, nobody's going to call me an unbiased source when it comes to evaluations of honesty of the Bush administration. Luckily, you no longer have to take my word for it. For example, David Corn has written a meticulously researched must-read called *The Lies of George W. Bush*. And in September 2003, *The Washington Monthly* magazine put together a panel of experts to study the last four American presidents and determine who was responsible for telling the biggest lies.[12]

They looked at Clinton's lying about sex, Reagan's lying about arms for hostages and welfare claims, George H. W. Bush's request that we read his lips. But they concluded that George W. Bush blew them all out of the water with his lies about deficits, tax cuts, and weapons of mass destruction.

I suppose George W. Bush should be proud. There's finally a measure by which he's number one.

When I reported this on *Crossfire*, Tucker Carlson, my co-host, responded that he was amazed at the lengths I would go to prove that someone else lies as much as Bill Clinton. That's always the Republican response—Clinton lied about sex. Republicans simply can't get over that. I think it comes down to this: Democrats lied about something we really like: sex. Republicans lie about something they really like: war and money. The difference is nobody gives a damn when you lie about your own sex, but it matters when you lie about a war that other people have to go fight and money that other people end up losing.

After 1992, I started spending a lot of time going to seminars for campaign managers and press secretaries and telling them my philosophy on dealing with the press. I told them that I had three hard and fast rules: Cooperation is better than intimidation; it doesn't pay to lie because lying hurts your credibility in the long run; and don't gripe too much about bad stories.

This administration has proven me not just wrong but colossally wrong, on all counts. They intimidate the entire media. You write a bad story, you get cut off. You make someone look bad, you don't get any more interviews. The White House press corps has been slapped around more than one of Mike Tyson's girlfriends. The problem is that none of this sorry bunch of crayon scribblers has the balls to fight back.

Because of this, the Bush administration is free to lie, repeatedly, without consequence. And when someone in the press calls them halfway to account, all they do is whine, complain, and make themselves victims of an imagined left-wing media bias.

As a result, no president has received more fawning coverage than this president—and he owes it all to intimidation, constant complaining, and lying.

What scares me is that all this lying works. The other night I was flipping through the channels, and I stopped to watch a little bit of *Hannity & Colmes* on Fox. I have to say, some of those right-wingers have moments where—while not great entertainers—they're talented demagogues. At the end of the show, they had the comedian Dennis Miller do a little commentary—and his topic was North Korea. Here's what he said: "Folks, there's only one reason North Korea has come to the table now and that's Iraq. Forget WMDs. . . . Pancaking Iraq got us six-way talks and six-way talks got us a valuable one-on-one date with Erin/North Korea where I'm pretty sure we reminded them to cool their nuclear jets or we just might have to beat them to the $e = mc^2$ punch."[13]

278 ■ JAMES CARVILLE

He neglected to say that when they got to that table, they told us they had nuclear weapons and they intended to keep making them. In fact, the message they probably got by watching us "pancake" Iraq was that if the United States comes knocking, you'd better have something big to answer the door with—namely, nukes. Now Dennis Miller is a smart guy. I used to think he was funny. Is he, like so much of this administration and its sympathizers, a committed conservative so blinded by ideology that he's incapable of seeing the truth? Is it that he, like so much of this administration and its sympathizers, is a garden-variety liar? Or is it something else?

I think it's something else. I have to believe it's that the lies are so pervasive, even smart people like Dennis Miller start believing them. I have to believe that all of George W. Bush's economic advisers and education advisers and military advisers are smart enough to see the truth, but they're not brave enough to admit it, so they loudly and boldly proclaim what they *hope* to be the truth and fool a pretty fair number of not unintelligent people in the process.

Therefore, I have to believe that if we put out the truth, daily and forcefully, even though a lie may be halfway around the world before the truth can get its boots on—the truth will eventually catch up.

13

A NOTE ON THE RELIGIOUS RIGHT AND POLITICS

The religious right spews a lot of hate, venom, fire, and brimstone when it talks about the direction of our country. To hear them tell it, Christ himself frowns upon social welfare programs and smiles on marginal rate tax cuts. All this righteous, moralistic, holier-than-thou, Bible-based outrage makes for great direct mail pieces. The problem with the New Testament is that every once in a while somebody actually picks the doggone thing up and reads it.

One of the people who seems to have done just that is Bob Riley, the conservative Republican governor of Alabama. Citing his Christian faith, he called for the largest tax hike in Alabama history, largely on the backs of wealthier taxpayers, for the benefit of the poor.

In explaining his tax plan, Riley wrote, "Alabamians are a faithful people who believe that creating a better world for our children and helping our neighbors are both sacred duties." He later told the *Birmingham News* that "Jesus says one of our missions is to take care of the least among us."[14] That tax plan lost, mainly because Republicans worked so hard against it. After all, they were terrified that people of faith in this country would see that Democrats tend to be more in tune with their values.

The great sportscaster Warner Wolf likes to say, "Let's go to the videotape." Maybe progressives should start making more members of the religious right "go to the scripture."

14

A NOTE ON FRIENDS

My momma always said to me, "Tell me who you go with, and I'll tell you who you are."

Here are five people I'm proud to "go with"—five folks who make me proud to be a progressive and five folks who make me *really* proud to be a progressive.

George McGovern: That's right, George McGovern. George McGovern's good name is often summoned by Republicans when describing a wing of our party that protests war, is wary of American might, and seeks to keep us clear of conflict. His antithesis, in Republican mythology, is Ronald Reagan—an actor who played a cowboy who played a president. Now, I'm sure that Ronnie was a good American and loved his country, but he never left Culver City during World War II. George McGovern, on the other hand, wasn't just a war hero—he was maybe one of the *greatest* heroes of World War II. As a bomber pilot, McGovern flew thirty-five missions, brought his damaged plane home safely every time, was awarded one Distinguished Flying Cross and nominated for another. He was so accurate that his squadron effectively closed down the oil refineries in Eastern Europe and Germany, essentially grounding the German air force. Heck, Stephen Ambrose wrote a book about what a hero he was (*The Wild Blue: The Men and Boys Who Flew the B-24s Over Germany, 1944–1945*) and said that he can't imagine we would have won the war without McGovern's 455th Bomber Group. George McGovern earned the right to say whatever he damn well wanted about the direction of America—and it should be a source of pride to our party when he said, "The highest patriotism is not a blind acceptance of official policy, but a love of one's country deep enough to call her to a higher standard." Unlike many of his right-wing critics, George McGovern has been married to the same woman for over fifty years. George McGovern's good name, his politics, and the modest but heroic life he lived should not be a source of shame, but rather a proud demonstration that you don't have to be an ultrahawk to be courageous and patriotic.

Nancy Pelosi: Nancy Pelosi is another bogeyman (or bogeywoman) the Republicans like to point to as a demonstration of out-of-touch Democratic values. For years, they've been snarling at her heels, determined to cast her as some leftist California quack. After all, she represents San Francisco and, god forbid, has been an unwavering supporter of gay rights and AIDS research. What they don't say is that this is a woman who was largely a stay-at-home mom who refused to run for office until she was forty-seven, when the youngest of her five children (four daughters, one son) was a senior in high school. See, unlike some who preach family values, she wasn't busy feeding $500 tokens into a slot machine at 3:00 A.M.; she was busy feeding her kids. Today, she is the highest-ranking woman in the history of the U.S. Congress. We should be proud of her as a mother, a leader, and a pioneer. Personally, I'll take someone who lives her values over someone who just preaches theirs any day of the week.

Marian Wright Edelman: Marian Wright Edelman is the founder of the Children's Defense Fund. The CDF serves as a voice for poor, minority, and disabled children in this country. If you've ever heard her speak, she will inspire you to go out and do a good deed that minute. I've always loved her saying that "you just need to be a flea against injustice. Enough committed fleas biting strategically can make even the biggest dog uncomfortable." She's been given the MacArthur "genius" award and more than sixty-five honorary degrees. In fact, the only thing ever taken from her was her slogan, "Leave no child behind." George Bush stole it outright (see the education chapter for more). It's a shame he didn't steal some of her intelligence or compassion.

Bob McIntyre and Bob Greenstein: These two guys are both absolutely nonpartisan, so I don't want to get them in any trouble for mentioning them here. But they are progressive thinkers who have dedicated their lives and careers to making this country a more fair place. How do they do it? By being relentlessly honest and factual. Bob Greenstein heads an organization called the Center on Budget and Policy Priorities, an organization that uses smart people and one of the most sophisticated budget models to evaluate the impact of budget and tax proposals on average people. Even Republicans concede that the information he puts out is always right. Bob McIntyre heads a group called Citizens for Tax Justice. He's dedicated his career to making our tax laws more fair by getting the wealthy and corporations to pay their fair share and by waging daily battle with the armies of special interest lobbyists and all their misinformation. Both of these guys are working miracles on a shoestring, so if you want a place to send some money that you know will be well spent, consider supporting these guys. Citizens for Tax Justice can be found at www.ctj.org. The Center on Budget and Policy Priorities is at www.cbpp.org.

And here are five people who today's Republicans "go with"—five people who make me *really* proud to be a progressive

Tom DeLay: Tom DeLay says the most important thing we can do in a time of war is cut taxes, he's argued that unions are as dangerous as terrorists, he's paid back contributors with regulatory relief,[15] and when it was discovered that 6.5 million low-income families were left out of the increase in the child tax credit in the most recent tax bill, Tom DeLay was the one who stopped them from getting help. In his words, "There are a lot of other things that are more important than that."[16] And for this, Republicans in the House have elected him their majority leader.

But the thing he does that I find most disgusting is his constant questioning of people's patriotism. He is the chief of what I call the patriotically correct police. Now, I've always said that work is dignity, and you never mock a man for the work he does—but this man was an exterminator who never wore his country's uniform. How can Tom DeLay question anybody's patriotism when the most dangerous thing he ever faced was a termite?

Rick Santorum: Honestly, Rick Santorum has no shame. He says he's for tort reform and then he and his wife sue their chiropractor for more money than he feels anyone else is entitled to (see the chapter on tort reform).

He's talking with a reporter, and he feels compelled to equate homosexuality to pedophilia and bestiality. Heck, he actually used the expression "man on dog." Now I have no idea what man on dog is, but I'll tell you this, you have to suspect that someone who conjures the term "man on dog" with utter ease is a guy who might have spent some time actively searching for just that thing on the Internet.

He practices the most ruthless, gutless, brainless form of politics and has the gall to call Tom Daschle a "rabid dog." The guy has a serious hang-up about dogs.

And Rick Santorum is not a minor figure in the Republican Party—he has been elected by his fellow Republican senators to be their number three ranking leader.

The greatest thing said in this millennium, and I know that we're only a couple of years into it, was said by Bob Kerrey, the former Democratic senator from Nebraska. I'm sure in the next 997 years, someone will beat it, but until they do, Kerrey's got the lead. Here's what he said: "Rick Santorum is Latin for 'asshole.' "

Bill Bennett: Bill Bennett has made himself rich and famous by making himself a national spokesman on morality and personal responsibility. He was Ronald Reagan's secretary of education, where he blasted schools and students for failing to meet high standards. As drug czar under George H. W. Bush, he argued that people have a moral responsibility to own up to their addiction. After leaving office, he wrote a best-seller called The Book of Virtues. But for Bill, it was never enough to extol virtues; he sowed self-righteous anger at those who couldn't control their appetites. A more recent book, The Death of Outrage, expressed his anger that the public failed to take Bill Clinton's sins more seriously.

Turns out big Bill ain't as virtuous as one might think. Since the early 1990s, he's been a high-rolling gambler who has lost about $8 million during that time. Casino sources report seeing him playing the $500-a-pull slots, mostly between midnight and 6:00 A.M. As someone who isn't afraid to admit that he enjoys gambling now and again,* I can tell you that someone pulling $500 slots at 3:00 A.M. is a man who sits at the very top of the degenerate gambler pyramid. I can also tell you that someone who plays video poker and slots is never going to break even—as Bennett claims he does—because the machines are designed with the odds against you. Play enough, and they will always take your money. That's why they're called one-armed bandits, stupid.

While Bill's been sneaking into casinos during the dead of night, his organization, Empower America, has been railing against lawmakers who "pollute our society with a slot machine on every corner." In fact, he wrote an introduction to one of their reports, in which he stated that 5.5 million American adults are "problem" or "pathological" gamblers. Bennett says he's neither, because he says his habit doesn't disrupt his family life. Never mind that there's no way in hell a guy who blows $8 million isn't a "problem" or "pathological" gambler, but as one casino source puts it, "There's a term in the trade for this kind of gambler. We call them losers."

During the Clinton impeachment, one of Bennett's favorite things to say was, "This much we know . . ." and then follow it with a litany of Clinton's wrongs.

Well, this much *we* know: Bill Bennett is worse than a loser, he's a sanctimonious hypocrite.[17]

Michael Savage: If you don't know Michael Savage, he's the guy I

---

* My games are craps and sports betting.

like to call the intellectual godfather of modern conservatism. He founded a group called the Paul Revere Society, which "stands for the reassertion of our borders, our language, and our culture." His talk show is syndicated on more than three hundred stations, and his book, *The Savage Nation*, was a #1 bestseller. He preaches the most hateful, virulent, and popular brand of right-wing tripe you'll ever hear. But you won't be seeing him on TV anymore. That's because this towering giant of twenty-first-century conservatism was fired by MSNBC because he had this to say to a caller to his show who identified himself as gay: Quote—"You're one of the sodomites. You should only get AIDS and die, you pig."

Although it's a relief to finally see someone who lost his job but doesn't have the Bush economy to blame, it's a shame that Savage loses his job while Santorum keeps his. But the real shame is that legions of conservatives continue to worship the guy for his stupidity, intolerance, and bigotry.

Paul Johnson: Paul Johnson's is not a name that you think of a lot when you think of right-wing Republicans, but he actually predates Bill Bennett in the right-wing Hypocrite Hall of Shame. Paul Johnson is essentially the Republican court historian. Nixon used to send out Johnson volumes for Christmas. Oliver North loves him. Whenever Vice President Dan Quayle needed to name a book he had read, he cited Johnson's *Modern Times*. (When he was asked what it was about, Quayle called it "a very good historical book about history.") That book, by the way, called the New Deal an example of government run amok, Watergate a liberal conspiracy, and Reagan the ne plus ultra of leadership. Johnson's other writing is all about "family values" and "moral uprightness"—he was one of Bill Clinton's harshest critics. And that's why it was no surprise that in 1998, his mistress of eleven years, sick of all his moralizing, exposed him not only as a philanderer but one who loved to be spanked. It almost seems that what conservatives really hate most in this world is themselves. And Paul, you've been a very bad boy. . . .[18]

PART SIX

"TO FORM A MORE PERFECT UNION"

* * *

This is a tough time, not just because we don't hold the House, the Senate, or the presidency. It's deeper than that. It's because every single one of our core beliefs is under relentless and—I hate to say it—effective assault. Who would have thought that after what this nation has gone through in the last three years—war, terrorism, and recession—we'd have to be arguing that in a time of sacrifice maybe wealthy Americans shouldn't be making out like bandits? Who would have thought that in the richest nation on earth, we'd face such opposition in standing up for core, decent, Christian principles such as health care for the poor or a decent education for everyone? Who could have predicted that after years of proving that environmental conservation and economic growth could go hand in hand, we'd be fighting off efforts to allow more pollution into our air, more arsenic in our water, and more cutting in our forests? Who would have thought that in a time when it's clear that if we're going to fight terrorism around the world we need allies around the world, we'd be begging this administration to work with other nations?

Right now, Republicans are cocky. They are actually mocking us. At a speech in Pennsylvania, Tom DeLay said, "A once mighty force has been reduced to a leaderless pack wandering around in the desert, united only by a burning hatred of George W. Bush. I speak of course of the national Democratic party." [19]

In his first speech as the new director of the Republican National Committee in July 2003, Ed Gillespie said that Republicans were "developing ideas. We're implementing solutions. And in the best American political tradition, we would welcome being challenged in the contest of ideas by a loyal opposition with an alternative agenda of its own. Unfortunately, that seems almost too much to ask these days."[20]

That's the verbal equivalent of cork-popping. They're so smug, so confident, so arrogant that they think they've left us on the canvas and they're wishing someone—anyone—will step into the ring and throw a punch. That's what the American people are waiting for, too. A truly national Democratic Party with a national message—one that speaks not only to the people who cheer the "transgender amendment" but to those who want a true alternative to what we've got today and a different vision for what we should be tomorrow.

In the face of this assault, getting angry is understandable—and easy. But getting active is what's effective. Nobody's going to do our work for us. Not the spineless press. Not people who are uninformed. Not Canada. It's up to us. It's in our hands.

One of my earliest memories is of going with my momma and my grandma to a place in Louisiana called Pierre Part to buy crawfish. The men working the little stand out by the dock were courteous to my momma and grandma and were talking about how they were going to give us a good price on the best of the catch and how well we'd be eating that night. Then they started talking to each other in French about how they were going to rip us off. Well, they didn't realize that my grandma and mother both spoke French—and the minute they heard what those dock hands were saying, they called them out on it. In French, my grandma said something to the effect of "I understand what you're saying," and my momma followed up with, "And, boys, it ain't gonna happen."

Right now, the Republican Party is like that crawfish stand. They tell Americans that they're going to give them everything, and then in a language not everyone understands—the language of policy—they work to fleece us.

Well, we speak their language, and we've got to call them out on it—just like my grandma did.

Here's nine ways you can do that:

1. **Put a member of Congress on the spot.** When Republican members of Congress get generic letters to their offices saying, "Why are you cutting education?" it just rolls off them like water off a duck's back. They believe they can act against their constituents with impunity, and that belief is reinforced by an entire ideological infrastructure that gives them talking points and issue briefs telling them that what they're doing isn't really all that bad. What they're not prepared for is the *specific* critique in their *local* news. So to really put a member of Congress on the spot, send a letter to the editor of your local paper explaining how his or her vote actually hurts your town or state. That'll get to them faster than an oil company lobbyist.

   Let me give you one example. A former intern of mine helped put together a series of letters to New Hampshire newspapers asking Congressman John Sununu why he was supporting a bill that allowed companies that got homeland security government contracts to incorporate offshore to avoid paying taxes. Those letters included mentions of specific New Hampshire companies, and guess what: Congressman Sununu changed his vote. Every time a Republican votes against the interest of his or her constituents, they should be similarly embarrassed.

2. **Educate yourself.** Republicans have built up a cottage industry of books, magazines, policy papers, and other written material that serves to advance their nutty views and specious arguments. That's why you need to arm yourself with facts and counterarguments. There are a lot of places you can do this, but as far as I'm concerned, the progressive must-read is a magazine called *The Washington Monthly.* You can read some of its stuff online and subscribe at washingtonmonthly.com.

3. **Defend your ideas.** You've just read a book full of ideas . . . you've got strongly held views. Don't keep 'em to yourself. Don't cede arguments with knuckleheads at cocktail parties and barbecues. You've got the tools: take 'em to task.

4. **Volunteer support for a public servant.** A lot of good public servants labor in obscurity—and a lot of bad ones give the good ones a bad name. If you see someone serving honorably, that's someone worth supporting with your time and energy.

5. **Participate.** Call or write your congressperson, go to a town hall or school board meeting . . . the vocal majority beats the silent majority every day of the week and twice on Sundays.

6. **Write a check.** I hate to say it, money talks. The least we can do is make it say the right things. Sit down, figure out what causes or candidates are important to you and how much you can afford to give, and write a check.

7. **Vote, and make sure a like-minded friend does, too.** I bet you didn't know that we have a way to have a national "recall" elec-

tion—it's called an *election*. If you didn't vote, and didn't make your like-minded friends vote, you have no right to come whining to me.

8. **Aggravate a Republican.** Every time I see a car with a BUSH-CHENEY sticker, one of my favorite things to do is pull up alongside them, motion for them to roll down the window, and when they do, I say, "Hey, I just thought you should know—somebody put a BUSH-CHENEY sticker on your car." This doesn't really help anything, but you'll find it very therapeutic.

9. **Be positive.** Don't just let people know when they're doing bad, let 'em know when they're doing good. Like I said in the beginning—we need more of my daddy's attitude and less of the cynical negativity that dominates so much political discussion today.

✯ ✯ ✯

So now you've plowed through this book and you're at the very end.

You've read more than forty policy ideas, you've heard scathing criticisms of the current administration, and you've seen a whole bunch of right-wing myths busted.

"James, all of this is well and good," you say, "but what's the *message*?" You're the guy who gave us "It's the economy, stupid."

You admonish us to communicate in simple, meaningful, direct terms.

You preach about how we live in a world of sound bites. Heck, you helped create a world of sound bites.

And yet, for all of this, what do we get? Some detailed six-page campaign finance reform proposal that will never pass, some Social Security proposals that will get us skewered, and a tax plan that'll make us a 40 percent party for years to come.

Again, you ask, "What's the message?"

"Where's the simplicity?"

"What's the sound bite?"

So, my dear reader, let's go back to that famous War Room wall in 1992, where we distilled the essence of Bill Clinton's message onto a dry-erase board.

We wrote down three things—three core concepts that defined our campaign:

1. Change vs. more of the same.
2. It's the economy, stupid. (Actually, if you look at that dry-erase board in the War Room, it just said, "the economy stupid"—but I'll take the legend over the fact every time.)
3. Don't forget health care.

Now we're in the year 2003, and I propose a little update. So let's pull up that old board, take out the eraser, and . . . drumroll, please.

Number 1 stays intact. The choice is still between change and more of the same.

Number 2 is a little too narrow for these guys. We're going to change that to It's the people, stupid—all of the people.

See, they're about people, too, just not all of them. If you're one of the wealthiest people in America, a member of the arsenic lobby or the drill anywhere, anytime posse, the corporate cheat club, or anyone who wants more money now at the expense of passing on our problems to our children later—they're for you.

For progressives, all of the people has to be *all of the people* . . . the eld-erly, the children, the black, the blue, the strong, the weak, the lame, the halt, the blind . . . *everybody.*

We can be justifiably scathing in our criticism that this admin-istration has not just neglected but also acted detrimentally to the interests of tens of millions of Americans. When we say, "It's the people, stupid—all of the people," we're really saying: Are we going to have a gov-ernment for a few of the people or for everybody? You know where I stand.

Number 3. Of course, health care is still a huge issue and growing bigger every day. We should look at how this administration's policies have meant that millions of people have lost their health insurance, and this president has offered basically nothing but a prescription drug ben-efit that by everybody's account is convoluted, inadequate, insufficient, and unworkable. All of that is legit, and all of that becomes part of num-ber 2. That way we'll use number 3 to move on to that foreign policy ground that Democrats ought to occupy forcefully and proudly. For number 3, we're going to steal a line from our good friends at State Farm and call for a good neighbor policy.

Even though America has the biggest and best house in the neigh-borhood, we have got to recognize that our house is safer when we join the neighborhood watch, when we don't speed down the street or throw our garbage out on other people's lawns. That's the only way we can get our neighbors to look out for us.

There you have it:

1. Change vs. more of the same.
2. It's the people, stupid—all of the people.
3. A strong America that's a good neighbor.

That's our message. That's the tip sheet for all of you who have had enough. That's how we meet the constitutional prescription for good government. Now it's up to us to bring that message to the American people and bring the candidates who represent it to victory. That's how you build a more perfect Union. That's how you fight back. That's how you respond when you finally decide you've had enough.

A SWEET ENDING–BREAD PUDDING

It'll be a sweet day when all of the Americans who have had enough start fighting back and start winning. Now that you've made it through to the end, you deserve something sweet, too.

Growing up in rural south Louisiana, we didn't have a lot of great dessert cuisine. Tiramisu and crème brûlée were in short supply. In fact, other than watermelon, the only thing I ever had for dessert until I was thirty was the one great dessert we did have—bread pudding.

This bread pudding recipe comes from Mrs. Gert Gueymard, who was my fourth-grade teacher. As a child, I called her Miss Aunt Gert. That's because she was so close to my family, I thought she was kin.

> 1 loaf French bread
> 1 quart milk
> 3 eggs
> 2 cups sugar
> 2 tablespoons vanilla
> 1 cup raisins
> 3 tablespoons butter

1. Soak bread in milk. Break into pieces with hands and mix thoroughly. Stir in eggs, sugar, vanilla, and raisins.

2. Pour mixture into buttered 9 x 13-inch baking dish. Set the dish in a pan of water and bake at 350°F for 45 to 55 minutes, until firm.

3. Allow to cool and spoon into individual cups or serve from casserole. Before serving, top with Whiskey or Rum Sauce and heat under broiler.

Whiskey or Rum Sauce

1 cup sugar
1 egg
1 stick butter, melted
Whiskey or rum (I prefer whiskey, but they each work fine)

1. Cream the sugar and egg.
2. Add melted butter and continue to blend.
3. Stir in whisky or rum to taste, until sauce is creamy and smooth.

Yield: 12 servings

NOTES

Introduction

1. Franklin D. Roosevelt, "A Call for Sacrifice," April 28, 1942.
2. Lynette Clemetson, "More Americans in Poverty in 2002, Census Study Says," *New York Times*, September 27, 2003, p. A1.
3. Ibid.
4. Ceci Connolly, "Census Finds Many More Lack Health Insurance," *Washington Post*, September 30, 2003, p. A1.
5. Michael E. Kanell, "Soaring Oil Costs, War Anxiety Trigger Wave of Unemployment," *Atlanta Journal Constitution*, March 8, 2003, p. 1A.
6. Edmund L. Andrews, "Economic Inequality Grew in 90's Boom, Fed Reports," *New York Times*, January 23, 2003, p. C1.

Part One: "The Common Defense"

1. Joby Warrick, "Biotoxins Fall into Private Hands; Global Risk Seen in S. African Poisons," *Washington Post*, April 21, 2003, p. A1.
2. Editorial: Securing Chemical Plants, *Milwaukee Journal Sentinel*, July 27, 2002, p. 12A.
3. President George W. Bush, remarks to new employees of Department of Homeland Security, February 28, 2003.
4. Jim VandeHei, "Bush Blames Hill Republicans; President's Homeland Security Explanation Creates Problems for Allies," *Washington Post*, February 28, 2003, p. A6.
5. Senator Hillary Rodham Clinton, remarks made at John Jay College of Criminal Justice, New York City, January 24, 2003.
6. Jim Morris, "Effort to Equip Planes with Missile-Defense Technology Gains Momentum," *Dallas Morning News*, September 28, 2003, p. 1A.
7. Jay Root, "Federal Agency Was Asked to Track Democrat's Plane," *Dallas/Fort Worth Star Telegram*, May 15, 2003, p. 10.

8. Richard Cheney, Address to the Southern Center for International Studies, August 30, 2000, Atlanta, Georgia.
9. Michael Elliott, "Special Report—The Secret History," *Time* magazine, August 12, 2002, p. 28.
10. Christopher Marquis, "How Powerful Can 16 Words Be?" *New York Times*, July 20, 2003, Sect. 4, p. 5.
11. Richard Leiby and Walter Pincus, "Retired Envoy: Nuclear Report Ignored; Bush Cited Alleged Iraqi Purchases, Even Though CIA Raised Doubts in 2002," *Washington Post*, Sunday, July 6, 2003, p. A13.
12. Ibid.
13. Sebastian Rotella, "Allies Find No Links Between Iraq, Al Qaeda," *Los Angeles Times*, November 4, 2002, p. 1.
14. Walter Pincus, "Oct. Report Said Defeated Hussein Would Be Threat," *Washington Post*, July 21, 2003, p. A1.
15. Daniel Benjamin, "Condi's Phony History—Sorry, Dr. Rice, Postwar Germany Was Nothing Like Iraq," *Slate* magazine, August 29, 2003.
16. Maureen Dowd, "Let's Blame Canada," *New York Times*, July 11, 2003, Sect. 4, p. 11.
17. Daniel Bergner, "Where the Enemy Is Everywhere and Nowhere," *New York Times Magazine*, July 20, 2003, p. 38.

Part Two: "The General Welfare"

1. Calculations made from February 2001 until the end of June 2003: 880 days; values are averaged.
2. Wilshire.com and world-exchanges.org/wfe/home.asp
3. www.democrats.org/news/200309230001.html
4. Bureau of Labor Statistics reports: http://www.bls.gov
5. www.nber.org/cycles/November2001
6. *Exploding Deficits, Declining Growth*, Committee for Economic Development, March 2003, p. 1.
7. www.cbpp.org/8-26-03bud.htm
8. Dana Milbank, "Seek and Ye Shall Not Find," *Washington Post*, March 11, 2003, p. A21.
9. Jonathan Chait, "Red Handed: The Deficit Gets Worse, and So Does Bush," *New Republic*, May 13, 2002, p. 12.
10. Al Gore, Speech to the Economic Club of Detroit, May 1998.
11. *Exploding Deficits, Declining Growth*, pp. 5–9.
12. John Cassidy, "Bushonomics," *The New Yorker*, May 12, 2003, p. 37.

13. Robert S. McIntyre, "Déjà Voodoo Economics?" *The American Prospect* (May 2003): www.prospect.org/print/V14/5/mcintyre-r.html

14. Alan Fram, "White House Says It Will Cut Record Projected Deficits in Half," Associated Press, July 15, 2003.

15. Cheney, remarks to the U.S. Chamber of Commerce, Washington, D.C., January 10, 2003.

16. Senator Tom Daschle, Speech to the Senate, November 14, 2001.

17. Ray Boshara, "The $6,000 Solution," *Atlantic Monthly* (January 2003), p. 95.

18. Bennett Roth, "Bush's Fiscal Skills Fall Short, Gore Says," *Houston Chronicle*, July 16, 2000, p. A4.

19. Texas Government Legislative Report, July 13, 2000: www.tgslc.org/lege_report/index.cfm

20. Stateline.org report on State Budget Gaps, February 11, 2003.

21. G. Robert Hillman, "VP, Governor Spar Over Texas Budget Shortfall," *Dallas Morning News*, July 14, 2000, p. A1.

22. Joel Friedman, Richard Kogan, and John Springer, "A Brief Overview of the Administration's Tax Cut Agenda," Center on Budget and Policy Priorities, March 20, 2003: www.cbpp.org/2-14-03tax.htm

23. Joel Smith, "Executive Pay Up in Down Time," *Detroit News*, May 4, 2003, p. 1B.

24. Bureau of Labor Statistics, March 7, 2003.

25. *Crossfire* transcript, CNN, April 30, 2003.

26. Bush, remarks to the people of Omaha, Nebraska, February 28, 2001 (italics added).

27. Bureau of Labor Statistics, 2003; AFL-CIO, January 27, 2003.

28. Bush, remarks at the Children's Healthcare of Atlanta Hospital, Atlanta, Georgia, March 1, 2001.

29. Bush, remarks on the economy to small-business owners, White House Rose Garden, April 15, 2003.

30. Lawrence Mishel, Testimony before House Education and Workforce Committee, February 12, 2003.

31. Bush, State of the Union address, January 28, 2003.

32. NBC Nightly News, January 13, 2003.

33. Citizens for Tax Justice fact sheet, January 27, 2003.

34. Bush, remarks to the Economic Club of Chicago, January 7, 2003.

35. Center on Budget and Policy Priorities fact sheet, January 6, 2002: www.cbpp.org

36. Bush, remarks to the Economic Club of Chicago, January 7, 2003.

37. William Gale and Janet Holtzblatt, "On the Possibility of a No-Return Tax System," *National Tax Journal*, September 1997, pp. 475–85.

38. "Auditing the Poor: The Bush Administration Is Cracking Down on Households Claiming the Earned-Income Tax Credit," *Albany Times Union*, April 30, 2003, p. A12.

39. Kelly St. John, "Supreme Court to Hear Case on S.F. Restaurant: IRS Says Wait Staff Underreported Tips," *San Francisco Chronicle*, February 12, 2002, p. A10.

40. Editorial, "Skewed Tax Prosecutions," *Louisville Courier-Journal*, April 18, 2003, p. 10A.

41. Richard Cay Johnston, "Very Richest's Share of Income Grew Even Bigger, Data Show," *New York Times*, June 26, 2003, p. A1.

Part Three: "Secure the Blessings of Liberty . . ."

1. *National Assessment Shows Encouraging Trends in Mathematics Performance*, August 24, 2000, National Center for Education Statistics: www.nces.ed.gov/pressrelease/rel2000/8_24_00.asp

2. Minority enrollment rates from *Status of Trends in the Education of Hispanics*, April 2003, National Center for Education Statistics, p. 136, Table 2.3a.

3. Minority dropout rates, ibid., p. 144, Table 3.3a.

4. African-American disparity rates, *The Condition of Education 2002: Trends in the Achievement Gap in Reading Between White and Black Students*, National Center for Education Statistics, p. 135.

5. www.nces.ed.gov/timss/results.asp

6. *Private Schools in the United States: A Statistical Profile, 1999–2000*: Department of Education: www.ed.gov

7. *Barriers, Benefits, and Costs of Using Private Schools to Alleviate Overcrowding in Public Schools*, U.S. Department of Education, Office of the Undersecretary, November 1998: www.aft.org/research/vouchers/research/usvoucher.html

8. Thomas Toch, "An Education Plan with the Right Goal, Wrong Yardstick," *Washington Post*, November 18, 2001, p. B5.

9. Michail Winerip, "What Some Much-Noted Data Really Showed About Vouchers," *New York Times*, May 7, 2003, p. B12.

10. Richard Cohen, "Houston's Disappearing Dropouts," *Washington Post*, September 4, 2003, p. A21.

11. Thomas Toch, "Divide and Conquer," *Washington Monthly*, May 2003, pp. 20–26.

12. Marge Scherer, "On Savage Inequalities, a Conversation with Jonathan Kozol," *Educational Leadership*, vol. 50, #4 (January 1993), pp. 4–10.

13. Editorial, "Bonn Meeting Was a Rebuke for Bush," *Dallas/Fort Worth Star Telegram*, July 25, 2001, p. 10.

14. Andrew C. Revkin with Katherine Q. Seelye, "Report by the E.P.A. Leaves Out Data on Climate Change," *New York Times,* June 19, 2003, p. A1.

15. Democratic Policy Committee environmental monitor, Natural Resources Defense Council, "The Bush Record": www.nrdc.org/bushrecord/default.asp

16. www.ase.org/powersmart/

17. www.ase.org

18. www.ucusa.org

19. Union of Concerned Scientists: www.ucusa.org

20. www.epa.gov/history/publications/train/08.htm

21. www.coveringtheuninsured.org

22. M. Charles Bakst, "In GOP Primaries, Both Bush, McCain Are Looking Smaller," *Providence Journal,* February 22, 2000, p. 1B.

23. "Health Insurance Coverage: 2001," *2001 Current Population Report* (September 2002), U.S. Census Bureau: www.coveringtheuninsured.org

24. Institute of Medicine, *Care Without Coverage: Too Little, Too Late,* Committee on the Consequences of Uninsurance, Board on Health Care Services (Washington, D.C.: National Academy Press, 2002), p. 162.

25. E. Warren, T. Sullivan, and M. Jacoby, "Medical Problems and Bankruptcy Filings," *Norton's Bankruptcy Adviser* (May 2002).

26. Greg Schneider, "Pension Needs Fueling GM's Sales Push Rivals Feel Forced to Match Offers," *Washington Post,* June 25, 2003, p. E1.

27. Todd Gilmer and Richard Kronick, "Calm Before the Storm: Expected Increase in the Number of Uninsured Americans," *Health Affairs* (November–December 2001), pp. 207–10.

28. John Kerry, "Affordable Health Care for All Americans," remarks at Mercy Medical Center, Des Moines, IA, May 16, 2003.

29. Elliott S. Fisher, David E. Wennberg, Thérèse A. Stukel, et al., "The Implications of Regional Variations in Medicare Spending. Part 2: Health Outcomes and Satisfaction with Care," *Annals of Internal Medicine,* vol. 138, #4, February 18, 2003, pp. 288–98.

Part Four: "Establish Justice"

1. National Election Studies Guide to Public Opinion and Electoral Behavior: www.umich.edu/ŝtnes/nesguide/toptable/tab5a_5.htm

2. www.opensecrets.org/

3. Jeffrey McMurray, "Democrats Raise Influence Peddling Charge," Associated Press, May 14, 2003.

4. www.opensecrets.org/payback/issue.asp?issueid=CFR&CongNo=107

5. This information is adapted from Common Cause's *Pocketbook Politics: How Special Interest Money Hurts the American Consumer,* February 24, 1998: www.common cause.org/publications/pocketbooktoc.htm

6. www.walmartstores.com

7. This information is drawn from the excellent report, *Executive Excess 2002—The Ninth Annual CEO Compensation Survey* by Scott Klinger, Chris Hartman, Sarah Anderson, et al., Institute for Policy Studies and United for a Fair Economy, August, 26, 2002, pp. 1–26.

8. Ibid., p 1.

9. Knut Royce, "Bush's Insider Connections Preceded Huge Profit on Stock Deal," Center for Public Integrity, April 4, 2000: http://www.publicintegrity.org

10. Tom Raum, "Bush Presses Attack on Gore," Associated Press, September 6, 2000.

11. Charlotte-Anne Lucas, "Richards Wants Bush to Reveal Documents from SEC Inquiry: GOP Challenger Denies Insider Trading with Harken Energy Stock," *Dallas Morning News,* October 11, 1994, p. 22D.

12. "O'Neill Urges CEOs to Criticize Unethical Peers," Bloomberg News in *Los Angeles Times,* June 19, 2002, Sect. 3, p. 5.

13. Bush, remarks on Wall Street, July 9, 2002.

14. "George Bush, Enron Party Animal," *New York Post,* December 18, 2002; *Wall Street Journal,* May 10, 2002.

15. Peter Eisler, Julie Appleby, and Martin Kasindorf, "Hype Outraces Facts in Malpractice Debate," *USA Today,* March 5, 2003, p. 1A.

16. Bush, remarks at the University of Scranton, January 16, 2003.

17. CA Proposition 103 Enforcement Project Study, 1995—AMA, 2002.

18. "Nevada's New Liability Program Won't Offer Immediate Results," *Best Week Insurance News and Analysis,* August 26, 2002.

19. *Medical Malpractice Insurance: Stable Losses/Unstable Rates,* Americans for Insurance Reform, October 10, 2002, available on www.insurance-reform.org

20. Congressional Budget Office, September 25, 2002: www.cbo.gov

21. Peter Eisler, Julie Appleby, and Martin Kasindorf, "Hype Outraces Facts in Malpractice Debate," *USA Today,* March 5, 2003, p. 1A.

22. Amy Keller, "Democrats Attack Santorum Over Suit," *Roll Call,* December 16, 1999, p. 1 and James O'Toole, "A Punk Among Solons No More, Santorum Is at Home in the Senate," *Pittsburgh Post-Gazette,* October 22, 2000, p. A10.

23. Sidney M. Wolfe, "Bad Doctors Get a Free Ride," *New York Times,* March 4, 2003, p. A25.

24. Ibid.

Part Five: "Insure Domestic Tranquility"

1. 2003 Trustees Report: www.SSA.gov
2. www.Commoncause.org
3. Campaign for America's Future: Bush Social Security Commission Members: Who Are They?: www.ourfuture.org/docUploads/20020116132652.pdf
4. Hans Riemer, "Institute for America's Future: Bush Social Security Commission Proposes Benefit Cuts to Pay for Privatization," December 6, 2001: www.ourfuture.org/docUploads/20011207121150.pdf
5. Robert Pear and Robin Toner, "Bush Drug Proposal in Medicare Plan Faces Stiff Battle," New York Times, May 21, 2003, p. A28.
6. Bush, speech in Minneapolis, July 11, 2002.
7. Jane Bryant Quinn, "Bad Medicine for Medicare," Newsweek, June 9, 2003, p. 39.
8. Statement of Judy Feder, Georgetown University Dean of Public Policy, House Budget Committee Hearing, February 26, 2003.
9. Elizabeth A. McGlynn, et al., "The Quality of Health Care Delivered to Adults in the United States," New England Journal of Medicine, June 26, 2003, pp. 2635–45.
10. www.dartmouthatlas.org
11. General Accounting Office, "Comparison of Medicare and VA Payment Rates for Home Oxygen," May 15, 1997, updated April 1999.
12. The Mendacity Index, Washington Monthly Staff, The Washington Monthly (September 2003), pp. 27–29.
13. Dennis Miller, "Eliminating the Axis of Evil," Fox News, September 30, 2003.
14. Oliver Libaw, "Matthew 1040 a Biblical Tax Policy? One Governor Says Yes," July 2, 2003, www.ABCNews.com, quoting Birmingham (Ala.) News.
15. Pete Yost, "Utility's Documents Lay Out Donations to Republicans Meant to Win Law Exemption," Associated Press, June 6, 2003.
16. David Firestone, "DeLay Rebuffs Move to Restore Lost Tax Credit," New York Times, June 4, 2003, p. A1.
17. "The Bookie of Virtue," Josh Green, The Washington Monthly (June 2003), p. 8.
18. Assembled from Christopher Hitchens, "The Rise and Fall of Paul 'Spanker' Johnson," Salon magazine, May 28, 1998, and Jacob Weisberg, "The Courtly Contrarian," New York Times Magazine, March 15, 1998, p. 34.
19. Justin Quinn, "Tom DeLay Visits, Rips Democrats as 'Unfit,' " May 6, 2003, Intelligencer Journal, p. A1.
20. Remarks by Ed Gillespie, Republican National Committee Chairman Elect, in New York City, July 25, 2003.

Made in the USA
San Bernardino, CA
08 May 2013